Science and Technology Illustrated

The World Around Us

Science
Technology

The World Around Us

and
Illustrated

17**68**

Encyclopaedia Britannica, Inc.

CHICAGO

AUCKLAND · GENEVA

LONDON · MANILA

PARIS · ROME

SEOUL · SYDNEY

TOKYO · TORONTO

© Gruppo Editoriale Fabbri S.p.A., Milan, 1983

© 1984 by Encyclopaedia Britannica, Inc.

Copyright Under International Copyright Union

All Rights Reserved Under Pan American and Universal Copyright Convention
by Encyclopaedia Britannica, Inc.

Library of Congress Catalog Card Number: 84-80129

International Standard Book Number: 0-852229-425-5

English language edition by license of Gruppo Editoriale Fabbri

Title page photograph courtesy of Hale Observatories;
California Institute of Technology and
Carnegie Institution of Washington

Printed in U.S.A.

Volume 16

Contents

7

Maps and Mapmaking

When we look at a map, we think we are seeing a precise representation of the world or some part of it. Like a painting of a human face, however, a map is liable to interpretation or caricature. The great advantage of maps, in fact, is that they are abstract and distorted, and can be manipulated to perform a variety of functions. Satellite photographs show the world more closely as it really is, but they are often confusing in their detail. Maps drawn by skilled cartographers graphically organize this geographic information with colors, symbols, words, and lines, so that we can understand it better.

By the addition of black borders, for example, a political map can indicate boundaries between nations, states and provinces, counties, townships, districts, and other jurisdictions. By using lines and colors associated with specific elevations, a relief map can visually convey the physical or topographic characteristics of a given area. With standardized symbols such as arrows (wind flow) and isobars (lines that connect points of equal atmospheric pressure), a weather map—an example of a scientific map—depicts natural phenomena. A celestial map is a graphic representation of the stars. With compass points and coordinates, a nautical chart helps a mariner navigate across the open sea. These are just a few examples of the many kinds of maps that are made.

Drawn to Size

All maps are drawn to scale, meaning that they are miniaturized versions of the areas they represent. Scale is typically expressed as a numerical ratio, such as 1:1,000,000. This means that one unit of map measure equals one million units of that measure in nature—(an inch, for example is about 16 miles in this case, or 1 millimeter equals a little over 10 km). Maps that cover large areas are said to be small-scale, while maps showing greater detail in a smaller area are said to be large-scale. The numerical ratio is always in the opposite sense.

Early in the history of mapmaking, scholars concluded that the Earth was a sphere; this theory provided the mathematical foundation for cartography, the art and science of drawing maps. A sphere can be divided into precise geometrical segments by means of a grid. Those lines—meridians, or longitudes, and parallels, or latitudes—are the basis of all maps, whether they represent a large or small part of the globe. The grid system works like this:

Because the Earth is a sphere, it is possible to draw a circle around the middle of the sphere, dividing it into two equal parts. The ancients called this circle the

One of the first methods of mapping the surface of the Earth was to draw directly on a sphere. Although this was accurate for an overview, it was inefficient for displaying detail and, in addition, inconvenient for storage and transportation. All successive maps are based on the principle of representing the spherical surface of the Earth on a form that can be flattened. *Right:* Mercator method consists of projecting the surface of the Earth onto an imaginary cylinder that is tangent to the equator. The defect of the Mercator projection is that it shows the polar zones as being disproportionately large. However, detailed maps of relatively small areas can be very accurate when drawn in Mercator projection.

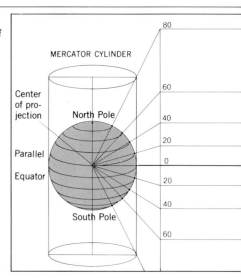

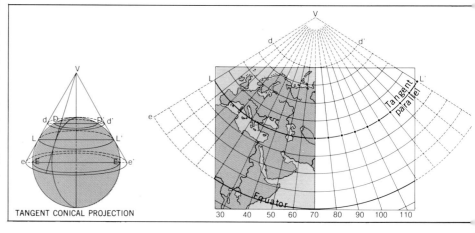

TANGENT CONICAL PROJECTION

equator. Like any other circle, the equator can be divided into 360 degrees. One point on the equator, by international convention, marks the location of the prime meridian. This is a line that runs from the North Pole to the South Pole, passes through the Royal Observatory in Greenwich, England, and intersects the equator perpendicularly at 0°.

From Degrees to Grids

Each degree east or west of the prime meridian marks a measure of longitude, up to 180° east or 180° west. Each degree of any meridian circle north or south of the equator marks a measure of latitude, from 0° at the equator to 90° north and 90° south. The latitude line 40° north, for example, runs through Philadelphia, Pennsylvania, and Beijing, China, among other places, girdling the globe in a circle that is always parallel to the equator. Each of these circles of latitude is smaller than the equatorial ring. When these measurements are depicted on a globe as lines, the world is covered by a grid, and any location on the globe can be pinpointed by its latitudinal and longitudinal coordinates.

When this grid is transferred to a piece of paper—a process known as projec-

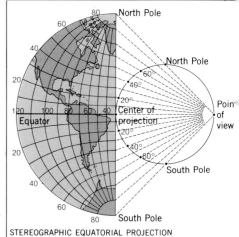

STEREOGRAPHIC EQUATORIAL PROJECTION

Above, center: Conical projection. The map is drawn on a cone whose axis coincides with that of the Earth and whose base is tangent with a given parallel. Conical projection is most accurate along the given parallel, progressively less so as one moves north or south.

Directly above: Map drawn on stereographic equatorical projection.

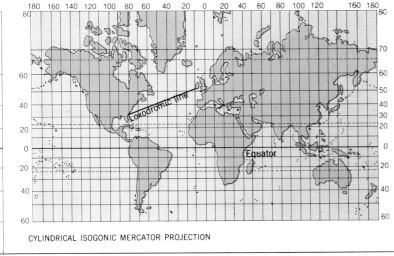

CYLINDRICAL ISOGONIC MERCATOR PROJECTION

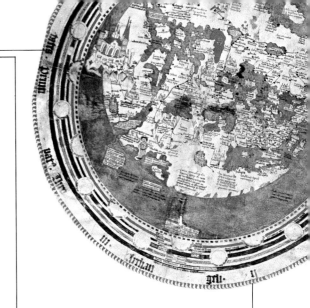

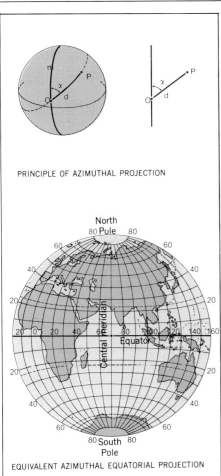

PRINCIPLE OF AZIMUTHAL PROJECTION

EQUIVALENT AZIMUTHAL EQUATORIAL PROJECTION

Above: Azimuthal projection. As shown in the diagram above the projection, a point of origin (*O*) is selected on the globe and a meridian line is established (*m*). To locate a second point (*P*), a great circle is drawn passing through both *O* and *P*. The angle of the great circle with the meridian and the distance from *O* to *P* are measured and transferred to the flat map.

Right: At top, antique map drawn in stereographic projection. At center, example of how areas appear different depending upon the projection used to make the map. On a globe, these 2 areas would be identical.

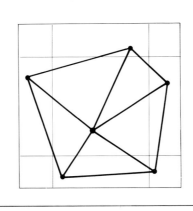

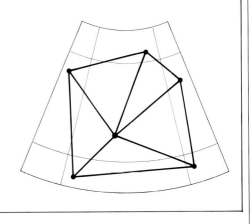

tion—any location on the curving globe can be plotted on the flat paper. There are hundreds of different styles of projections, but the three that are most commonly used are cylindrical, conical, and azimuthal. To get a basic idea of projection, imagine the Earth as a glass globe with a light located precisely in its center. If the globe is painted with dark lines to represent latitude, longitude, and continents, these lines appear as shadows when the globe is placed near a piece of paper. The shape of the shadows (and the type of projection) depends on the way the paper is positioned relative to the globe.

Types of Projection

Cylindrical projection can be pictured by imagining this glass globe as being inside a cylinder of paper. This projection, also known as the Mercator projection, has the effect of turning the curving meridian lines of the globe into straight, parallel shadow lines on the paper. The Mercator projection is used in nautical charts.

Similarly, a conical projection can be pictured from the shadows cast on a cone of paper placed over a section of our hy-

pothetical glass globe. A common example is a map showing the Earth viewed from the North Pole. The third type of projection, azimuthal, can be pictured when the piece of paper stands flat against the glass globe. Different types of azimuthal projection result, depending on the location of the light source within the globe, on its surface, or behind the globe. All projections are mathematical solutions to visual problems; the glass globe is merely an aid to help imagine this crucial transfer process.

No projection presents a completely uniform picture. Some ensure that all lines from the center of the map accurately reflect distance (equidistant projection), some are true to the amount of area shown (equal-area projection), and some are faithful to the shapes of the land masses depicted (conformal projection). Once the system of projection is worked out, mapmakers can plot geographical features, select color tints, add lettering, draw in boundaries, and send the finished manuscript off to the printer.

See also CARTOGRAPHY.

Margarine

Margarine may seem like a newfangled substitute for butter, but in fact, it was invented in 1869 by a French chemist, Hyppolyte Mège-Mouriés, who thereby won Napoleon III's contest for the invention of an inexpensive butter substitute.

Ingredients

Margarine consists of fats or oils dispersed in an aqueous phase (a waterlike base), containing milk products dispersed in fats or oils, and flavoring. In its early years, margarine was often made with an-imal fats—Mège-Mouriés's concoction contained lard—but the great interest in polyunsaturated fats and oils for health reasons has popularized the American shift to vegetable oils such as corn, safflower, soybean, cottonseed, and peanut oils. In Europe, however, lard and whale oil are still used.

According to U.S. regulations, margarine must contain not less than 80 percent fat, except for the low-calorie types on the market. The aqueous phase can be water, milk, or a vegetable-protein solution, and it must be pasteurized. Vitamin A, which is soluble in fats and oils, is added so that the finished product contains no less than 15,000 international units per pound (0.45 kg). Sometimes salt (or, for those on low-sodium diets, potassium chloride), nutritive sweeteners, emulsifiers for proper blending, preservatives, colorings, and flavorings are added (*also see* PROCESSED FOODS and FOOD ADDITIVES).

During World War I butter was in short supply, and in the United States blocks of white margarine were sold with small packets of yellow dye that home cooks stirred together in the kitchen.

The "polyunsaturated" vegetable oils in margarine are hydrogenated, so called because hydrogen is bubbled through them,

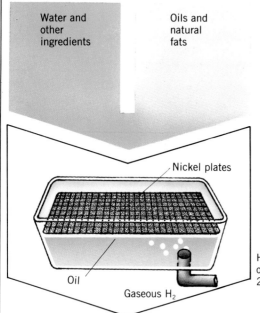

Water and other ingredients

Oils and natural fats

Nickel plates

Oil

Gaseous H₂

Hydrogenation of oil 200-220°C. 150 mmHg

Left and below: Stages in the production of margarine. The most important phase is hydrogenation, which occurs in closed containers. This involves the addition of gaseous hydrogen in the presence of catalysts (usually nickel) that do not react directly with the principal ingredient, vegetable oil. The process also reduces the tendency toward oxidation of the lipids. The structure of the unsaturated fatty acids is changed, too—the normally occurring *cis*-form is changed to a trans-isomer.

EMULSIFICATION OF MIXTURE

CRYSTALLIZATION

Cold drum (15°C.)

LAMINATION AND AGING

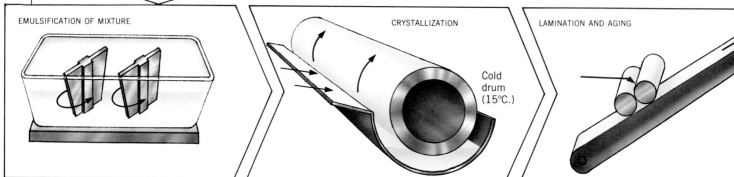

AVERAGE FATTY ACID COMPOSITION OF VARIOUS MARGARINES		UNSATURATED FATTY ACIDS			SATURATED FATTY ACIDS
		Mono-un saturated	2 double bonds	Polyunsaturated	
TYPES OF SOLID MARGARINE	Vegetable	35-66	12-48	0.5-4	17-25
	Mixed vegetable and animal	52-57	2-11	0-0.5	36-41
	Semisolid	22-48	25-65	0.5-3	15-23
	Spreadable	14-36	42-75	0.5-5	10-17

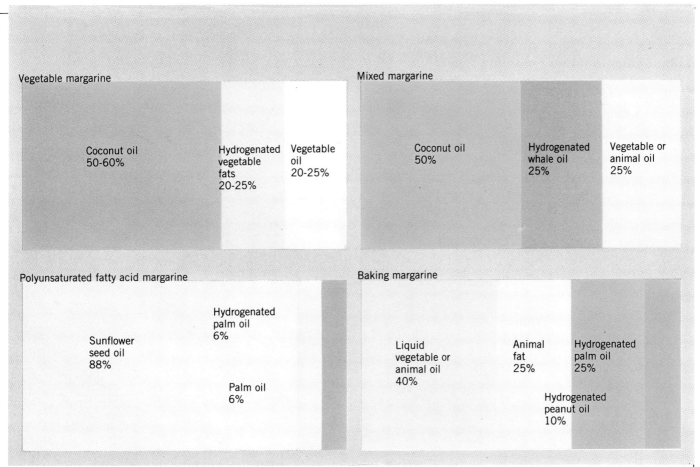

Vegetable margarine

Coconut oil 50-60%

Hydrogenated vegetable fats 20-25%

Vegetable oil 20-25%

Mixed margarine

Coconut oil 50%

Hydrogenated whale oil 25%

Vegetable or animal oil 25%

Polyunsaturated fatty acid margarine

Sunflower seed oil 88%

Hydrogenated palm oil 6%

Palm oil 6%

Baking margarine

Liquid vegetable or animal oil 40%

Animal fat 25%

Hydrogenated palm oil 25%

Hydrogenated peanut oil 10%

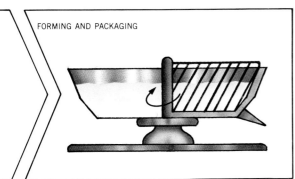

FORMING AND PACKAGING

The lipid phase of margarine preparation involves mixing natural ingredients in proportions that depend upon the consistency or nutritive value desired. The water phase mixture consists of water, food coloring, preservatives, and flavoring. The 2 phases are mixed together with emulsifiers, which ensure proper dispersion of the water phase throughout the lipid phase. The mixture then passes around a cold rotating drum and solidifies. It is scraped off in a sheet, allowed to age, and formed and packaged. There are several different types of margarine, based on the initial ingredients used and the degree of hydrogenation. Besides the traditional margarine prepared from hydrogenated fats and vegetable oils such as coconut and palm, many commercial margarines are highly unsaturated, containing over 80% unsaturated fatty acids.

filling the unused carbon bonds with hydrogen atoms, which raises the melting point closer to that of butter and prevents the margarine from going rancid by leaving fewer unoccupied spots to which oxygen atoms in the air can attach.

There is a growing concern about another change that takes place when polyunsaturated fats are hydrogenated—the phenomenon is the formation of mirror-image forms of molecules known as isomers. These molecules are large and complex in shape. They must have a specific configuration to fit into the body's machinery. Just as a pair of gloves share certain identical features but cannot be interchanged, the healthy *cis*-form of a fat can be converted to the look-alike *trans*-shape, which cannot properly fit into the

body's biochemical processes and therefore may "gum up the works," contributing to degenerative diseases like hardening of the arteries.

Manufacture

Mège-Mouriés's margarine was produced in the butter-churning equipment of his day. In the United States, the process was simplified so that the melted-fat mixture was churned with milk and salt, chilled with cold water until it solidified, then kneaded and packaged. Today, the process is not very different. In one supply tank are the oil components—oil and oil-soluble ingredients like vitamins—while the aqueous solution is in another (the water or milk, salt, and emulsifying agent). The two parts are each premixed

in the right proportions, then blended together and pumped through a chilling machine. The mixture is cooled rapidly until it is cold but still liquid, then is allowed to rest until it is firm enough to be shaped in bars and wrapped.

If the margarine is destined either for 50-pound (22.7 kg) cans to be used in bakeries or for 1-pound (0.45 kg) tubs to be sold as "soft margarine," it is whipped. Another new form of margarine—which has no real counterpart to butter—is fluid margarine, produced according to a different oil formula and designed to be dispensed from a "squeeze" bottle.

Marine Biology

Since ancient times, man has been inspired and fascinated by the world below the surface of the ocean. Although archaeologists have found Assyrian bas-reliefs of men swimming underwater breathing through goatskin bellows and Leonardo da Vinci made sketches of diving lungs, it was not until the 17th century that the invention of the diving bell enabled man to spend more than a few minutes at a time underwater. One of the earliest, and still indisputable, findings of the relatively young science of marine biology—the study of life in the ocean—is that the sea is one of the most complex ecosystems in the Universe. The most recent deep-sea explorations, though, have yielded surprising discoveries that challenge not only long-standing theories regarding the conditions necessary for life on Earth, but also offer evidence that life here may not have begun in the shallows, as scientists have generally believed, but may well have its source in deep-sea vents located nearly 2 miles (3,000 m) beneath the surface.

Plumbing the Depths

The first diving suit to make it from the "drawing board" into the water required the diver to remain attached to his ship, from which his air supply was fed to him through a long rubber hose. Then, in the 1940s, Jacques Cousteau and Émile Gagnan developed the first SCUBA (self-contained underwater breathing apparatus), designed to allow the diver to go down without cables and to breathe with the minimal encumbrance of an air tank (which becomes weightless underwater) strapped to his back and the head of an air hose in his mouth. Cousteau and his crew knew that the scuba would revolutionize marine biology. Serendipity hastened to prove their point, however, for on one of their earliest expeditions, they discovered a school of monk seals supposedly extinct since 1690.

Though the invention of the scuba was a quantum leap for shallow-water biology, it does not permit divers to descend more than a few hundred feet. Auguste Piccard's 1948 invention of the bathyscaphe opened the ocean to a depth of nearly 5,000 feet (1,500 m). Much like an underwater dirigible, the bathyscaphe consists of a pressurized steel cabin, heavier than water, and a float, which is filled with fluid that is lighter than water, and thus can provide lifting power when the craft is underwater. The bathyscaphe descends beneath the surface when its ballast tanks are opened and the air therein is replaced by water.

World War II saw the invention of the two-man submarine, which served as a design model for the first series of diving saucers made in 1959. Resembling "flying saucers," the most advanced of these vehicles (now called submersibles) enables a biologist to work at 10,000 feet (3,000 m) below the ocean's surface.

Important as they are, the bathyscaphe and submersible allow biologists to work underwater for only limited periods of time. A series of "Conshelf" projects (so named because research/living stations were placed on the continental shelf) was directed by Jacques Cousteau during the 1960s and 1970s. Conshelf I, which took place in 1965, enabled two divers to live for a week at a depth of about 35 feet (11 m). By Conshelf II, six "oceanauts" could live for an even longer period of time at a depth of 369 feet (112.47 m). Not only were these scientists able to make the

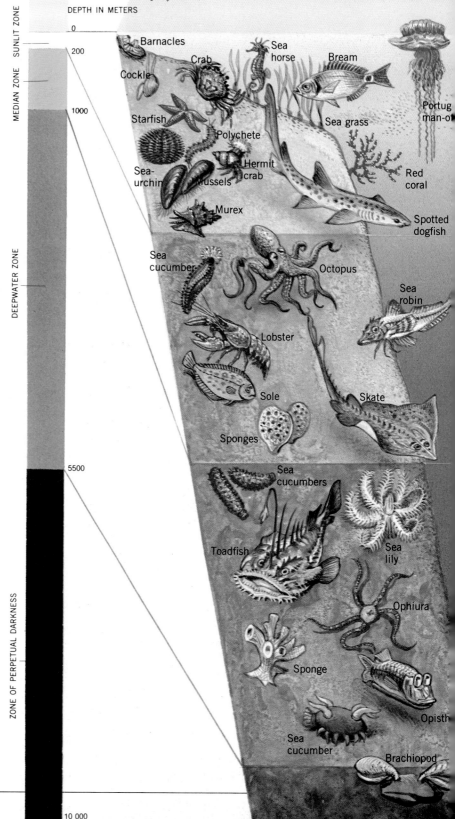

lengthiest observations of underwater life hitherto attempted, but they also were able to live comparatively normally—eating, sleeping, exercising, even playing chess. Since then, submersible design has been refined even further, and though these vehicles are very costly, they are nonetheless employed commercially, especially in the offshore oil industry.

The qualities of the ocean's waters at different depths determine the types of life at each level. The vast majority of all marine life exists relatively near the surface, where sunlight penetrates and the waters are rich with oxygen and nutrients. Below this layer there is no light. Nutrients are present in the form of decomposing elements drifting down from above and as living marine life. The forms of life in this zone of perpetual darkness have evolved strange shapes and capabilities: some even give off their own light, a phenomenon called bioluminescence. *Below:* Some of the marine creatures found at different depths of the ocean.

Jellyfish
Swordfish
Blue shark
Plankton
Anchovies
Remora
Tuna
Mackerel
Hammerhead shark
Squid
Dolphin
Sea turtle
Ribbon fish
Bonito
Giant squid
Toothed whale
Lantern fish
Shrimp
Vampire octopus
Tripod fish
Silver hatchetfish
Lantern fish
Viperfish
elanocete
Pennatulacea
Sea Lily

Life in the Depths

Documenting the distribution of life in the ocean and observing particular patterns of marine behavior constitute major provinces of marine biology. The 1981 American *Oasis* expedition, manned by scientists from the Scripps Institute of Oceanography, the Woods Hole Marine Biological Laboratory, and several major universities, proved to be a bellwether deep-sea exploration and a turning point not only for marine biology but also for allied disciplines as well. The *Oasis* crew was stationed at the East Pacific Rise (off the coast of California) 21°N of the equa-

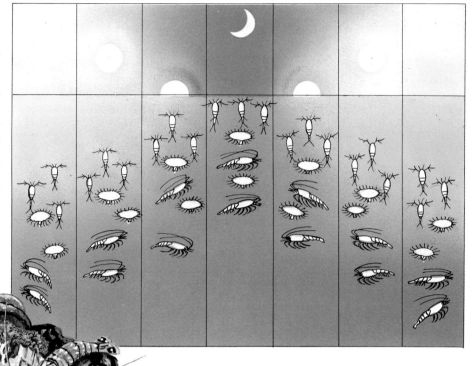

Left: Examples of bottom-dwelling marine life found in shallow tropical waters.

Above: Effect of the Sun on distribution of marine shrimp. During the middle of the day, the Sun's radiation is strong, so that light and heat reach deep into the ocean. The shrimp, which require warmth, can descend to greater depths. Conversely, at night, when the waters cool, the shrimp rise closer to the surface. Note that the immature shrimp always remain closer to the surface than the adults.

tor. Scientists who participated in the *Oasis* Expedition have described surface waters that were steely, harshly glaring, and apparently a fitting cover for vast stretches of eerily still, sparsely populated stretches along the bottom. The ocean surface, however, could not have been more deceiving. About 3,300 yards (3,000 m) below the surface, in vents fed on gases (hydrogen sulfide, primarily) emanating from a split in the earth's upper mantle, *Oasis* scientists turned up teeming colonies of giant clams, crabs, mussels, and worms, in addition to species that were hitherto unknown. This would have been surprise enough, but the vents have temperatures of up to 360°F. (182°C.) and pressures greater than 200 times that on the Earth's surface. Before this expedition, scientists believed that such temperatures were invariably lethal to life on Earth. Experts have concluded that the combination of high pressures and high temperature is a crucial factor for survival in the vents, for if the pressure were normal, the water would boil away into vapor.

The vents also contradict the classical notion that not only is temperature low at great depths, but food supply as well, with the result that deep-sea species have metabolic rates much slower than those of surface species. The *Oasis* team found that vent species respire, digest, excrete, and reproduce at rates comparable to those of animals in shallow waters. The explanation is that vent animals, unlike other marine species, do not rely on the bits of food that float downward from shallow waters, where photosynthesis is the driving life force. Rather, vent animals are chemosynthetic, which means that they use chemicals (in this case, hydrogen sulfide), as opposed to light, as the energy source in their production of usable organic compounds. When first advanced, this theory—logical though it seems—befuddled scientists even further, for hydrogen sulfide is a deadly poison to all organisms save those dwelling in the vents. Suspecting that vent species had evolved an adaptation that ensured the production of cytochrome oxidase (the enzyme that consumes oxygen in the metabolic process except in the presence of hydrogen sulfide), scientists began by isolating and studying this enzyme. Their bewilderment was compounded when they

found no such adaptation. Later experiments, however, revealed that vent species have a blood protein that regulates the travel of hydrogen sulfide through their systems. This protein—the only one known to perform in this manner—holds the sulfide until cytochrome oxidase has completed its work; it then releases the sulfide to the specific enzymes that utilize it. The presence of this blood protein has made scientists reevaluate their supposition that life on Earth began in the shallows and gradually moved to the depths. This theory seemed correct when predicated on the notion that light is the ultimate energy source of the Earth's food chain. The fact of chemosynthesis in the depths, however, has made scientists think that these vents may have been the "bed" of all life on this planet.

Sampling Ocean Life

Marine biologists do not do all their ocean-life studies underwater. Especially when they are studying tiny and microscopic animals and plants, they collect water samples and examine them in permanent laboratories either on shore or on shipboard. Several instruments have been designed specifically for taking samples from the ocean floor. One example is the Petersen Grab, a jawlike apparatus that is lowered, in the open position, from the ship to the ocean floor. When it hits bottom, the impact trips a closing catch, and the "mouth" shuts. Samples are strained and separated through a series of sieves of diminishing density before the grab is brought to the surface. Marine biologists also gather bottom samples with a dredge consisting of a mesh bag affixed to a rectangular frame, which has blades for overturning bottom sediment. Because dredges move slowly, they cannot be used to capture darting or quick-swimming organisms. For these, trawls (weighted nets hauled by boats) are used.

Nets are used closer to the surface to sample zooplankton, or tiny sea animals such as protozoa, worms, and primitive mollusks. These nets can be hauled either vertically or horizontally and can be closed at various depth intervals to enable scientists to determine the relative distribution of a given species.

Applications of Marine Biology

Life in the ocean greatly affects life on land. Since we rely on the sea as a food and energy source, we have an increased responsibility to its ecological integrity. Knowing the distribution of fish is important to the fishing industry as well as to biologists. A serious decline in a given fish population could signal overly zeal-

ous fishing activity or an influx of predators, which scientists could then attempt to eliminate to protect a valuable species. Marine biologists can also help to enlarge fishing areas by introducing species into regions that are rich in the nutrients they require. Observing the ways in which fish react to stimuli is helpful in developing new fishing tactics, lures, and traps.

Marine biologists are playing an increasingly active role in conservation and pollution control. Though wastes may be dumped far offshore, marine animals, through migration and food chains (the documentation of which is done by marine biologists), can return the pollutants to the very waters we need to protect.

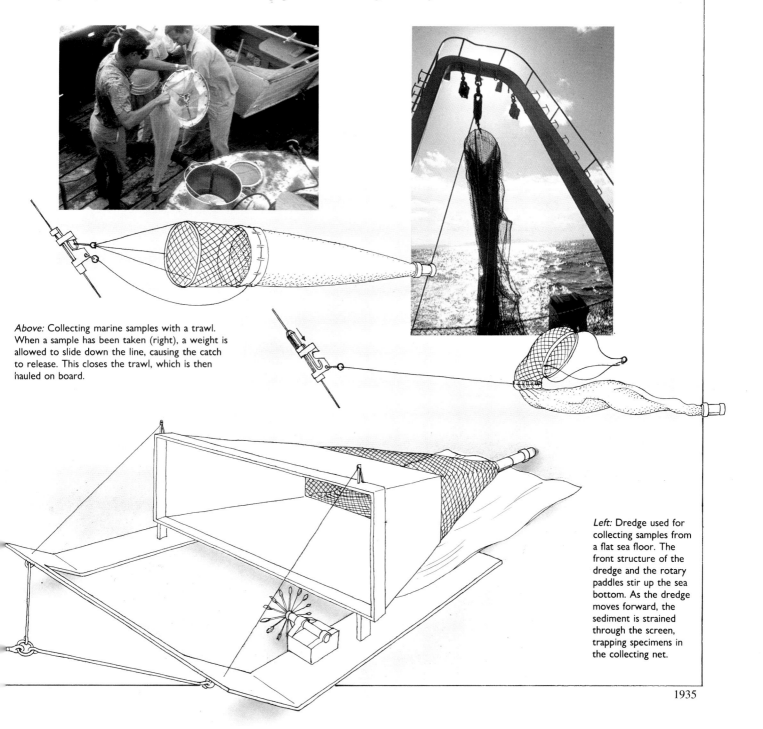

Above: Collecting marine samples with a trawl. When a sample has been taken (right), a weight is allowed to slide down the line, causing the catch to release. This closes the trawl, which is then hauled on board.

Left: Dredge used for collecting samples from a flat sea floor. The front structure of the dredge and the rotary paddles stir up the sea bottom. As the dredge moves forward, the sediment is strained through the screen, trapping specimens in the collecting net.

Mars

To ancient civilizations, it was the blood-red god of war. To author H. G. Wells, it was the home of macabre creatures intent on conquering Earth. To contemporary scientists, it is a place of planetwide dust storms, huge volcanoes, and canyons thousands of miles long.

It is the planet Mars, Earth's neighbor in space.

Mars and the Earth

Mars, the fourth planet from the Sun, has a highly elliptical orbit that brings it as close to the Sun as 128.4 million miles (206.7 million km) and as distant as 154.9 million miles (249.1 million km). The Martian year is about 687 Earth days, while the Martian day is only slightly longer than the days on our planet—24 hours and 37 minutes.

Mars is smaller than Earth, with a diameter of 4,210 miles (6,787 km), and only Mercury and Pluto are smaller. As a consequence, gravity on Mars is one third the intensity of gravity on Earth. This results in a very thin atmosphere—air pressure on the Martian surface is the equivalent of Earth's at an altitude of 15 miles (24 km). The sparse atmosphere makes Mars an extremely dry place and, combined with Mars' distance from the Sun, a very cold one as well. Though temperatures at the equator can reach 70°F. (21°C.) during the summer, the average surface temperature is 19°F. (−7°C.), and the lowest temperature recorded thus far on Mars was a bracing −275°F. (−175°C.).

Mars has two moons to Earth's one, but they are very tiny satellites indeed. Phobos measures about 14 miles (22 km) in diameter, and Deimos a mere 8 miles (13 km). Phobos orbits Mars in less than a third of one Martian day, resulting in a phenomenon unique in all the Solar System—from the surface of Mars, it seems to rise in the west and set in the east.

Mars and the Scientists

One of the seven planets visible to the naked eye, Mars has been known since antiquity, when its red hue earned it the name of the Roman god of war. It was often viewed as an ill omen.

For many centuries, it was believed that Mars and all the other planets circled the Earth (as did the Sun). But there was a problem—from time to time, Mars would seem to reverse direction as it moved against the unchanging background of the

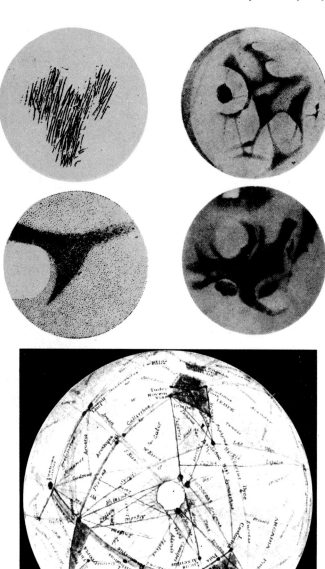

Left: Circles record the results of early telescopic observations of Mars, beginning with a sketch by the Dutch mathematician and astronomer Christian Huygens in 1659 (top left).

Below left: The confused details of the Martian planetary surface visible through early telescopes fueled speculation that the planet's surface might be covered by a network of canals. As shown in the antique map, these features were even given names.

Right: Artist's view of the surface of Mars. Though no human has yet set foot on the planet, it has been carefully studied by a series of sophisticated space probes. Those shown in the illustration are the Soviet Mars 3 and the U.S. Viking and Mariner 4 probes. The satellites visible in the background are Deimos and Phobos, the Martian moons.

stars. It wasn't until the 16th century that Polish astronomer Nicolaus Copernicus proposed that the planets, including the Earth and Mars, circled the Sun. The Earth, moving in a smaller and faster orbit, would periodically pass Mars and make it appear to reverse direction. This controversial theory was further refined by Johannes Kepler, who used observations of Mars compiled by Danish scientist Tycho Brahe to conclude that the orbits of the planets must be elliptical, not circular. Thus, the study of Mars played a central role in developing our understanding of the entire Solar System.

The refinement of the telescope in the 17th century changed Mars from a point of reddish light to an observable, if enigmatic, world. In 1659, the Dutch scientist and lensmaker Christian Huygens pro-

duced the first detailed drawings of the Martian surface. Huygens discovered such now familiar Martian landscapes as Syrtis Major, a dark, triangular region on the Martian equator, which we now know to be a giant plateau. By watching Syrtis Major, Huygens was able to clock the Martian day. He was also the first observer to note large white areas near the Martian poles.

In 1784, astronomer William Herschel suggested that these areas were polar ice caps. He also noted that these ice caps changed size during the year, indicating the existence of Martian seasons, and that there appeared to be clouds hovering over Mars, indicating an atmosphere.

In 1877, Earth and Mars were in their biannual "conjunction," when their orbits placed them directly opposite each other

in space, making for ideal observation. Italian astronomer Giovanni Schiaparelli reported seeing a network of thin lines crisscrossing the face of Mars. He dubbed them *canali,* which was translated as "canals" by English-speaking astronomers—and thus began a controversy that would last for decades.

In a series of books, the American Percival Lowell popularized the notion that these "canals" were built by a race of superengineers, who were attempting to distribute the water from the Martian polar caps across the entire planet. His ideas were challenged by many. Alfred Wallace (codiscoverer of the theory of evolution) believed that Mars was too cold and too dry to support any life at all. Many astronomers reported that they could not see any canals, and even those who did

Left: Cutaway view of Mars intended to show the planet's internal structure. The planetary core is thought to be composed of melted iron and iron sulfates. According to the model, the mantle of the planet is composed mainly of iron and magnesium silicates, while the crust is a thin layer of aluminum- and silicate-based minerals.

Below: The eroded appearance of some Martian surface features, like the canyon in the photograph, suggests that water may once have been plentiful on the planet.

Right: Artist's reconstruction of Mount Olympus, an enormous Martian volcano roughly 3 times as tall as Mount Everest.

Below right: Photograph taken on the surface of Mars by the Viking space probe. The reddish color of Martian rock is thought to indicate the presence of iron deposits.

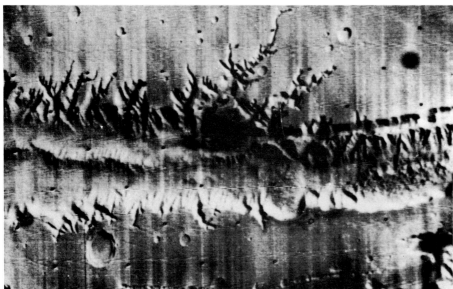

so drew such different maps of these canals that there was a growing suspicion that the canals were an optical illusion caused by the difficulties of looking at the red planet through Earth's atmosphere.

The mystery of the canals was not finally solved until the development of space exploration.

Mars and the Robot Explorers

By the time the United States and the Soviet Union began sending unmanned satellites to Mars during the 1960s, few scientists still believed in canals. But there remained a strong belief in the prospect of plant life, however primitive, on the Martian surface.

The first probes were not very encouraging. Mariner 4, which in 1965 became the first craft to complete a mission to Mars, flew past the planet and sent back 21 pictures of a cratered, Moonlike Mars without a trace of life or canals, and with an atmosphere even thinner than had been expected. The next three Mariner "fly-bys" confirmed this view. (Russian space efforts directed toward Mars were plagued by technical failures and returned little information of value.)

But Mariner 9, which went into orbit around Mars in 1971, showed that its predecessors had photographed only the least exciting portions of the planet. After a huge Martian dust storm subsided, Mariner 9 sent back photographs of volcanic mountains such as Olympus Mons, three times the height of Mount Everest; enormous canyons like Vallis Marinaris or Mariner Valley, 2,500 miles (4,000 km) long and 20,000 feet (6,100 m) deep—twisting features that many scientists believe are ancient, dried-up river beds.

There were still no signs of life. But the indications that Mars may have had rivers, perhaps even oceans, in former times still held out the hope that life may have established a foothold on the planet before today's harsh conditions set in.

Those hopes were more or less ended in 1976, when the United States landed two unmanned space craft on the surface of Mars. Viking I and II sent back awesome photographs of the red Martian landscape under pink skies, confirmed that the ice caps were made primarily of water (and not carbon dioxide, as some had

thought), and that there were only scant traces of oxygen in the atmosphere.

The three experiments on each craft designed to look for microscopic life gave results that were either ambiguous or negative, and most scientists no longer believe that there is any life on Mars. Some still hold out the possibility that life may exist in isolated locations or "microenvironments." If this is so, such discoveries must wait for future missions to the red planet, which is most likely the next world that will be visited by human beings and not merely their mechanical emissaries.

Marsupial

In many parts of the world, but especially Australia, Tasmania, and New Guinea, some of the animals are of a primitive order of mammals known as marsupials. Like other mammals, they are hair-bearing, breast-feeding, warm-blooded vertebrates. They differ principally in the way in which their young develop in the uterus. Placental mammals, which are the most prolific of all mammals, retain their young within the mother's womb, connected to it and nourished through an organ known as the placenta.

Marsupials do not have a placenta; there is little close connection between the mother's tissues and those of the growing fetus. Marsupial embryos get their food supply from their own surrounding yolk sacs, small organs that cannot support the unborn young for very long. Consequently, marsupials have very short gestation periods, ranging from 8 to 40 days. When its scanty food supply is all used up, the marsupial is born, at a stage of development parallel to that of a mature placental fetus.

The newly born marsupials are absolutely defenseless, and because they have had so few days to develop, they are quite minuscule. Needless to say, their fatality rate after birth is quite high. The 9-foot-tall (about 3 m) red kangaroo, for example, is just an inch (2.54 cm) long when it is born! Its mother licks a trail from her vagina to a flap of stomach skin called a pouch, which covers her nipples (mammary glands). If it is hardy enough, the

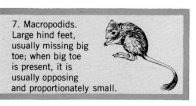

1. Marsupials. Mammals bearing live young; mammary glands contained in an abdominal pouch.

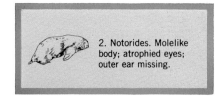

2. Notorides. Molelike body; atrophied eyes; outer ear missing.

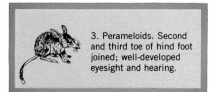

3. Perameloids. Second and third toe of hind foot joined; well-developed eyesight and hearing.

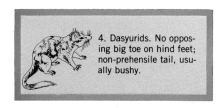

4. Dasyurids. No opposing big toe on hind feet; non-prehensile tail, usually bushy.

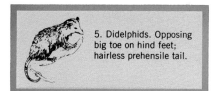

5. Didelphids. Opposing big toe on hind feet; hairless prehensile tail.

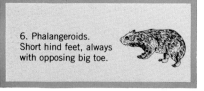

6. Phalangeroids. Short hind feet, always with opposing big toe.

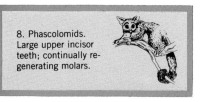

7. Macropodids. Large hind feet, usually missing big toe; when big toe is present, it is usually opposing and proportionately small.

8. Phascolomids. Large upper incisor teeth; continually regenerating molars.

Marsupials are divided into 7 major groups, as shown on the chart. *Below:* From left, marsupial mole, found in southern and western Australia; rabbit bandicoot, also found in southern and western Australia; and spot-tailed eastern kit, native to southeastern Australia and Tasmania. Drawings show distinctive features of each.

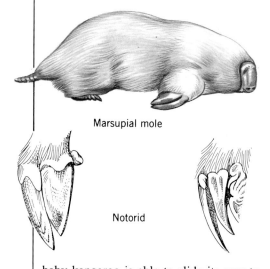

Marsupial mole

Notorid

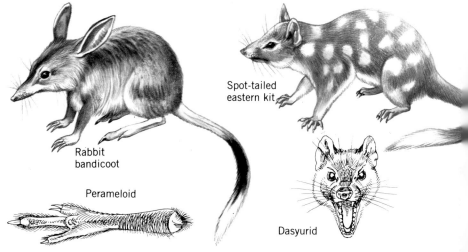

Rabbit bandicoot

Perameloid

Spot-tailed eastern kit

Dasyurid

baby kangaroo is able to slide its way to the pouch, crawl in, and attach its mouth firmly to a nipple. It will not let go for about 6 months; when the baby's head can stick out over the pouch, it is ready to hop along on its own.

While most marsupial females have pouches, a few—such as the South American rat opossum—lack them. These small rodentlike marsupials, which delight in hanging upside down, carry their young attached to their exposed nipples. The opossum family is one of only two marsupials in the Americas today.

Marsupial Characteristics

Marsupial body systems are basically the same as those of placental mammals. Their brains, however, are much smaller, and as a result, marsupials are relatively unintelligent mammals. Another predominant characteristic of marsupials is their large, sharp claws, handy for burrowing and climbing. The tail of a marsupial is also very important. Large creatures such as kangaroos and wallabies have huge, fat tails that serve as balancing mechanisms

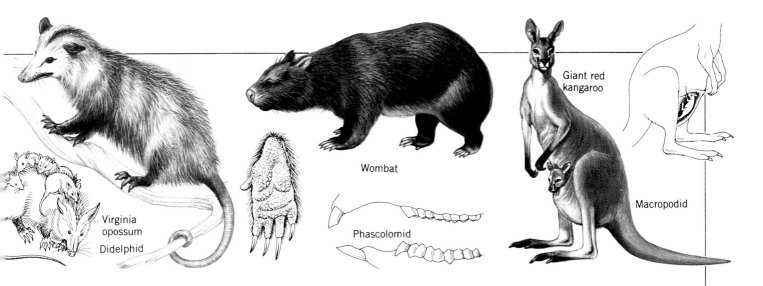

Giant red kangaroo

Wombat

Virginia opossum

Didelphid

Phascolomid

Macropodid

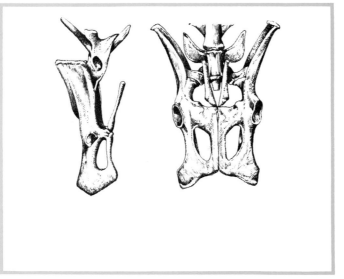

Above: From left, Virginia opossum, carrying her young on her back; Tasmanian wombat; and a giant red kangaroo, the most familiar of the marsupials. Note the baby kangaroo, called a joey, in the mother's pouch. Black-and-white drawings highlight distinctive features of each family.
Below: Koala bears.

The pelvis of marsupials has 2 spurs of bony cartilage not found in other mammals. These bones extend forward from the pelvic bone and help to protect the young in the pouch.

for their heavy bodies when they hop. Smaller, arboreal marsupials often have prehensile, or grasping, tails by which they can hang.

Most marsupials are herbivorous (plant-eating) animals. But occasionally they have adapted to an omnivorous diet, eating small birds and insects as well as plants when the vegetation is seasonally low.

While marsupials now comprise less than 5 percent of the entire mammalian population, scientists believe that they were once as plentiful as the placentals. Because of the high fatality rate inherent in their means of reproduction, they probably ceased to exist wherever they lived in competition with placental mammals. Eons ago, marsupials were abundant in North America and Europe, where they are now virtually extinct, except for the opossum. Scientists speculate that few placentals developed in Australia and because of this, marsupials continued to flourish there, isolated and protected.

There are about 240 species of marsupials—quite a variety, considering their limited geographical distribution. They can be as small as the pint-sized shrew or as large as the 200-pound (90-kg) red kangaroo. One of the most popular marsupials, the sleepy-looking koala bear, has one of the most finicky appetites known to the mammalian world. These shy Australian tree dwellers feast solely on the leaves of a particular species of eucalyptus tree and would rather starve than eat anything else.

Mass

Imagine a space capsule far out in space, among the stars, where any gravitational fields are extremely weak. The astronauts inside the capsule are able to float in midair, send small objects to each other across the room with light taps, and propel themselves about by simply pushing with their hands. These antics show that weight is not a permanent attribute of an object. An object that weighs a certain amount on Earth will weigh significantly less on the Moon, where the gravitational force is only about one-sixth as strong. And the object will weigh almost nothing at all in the near zero-gravity conditions of our space capsule, far from any celestial body. This is because weight is determined by gravitational force.

Yet, such objects, as well as the astronauts themselves, still contain the same amount of matter. The matter, known as mass, still offers inertia, or resistance to being moved, if it is motionless, and resistance to being stopped if it is in motion. While it is an easy matter for astronauts to set pencils and other small objects in motion, it requires somewhat more force to set more massive objects, including themselves, in motion. When the first space station is under construction, powered machinery will be needed to move some of the apparently weightless but still massive girders about.

How Mass Is Measured

There are two ways of measuring the mass of an object. One is to measure it on a simple balance, of the kind that statues of Justice traditionally carry, to see how it compares with other masses. Just as a standard unit of length must be chosen for a measuring stick, so must a standard mass be chosen for such a balance. By international agreement, the standard mass is called a kilogram, and the standard kilogram mass is a platinum-iridium cylinder kept at Sèvres, France. Other units of mass are defined with respect to this one; a pound, for instance, is 453.592 grams. The mass of an object measured this way is called its gravitational mass.

When the mass of an object is measured by how much resistance it offers to changing its motion, it is called the inertial mass. Newton and other scientists of his time realized that the inertial mass and the gravitational mass of an object were proportional, and no basic differences between them could be found. It was left to Albert Einstein, in the 20th century, to prove that gravitational mass and inertial mass are identical.

Mass-Energy

Until the work of Einstein, scientists considered mass and energy to be distinct, which indeed seems to be confirmed by experience. The energy expended in throwing a stone or in driving an automobile does not seem to make these objects more massive in any way. In 1905, however Einstein concluded that under certain conditions mass is converted into energy, and vice versa, and that the relation governing these conversions is given by the equation $E = mc^2$ (energy equals mass times the speed of light squared). Mass and energy, in other words, are different aspects of the same thing, called mass-energy.

The connection between mass and energy is more apparent when objects travel at high speeds. The higher their energy of motion, the more mass they acquire and the harder it is to change their motion. For this reason, scientists distinguish between an object's rest mass, or mass at zero velocity, and an object's relativistic mass, or mass while in motion. The interconversion of mass and energy can be observed in particle accelerators, where tiny particles are converted into energy and vice versa. Particle physicists often refer to a particle by its energy—the energy equivalent of its rest mass—rather than its mass. Mass, once considered by scientists to be unchangeable and eternal, is now known to be one aspect of a more general entity called mass-energy.

See also PARTICLE PHYSICS; RELATIVITY (SPECIAL AND GENERAL THEORY).

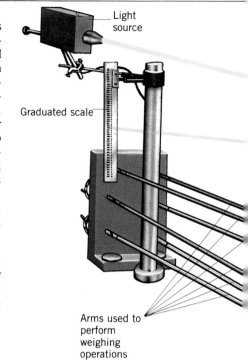

Light source

Graduated scale

Arms used to perform weighing operations

Below: Table of the relative gravity on planets in the Solar System in relation to that of Earth (Earth = 1) and the weight of a person on that planet (weight on Earth = 155 pounds, or 70 kg.). Only weight varies; mass remains the same.

Planet	Gravity	Wt. on Earth (Kg)	Wt. on Planet (Kg)
Sun	27.9	70	19.53
Mercury	0.37	70	25.9
Venus	0.88	70	61.6
Mars	0.38	70	26.6
Jupiter	2.6	70	182
Saturn	1.15	70	80.5
Uranus	1.17	70	81.9
Neptune	1.18	70	82.6
Pluto	0.5	70	35
Moon	0.16	70	11.2

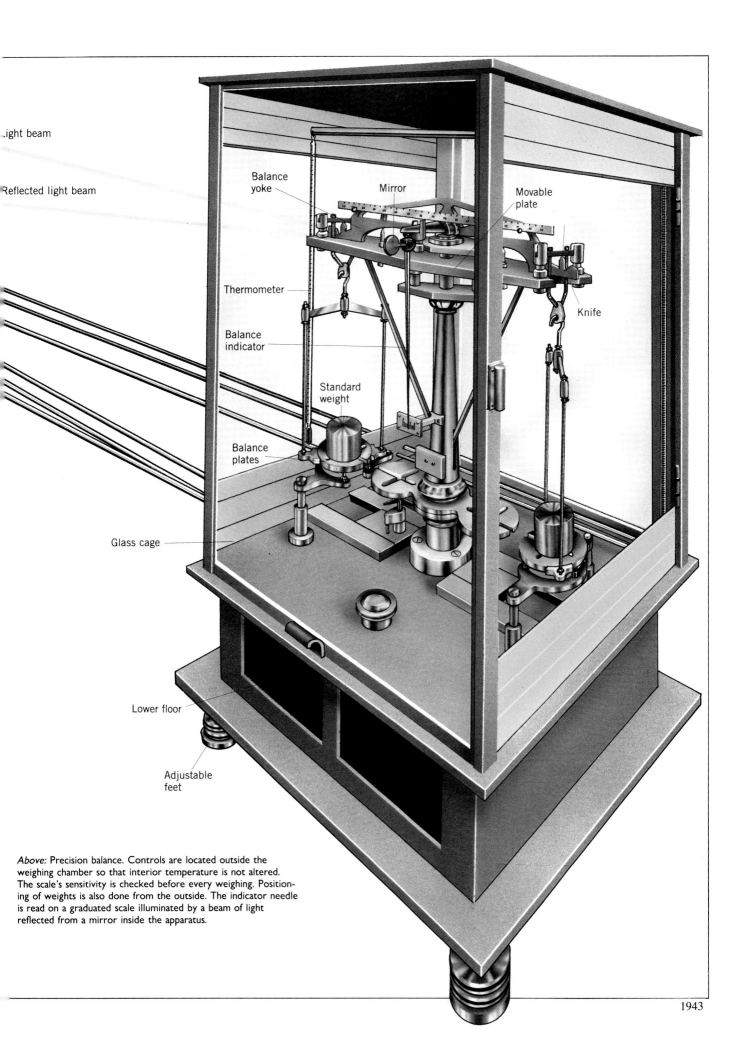

Light beam

Reflected light beam

Balance yoke

Mirror

Movable plate

Thermometer

Knife

Balance indicator

Standard weight

Balance plates

Glass cage

Lower floor

Adjustable feet

Above: Precision balance. Controls are located outside the weighing chamber so that interior temperature is not altered. The scale's sensitivity is checked before every weighing. Positioning of weights is also done from the outside. The indicator needle is read on a graduated scale illuminated by a beam of light reflected from a mirror inside the apparatus.

Mathematics

Mathematics is of key importance to most aspects of modern life. In such diverse fields as operations research and animal husbandry, mathematical techniques are used in the operation and control of complex systems. Mathematics, in fact, has often been called the language of science. It is not unusual for a scientist to ask a mathematical colleague to provide techniques that manipulate data in a desired way. For example, this was often the case in the very difficult evolution of quantum theory.

Of course, mathematicians are free to pursue their research far past the point at which it is useful to the scientist. And sometimes scientists find that the "language" they need to express new theories was formulated years before, by mathematicians who gave no thought to how their findings might be applied. For instance, in his theory of relativity, Einstein made use of an obscure branch of mathematics called tensor calculus, developed about 5 years earlier by G. Ricci and Tullio Levi-Civita.

Thus, mathematics has a dual nature. Although it can be usefully applied to the world, in essence it is independent. At its most fundamental level, the work of mathematicians is complete in and of itself. For this reason, in this article we will not examine what is done with mathematics, but, rather, what mathematicians do.

At large universities, there are dozens of courses offered by departments of mathematics—testimony to the great diversity of subjects that come under the general heading of mathematics. Although the divisions are by no means firm, we can, for the sake of convenience, divide the wealth of mathematical knowledge into three broad areas: geometry, algebra, and analysis.

Geometry

Geometry may have been born from attempts to fix boundaries for plots of land. The idea of a straight line, for example, might have sprung from ropes stretched between two stakes. The ancient Greeks realized the necessity of treating such concepts as line and point in an abstract way—as idealizations never to be found in actual objects. Thus, geometry became a system of reasoning about these abstract concepts. A summary of ancient Greek geometrical knowledge was made by Euclid in the 3rd century B.C. For centuries, Euclid's seemed to be the only possible geometry, the perfect theory of space.

In the early 19th century, however, N. I. Lobachevsky and J. Bolyai independently introduced non-Euclidean geometry, a subject that had also been explored

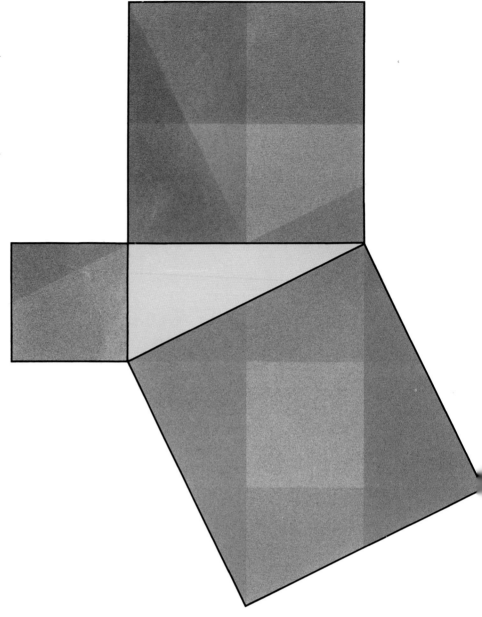

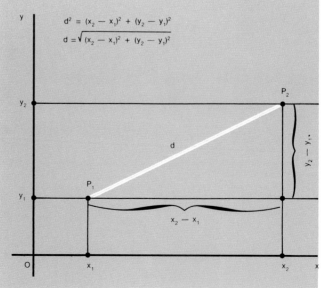

$$d^2 = (x_2 - x_1)^2 + (y_2 - y_1)^2$$
$$d = \sqrt{(x_2 - x_1)^2 + (y_2 - y_1)^2}$$

The Pythagorean theorem states that the square constructed on the hypoteneuse of a right triangle is equal in area to the sum of the squares constructed on the other 2 sides. Versions of the diagram above have been offered as proof of the theorem since the 6th century B.C., when it was introduced.

The use of x and y coordinates to define points in a geometrical figure was a product of the 16th century and is the bridge that links geometry—the study of forms in space—with algebra, which studies equations defining numerical functions. *Left:* Graph shows how a line, which is a basic geometrical element, can be described as an algebraic function.

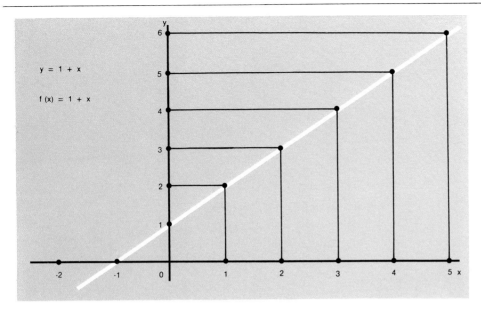

$$y = 1 + x$$

$$f(x) = 1 + x$$

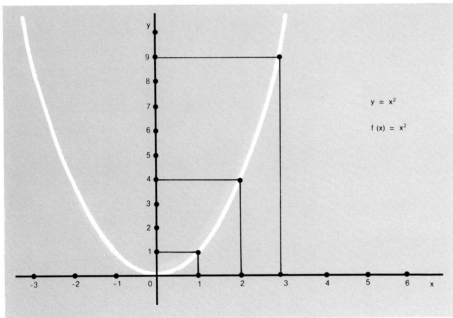

$$y = x^2$$

$$f(x) = x^2$$

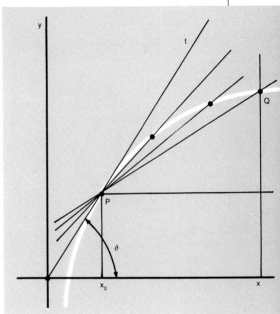

by the great mathematician Karl F. Gauss. By questioning one of Euclid's most basic assumptions—that a given line has one and only one parallel line through a given point not on the given line—these thinkers produced a very different system of abstract reasoning about points and lines. Taken as a description of the space we know, non-Euclidean geometry seems quite bizarre. The discoveries of 20th-century physics, however, have shown that it provides useful descriptions of very large as well as very small regions of space.

Algebra

Whereas geometry deals with points and lines, arithmetic deals with numbers. But if a simple arithmetic statement like 8 + 12 = 20 is not very interesting, it is in part because it is utterly specific. Algebra is concerned with equations—statements

The application of algebra to geometry by mathematicians like Fermat and Descartes enormously increased the power of mathematical abstractions to describe space. *Top:* Application of the Cartesian system, defining points on a line from the values of *x* and *y* coordinates.

Above: A parabola and the algebraic functions that describe its form. The curve in the chart at right typifies the use of differential calculus to describe the rate at which one variable changes with respect to another.

Right: Graphs of the assumptions underlying different systems of integral calculus—methods of calculation by successive approximation—developed by the French mathematician Augustin Cauchy and the German Georg Friedrich Riemann in the mid-19th century.

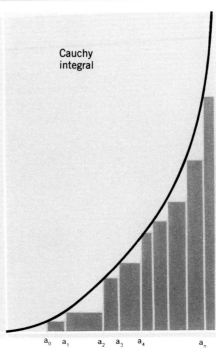

Cauchy integral

Riemann integral

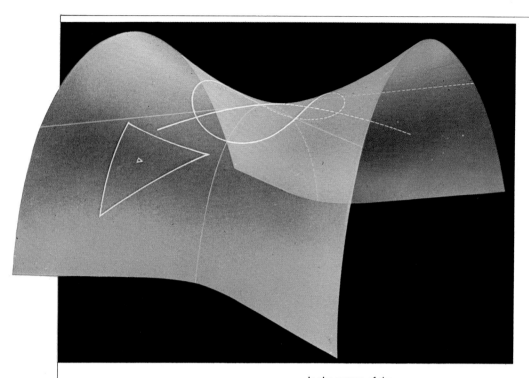

bers on the y counter are changing. In fact, for our given function, the speed of the changes in y will increase as x gets higher. We can then ask what is the rate of this change in the speed of the y counter.

To solve problems like these, we need the calculus, which was pioneered independently by Isaac Newton and G. W. Leibniz. Newton was working on a technique for calculating the velocity and acceleration of physical bodies, whose motions were expressed by making their location a function of time. The calculus has two main branches, differential and integral. Differential calculus takes a given function and calculates the rate at which one variable changes with respect to another. Integral calculus is the inverse of differential calculus—it takes a given rate of change of one variable with respect to another and determines the function that holds between them.

Integral calculus can also be used to calculate areas. It does this, in effect, by

that two things are equal—which have a high degree of generality, e.g., $ax + b = 20$. Here, a and b are called constants, and x is called a variable. The constants can be given any value we choose—their values are said to be known. But since the value of the variable depends on the values of the constants, we say that its value is unknown, at least until we solve the algebraic equation.

In the present example, if we say that $a = 4$ and $b = 12$, we get $4x + 12 = 20$; thus, $x = 2$. Algebra as a science is less concerned with solving specific equations than with developing techniques for solving equations that fit the same pattern. A more interesting algebraic result is the solution to the generalized equation $ax^2 + bx + c = 0$, whose solutions (called roots) are

$$x = \frac{-b + \sqrt{b^2 - 4ac}}{2a}$$

and

$$x = \frac{-b - \sqrt{b^2 - 4ac}}{2a}$$

One of the most important results in algebra is found in the work of Évariste Galois, who showed that there are no general solutions for equations involving a factor raised to higher than the fourth power (x^4, or $x \cdot x \cdot x \cdot x$, which, if $x = 2$, would equal 16).

Analysis

Some equations involve two (or more) variables. When one variable is defined in terms of the other—e.g., $y = 2x^2 + 4x + 3$—the equation is said to express a

In the course of the 19th century, different non-Euclidean geometries were developed by devising substitutes for Euclid's postulate that a given line has only one parallel through a given point not on the line. By postulating that the number of parallels may be infinitely large or that there may be none, there arose 2 new geometries, hyperbolic and elliptical. These geometries describe space in a different manner, as in the hyperbolic saddle above and on the surface of the sphere at right, on which no straight line can have a parallel.

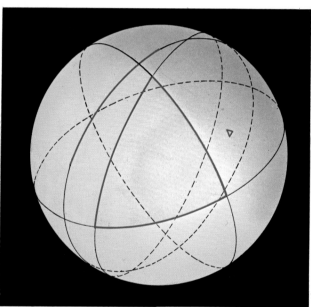

function; here we say that y is a function of x. Analysis is the branch of mathematics that studies the properties of functions. Analysis grew out of the calculus, which remains its best-known technique. We can come to understand the calculus by working with our given function.

Imagine that we have a machine that, when we put in a value for x, shows us the corresponding value for y. As we change x, the machine shows us the change in y. Thus, if we start with $x = 1$, the y counter will show, say, 9, and if we change x to 2, the y counter will move to 19. Let us say we increase x by one whole number each second. We might wonder, at any given moment, how fast the num-

adding together an infinite number of infinitely thin slices of the area (equivalent techniques are used to find lengths and volumes). This process involves what is called finding the limit of a sum. It was Leibniz who first concentrated on deducing the limits of sums by inverting the differential calculus.

Study of Abstract Structure

There are, of course, many other areas of mathematics, from the theory of numbers to probability and statistics. The question quite naturally arises, What makes all these things mathematics? Perhaps the most basic answer is that, at bottom, mathematics is concerned with the

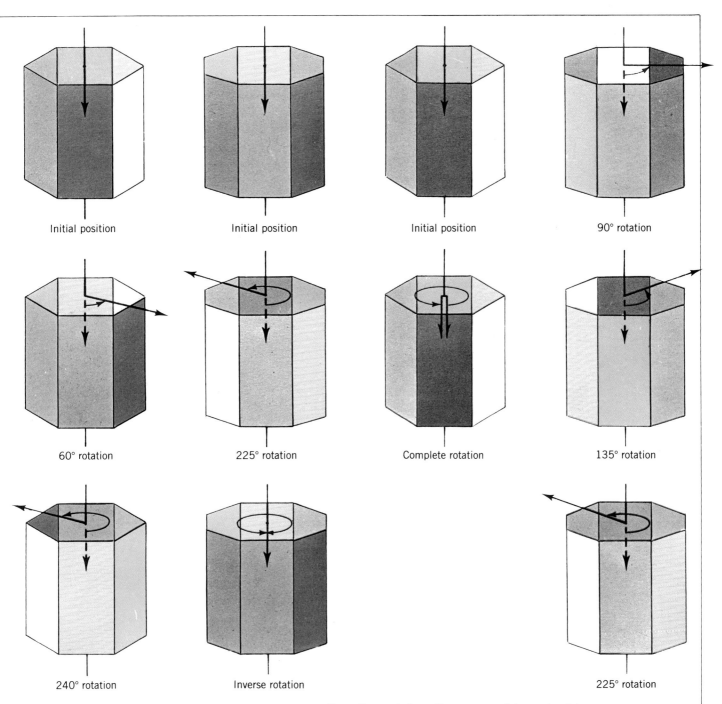

Initial position

Initial position

Initial position

90° rotation

60° rotation

225° rotation

Complete rotation

135° rotation

240° rotation

Inverse rotation

225° rotation

behavior and properties of abstract struc-tures. That is, mathematics can be said to study what happens when we have a col-lection of objects and a set of rules that relate the objects to one another. What in-terests the mathematician is the patterns in their relationships, as defined by rules that have been formulated by some of the greatest minds the world has ever known.

Above: Geometric forms illustrate some of the aspects of the theory of sets. The group is defined by a function that satisfies 3 requirements: the operation of the function on 2 elements of the set yield the value of a third element; there is a neutral element that, applied to another element, does not change its value; and each element has an inverse that, applied to the first, yields the neutral value. The rotation of the solids above illustrates this principle. The neutral value is 0° or 360°; that is, either a com-plete rotation of the form, which leaves its position unaltered, or no rotation at all. These alternatives have the same value.

Matter

"So poor is nature with all her craft," wrote Ralph Waldo Emerson, "that, from the beginning to the end of the Universe, she has but one stuff...to serve up all her dream-like variety. Compound it how she will—star, sand, fire, water, tree, man— it is still one stuff and betrays the same properties."

That "one stuff" is matter. The word comes from the Latin *materia* (related to *mater,* "mother"), meaning the stuff out of which something is made. Matter, then, is the building material of nature. It does not have to be made or produced, but is that from which everything else was, is, or ever will be produced.

The Nature of "Matter"

Although the concept of matter—the unalterable and simple substance that underlies all the change and variety of nature—seems at first glance to be self-evident, nothing could be further from the truth. Few concepts have undergone as much development and change as has "matter." Nearly all the assumptions that scientists took for granted about matter a mere 200 years ago, for instance—such as that it is unrelated to energy, or that the position of a tiny piece of matter can be determined with complete precision—today are known to be inaccurate. Basic questions about it have been hotly debated ever since the 6th and 5th centuries B.C., when the first Greek philosophers and scientists put forth various theories about the underlying nature of matter. Empedocles, for example, argued that earth, air, fire, and water make up all the familiar substances.

One such question, for instance, is whether matter can be divided again and again forever, or consists instead of certain basic units of matter, called atoms, which cannot be further divided (*atom* in Greek means "uncuttable"). The ancient Greek philosopher Anaxagoras maintained the first view, while Leucippus and Democritus held the second. Ever since then, philosophers and scientists have been found to argue both positions. The German philosopher Immanual Kant discussed this question at length and even claimed that it was possible to prove both that matter can be divisible infinitely and that the process of division must come to an end somewhere. Kant believed that this antimony, or inevitable contradiction, was the result of the limitations upon ordinary human reason, which was not capable of solving a problem pertaining to the realm of extremely tiny dimensions.

At the very beginning of the 19th century, the English chemist John Dalton re-

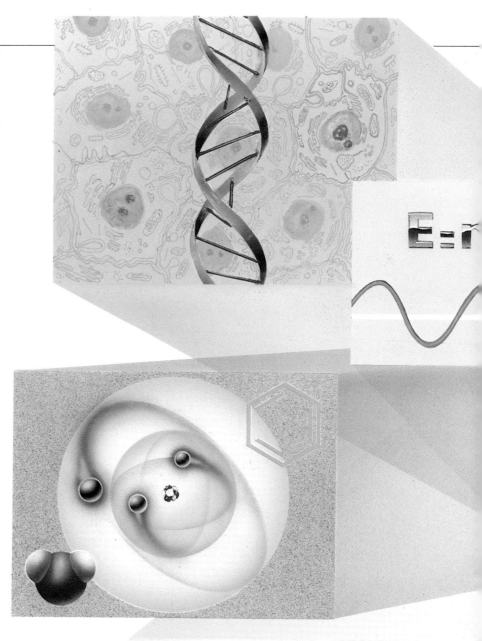

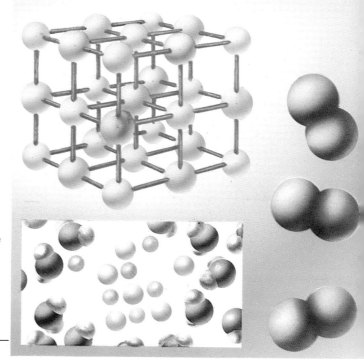

The nature of matter is, in a certain sense, the primary question that stands behind all scientific study. The illustrations on these 2 pages—which recall fields of research as diverse as genetics (with the double helix of the DNA molecule), theoretical physics (with Einstein's famous formula $E = mc^2$), astronomy, chemistry, and crystallography—point up the importance of a definition of matter as the basis of all concrete existence.

2

PHYSICAL PROPERTIES OF MATTER	
Mechanical	Density, ductility, hardness, compressibility, fragility, deformability, plasticity, elasticity, cohesion, viscosity, surface tension, porosity
Thermic	Specific heat, latent melting and boiling heat, caloric capacity, vapor tension, melting and boiling points, thermal conductivity, coefficient of thermal expansion, volatility
Electric	Conductivity, dielectric constant, polarity, thermionic effect, thermoelectric effect, ionizability
Magnetic	Paramagnetism, dimagnetism, ferromagnetism
Optical	Transparency, opalescence, refractivity, absorbance, luminescence, phosphorescence, fluorescence, photosensitivity, color
Radioactive	Half-life, decay constant, atomic activity

vived the view of Leucippus and Democritus in his attempts to explain chemical reactions, claiming that all matter was, in fact, composed of atoms. Since then, scientists have discovered that atoms themselves, far from being uncuttable, are composed of more elementary parts called particles, whose behavior is very different from that of objects with which we are familiar. Particles, in turn, may or may not be further divisible. (The story of how these particles behave is part of quantum mechanics.)

Matter Larger than Atoms

Although they are not the smallest bit of matter, atoms are nonetheless the basic building blocks of nature. There is no such thing as a piece of an element smaller than an atom of that element.

A basic type of atom, or the matter made of it, is called an element. there are 90 elements found in nature; about 16 more have been artificially created in laboratories. Atoms may link together in groups called molecules. Nearly all the matter around us consists of molecules. Water, for instance, is composed of molecules containing one oxygen atom and two hydrogen atoms. Small molecules have only a few atoms each; huge molecules called polymers may contain hundreds of thousands of atoms. A single molecule is extremely tiny; even the tiniest speck of dust that can be seen by the human eye contains many millions of them. A teaspoon of water contains more molecules than the Atlantic Ocean contains teaspoons of water.

The atoms and molecules in matter are in perpetual motion. In solids, they move about fixed positions, the way the tip of a slender reed may move in a slight breeze this way and that, yet always remain about the same place. In a solid, the fixed positions of atoms are found in regular patterns. A material whose atoms are located in regular patterns is called a crystal. Nearly all solids—even sand, rocks, and mountain ranges—are composed of crystals. While the crystal pattern of diamonds extends over distances large enough to see, the crystal pattern of most solids is broken and irregular, like jigsaw puzzle pieces in a pile. Noncrystalline solids are said to be amorphous.

The molecules in a liquid or gas are not located in fixed positions. They are free to wander about. In a liquid, the molecules exert an attractive force on each other, so that they remain close together as they wander about. In a gas, there is almost no such attraction, and the molecules fly about independently. The study of the behavior of matter in the form of

liquids and gases is called fluid physics. Most materials can exist as solids, liquids, or gases; these are known as phases or states of matter.

Many common types of matter, called colloids, consist of combinations of matter in different states. Sols, such as paint, and silt suspended in water, are both solids contained in liquids. Solid sols, such as colored gems, are mixtures of solids. Foams are gases suspended in liquids. Emulsions, such as milk, butter, and mayonnaise, consist of one type of liquid suspended in another; liquids dispersed in solids, such as jellies, are known as solid emulsions. Solids suspended in gases, such as smoke, are called solid aerosols, while liquids suspended in gases, such as clouds and fogs, are called liquid aerosols. Pumice is an example of a gas dispersed throughout a solid. Matter whose composition is uniform throughout is said to be homogeneous, while colloids and other matter whose composition is not uniform are said to be heterogeneous.

The structure of living matter is more complicated. The basic unit of living matter is the cell; the cell is the "atom" of biology. While some forms of life consist of only one cell, others consist of many

cells working together in larger groups, such as fibers and tissues. Each cell consists of a cell wall and a fluid inside it called protoplasm; each of these, in turn, is composed of molecules.

Matter Smaller than Atoms

Every atom is made up of three basic types of particles. Tiny, negatively charged particles, called electrons, whirl about a much more massive nucleus composed of positively charged particles, called protons, and neutrons, which have no charge. Nearly all the mass of an atom is concentrated in the nucleus, despite its small size. If an atom were expanded to the size of an auditorium, the nucleus would be the size of a tiny speck at the center. Most of the atom—and therefore most of matter—consists of empty space.

There are many other particles of matter besides the proton, neutron, and electron, which appear during radioactivity or during the nuclear processes that occur in the heart of the Sun. Particles are roughly divided into two broad classes—leptons (light particles), which include the electron, and hadrons (heavy particles), which include the proton and the neutron. (The

PHYSICAL THEORIES OF MATTER

RELATIVITY
MATTER = ENERGY

QUANTUM MECHANICS
MATTER = WAVE FORM

DIRAC EQUATION
ANTIMATTER

photon—the particle of light—is in a class by itself.) Hadrons, in turn, are composed of particles called quarks.

Properties of Matter

Every body of matter has a number of properties, both general and specific. The amount of space a body occupies is called its volume. The amount of matter in a body—always the same for the same body—is referred to as its mass. The mass per unit volume is called the density. Dependent upon mass is the weight of a body, which is the force of attraction between it and the Earth; this force is not constant, however, for it varies with the distance between the two, and a body will tip the scales with different weights on different planets. Every body resists to some degree any push or pull exerted on it; this resistance, called inertia, depends on the mass of the body.

The specific properties of matter are the result of its internal structure. These include hardness, for instance; when one substance can scratch another, it is said to have a greater hardness. Diamond is the hardest type of matter known, for it can scratch all other types of matter. Elastic bodies are those that have a tendency to resume their original shape after a force has been exerted on them and removed; steel wire and rubber are very elastic, whereas putty is not. The tenacity of a body of matter is its ability to resist being pulled apart. Steel has a high tenacity per unit area (or tensile strength); a piece of cake does not. If a body can be pounded into thin sheets, like gold or aluminum, it is said to be malleable; if it can be drawn into thin wires, it is said to be ductile. Other specific properties of matter include porosity (the ability of a body to allow another substance to pass through it) and the ability to conduct heat and electricity.

Matter, Energy, Waves

Until this century, it was believed that matter and energy were distinct things. Matter was anything that had mass and extension (volume), whereas energy was anything that caused changes in matter. Matter came in particles, energy in waves. A substance was either one or the other. Stones and trees were forms of matter; light, magnetism, and heat were forms of energy. Each class obeyed its own law, either the law of conservation of mass or the law of conservation of energy.

The work of 20th-century physicists has shown, however, that the boundary is not so clear after all. In 1905, Albert Einstein showed that matter and energy may be converted into each other under certain conditions, the conversion factor pro-

Left: Relationship among the principal theories that describe the nature of matter. The oldest of those shown is the special theory of relativity, which denies the distinction between matter and energy, paving the way for the other formulations.

Attempts to identify the smallest indivisible building block of matter have led to the creation of the field of particle physics. *Below:* Chart of the relationships among the different forms of known matter in terms of their particle structure.

STRUCTURE OF MATTER

MOLECULE

ATOM

HADRON, PROTON, NEUTRON

SUBATOMIC PARTICLES

LEPTON, ELECTRON, MUON, NEUTRINO

QUARK

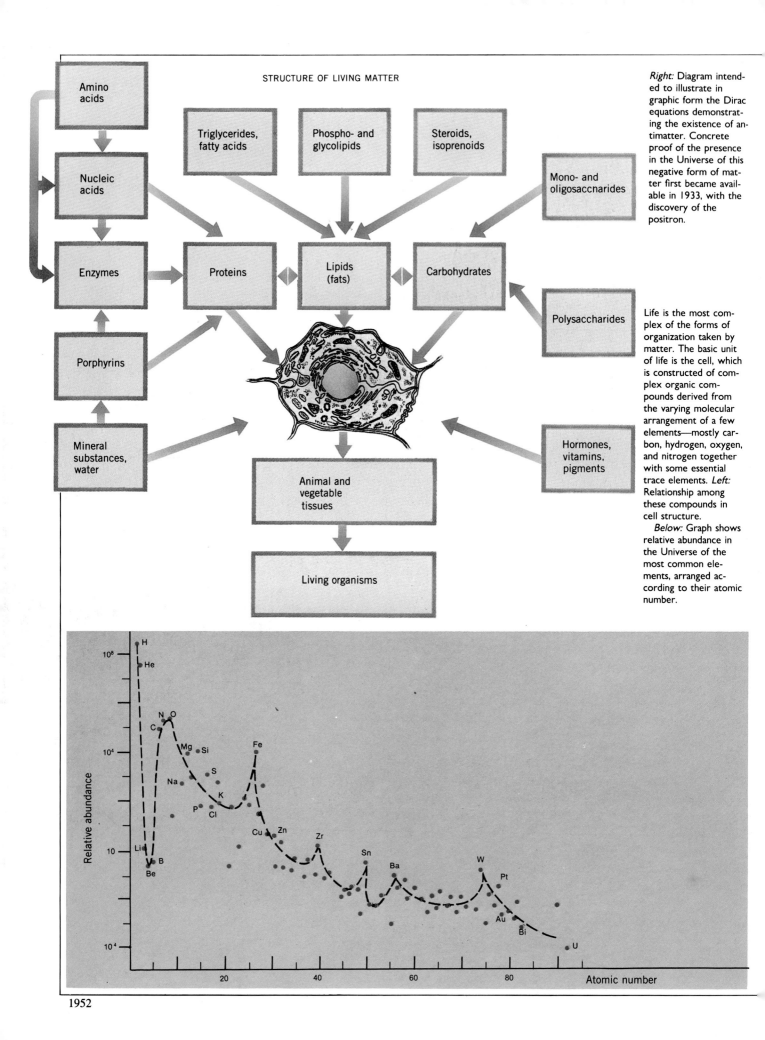

STRUCTURE OF LIVING MATTER

Amino acids

Nucleic acids

Triglycerides, fatty acids

Phospho- and glycolipids

Steroids, isoprenoids

Mono- and oligosaccnarides

Enzymes

Proteins

Lipids (fats)

Carbohydrates

Polysaccharides

Porphyrins

Hormones, vitamins, pigments

Mineral substances, water

Animal and vegetable tissues

Living organisms

Right: Diagram intended to illustrate in graphic form the Dirac equations demonstrating the existence of antimatter. Concrete proof of the presence in the Universe of this negative form of matter first became available in 1933, with the discovery of the positron.

Life is the most complex of the forms of organization taken by matter. The basic unit of life is the cell, which is constructed of complex organic compounds derived from the varying molecular arrangement of a few elements—mostly carbon, hydrogen, oxygen, and nitrogen together with some essential trace elements. *Left:* Relationship among these compounds in cell structure.

Below: Graph shows relative abundance in the Universe of the most common elements, arranged according to their atomic number.

1952

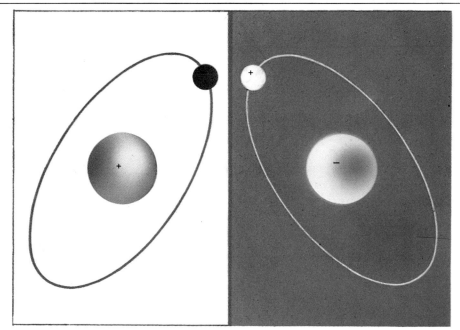

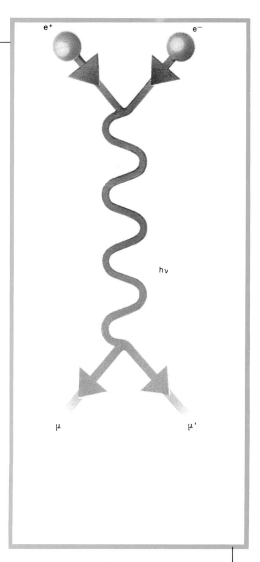

vided by the formula $E = mc^2$. Furthermore, Einstein showed that a given amount of energy could be thought of as having a certain mass. In 1925, the French physicist Louis de Broglie took Einstein's work one step farther. He proposed that each bit of matter should have its own wave, just as a bundle of energy has, and within 2 years the existence of electron waves was demonstrated. Everything in the Universe is therefore simultaneously both matter and energy.

Antimatter

Each subatomic particle has a set of properties, including electric charge, mass, and spin. For each particle of a given mass, spin, etc., there is another with the identical properties but with the opposite electric charge. Such a particle is called an antiparticle; when a particle and its antiparticle collide, the two annihilate each other, transforming both of their masses into energy. (Some uncharged particles, such as the neutron, also have antiparticles; for them, the property that is opposite is a complex one known as baryon number.)

Our world is made of matter; should antiparticles be created, as they are in certain nuclear reactions, they will rapidly encounter their counterparts and vanish in a blaze of energy. If left alone, however, antiparticles are as stable as particles, and antielectrons (positrons), antiprotons, and antineutrons could form antiatoms. Antiatoms, in turn, could combine to form antimolecules and larger units of antimatter—perhaps even antiworlds as large as our own. How much antimatter there is in the Universe is a mystery.

Right: Annihilation of an electron-positron in a collision with its antimatter equivalent. According to the Dirac equations, the collision results in the emission of a photon with energy equal to the sum of the energies of the incident particles. In some circumstances, such a photon decays to form two new particles.

Where Matter Is, and How Much

The matter in the Universe is found in celestial bodies—mostly stars, but here and there a planet, comet, or meteor—as well as in the thin interstellar matter scattered between. The matter in an ordinary star, such as our Sun, has a mass of about 4×10^{30} pounds (1.8×10^{30} kg). Our Galaxy alone contains around 100,000 million stars, so that the amount of matter in it has a mass of about 4×10^{41} pounds (1.8×10^{41} kg). There are 100,000 million galaxies thought to exist in the known Universe, making the amount of matter in its stars and galaxies about 4×10^{52} pounds (1.8×10^{52} kg).

Galaxies comprise only 0.1 percent of all space in the Universe. Scattered sparsely in between is a dust called interstellar matter, consisting of hydrogen and helium nuclei and occasionally nuclei of heavier elements. There is estimated to be about 123×10^{53} pounds (56×10^{53} kg) of it, meaning that the amount of interstellar matter exceeds the amount of matter in all of the galaxies of the Universe.

Matter and "Matter"

The instruments of 20th-century physicists reveal that, within the world of the atom, matter can change into energy, energy into matter, and particles into each other. Particles can even leap into being out of nothing at all. In such circumstances, questions such as What does matter consist of? and Can matter be divided forever? lose their meaning and cease to be questions to which experiments can supply an answer. Physicists have rediscovered the validity of Kant's conclusion that ordinary ways of understanding just do not apply to the world of the supersmall.

The study of matter in all its forms is called physics. The study of the ideas and principles involved in any knowledge about the world, or in any experience we may have, is called philosophy. The nature of matter is therefore—just as it was in ancient Greece—as much a philosophical question as a scientific one. For to talk about matter we must rely not only upon scientific data about its behavior and properties but also upon philosophical assumptions about what it is to be at all.

See also ANTIMATTER; ATOM; CELL; INERTIA; PARTICLE PHYSICS; QUANTUM MECHANICS; SOLID-STATE PHYSICS.

Matter, States and State Changes of

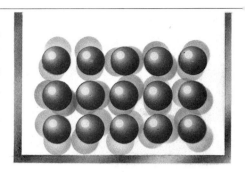

When iron rusts, gasoline burns, or hydrogen and oxygen combine to form water, a fundamental change in the original substances has occurred. It seems that the original materials have disappeared and that new ones with new properties have taken their place. Such a change is called a chemical change, and it cannot be reversed by ordinary means—by altering the temperature and pressure, for instance. In a chemical change, the atoms of the original materials have linked up with each other in new ways.

When ice turns into water or water into steam, a different kind of change has occurred. The basic substance is still intact, so the change can be reversed simply by changing the temperature or pressure—by freezing the water, for instance. This kind of change is called physical change, or a change of state. In a change of state, the atoms composing matter remain linked with each other in the same arrangements, called molecules; what has changed is the strengths of the bonds between the molecules. There are three basic states of matter—solid, liquid, and gaseous—and nearly every kind of matter can, in the proper conditions, appear in each form.

It was not until relatively recently that the nature of state changes was understood. In the 19th century, numerous theories were advanced to explain them. According to one, liquids and gases are composed of different types of molecules—liquidons and gasons. Today, however, we know that the same types of atoms and molecules are involved in each state; ice, water, and steam, for instance, are all composed of water molecules. The difference that alters the state of a substance lies in the strengths of the bonds between the molecules.

Solids

A solid is a rigid substance that has a definite volume and a definite shape. If you take a solid object from one container and place it in a larger one, both its volume and its shape remain unaltered.

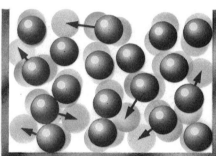

It might seem as if the atoms composing a solid do not move, are permanently affixed to each other. This is not the case, however. All atoms are in a perpetual motion, whether they are atoms of a solid, liquid, or gas. Whereas atoms in a liquid or gas wander, never remaining in the same place, the atoms of a solid vibrate about a fixed position; although they make tiny excursions, they never stray too far from that position. An atom in a solid acts as if it were bouncing around in a tiny box. The hotter the temperature of the solid, the more vigorously it moves about

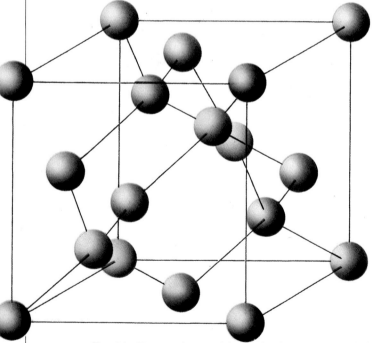

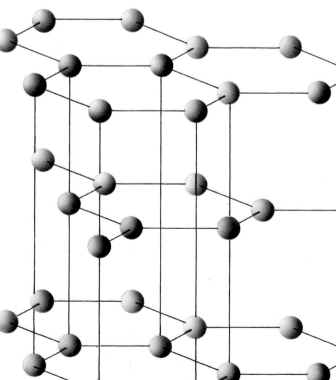

Top right: Diagrams show models of molecular motion in the 3 phases of matter. Top, in solid phase, atoms can only oscillate around their position of equilibrium. In liquid phase, center, molecules have freedom but are limited by intermolecular forces. In gas, bottom, molecules have greatest freedom of movement.

Above: The structure of 2 crystalline forms of carbon—at left, diamond; at right, graphite. This is an example of allomorphism, in which the atoms of an element bond in various ways to form crystalline structures with different characteristics. Diamonds are transparent and hard, while graphite is black and soft.

in the box. But even at the coldest possible temperature, absolute zero (0°K, −273.15°C., −459.67°F.), the atoms still have some kinetic energy (energy of motion), and their vibrations do not cease. Nonetheless, the object that is made is still rigid, not because of the absence of motion on the part of its atoms, but because of the existence of limits to the motion.

In a solid, furthermore, these points are arranged in patterns that are repeated over and over. A material built up from repeating atomic patterns is called a crystal, and its particular pattern of points is called its lattice structure. Ordinarily, we think of crystals as rare and precious things, such

as diamonds, whose structure can be seen by the naked eye. The crystal structure of most other solids, however, is detectable only under a microscope, for their crystal pattern is broken up like a jumble of jigsaw pieces.

There are certain rigid substances that are not crystalline—glass and certain kinds of plastics, for example. In these materials, the atoms are "boxed" in certain relatively confined spaces, as in crystals, but there is no lattice structure or repeating pattern. These types of materials are sometimes (particularly in the case of glass) called supercooled liquids.

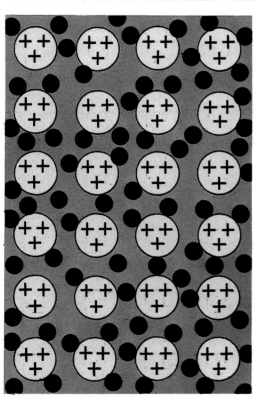

Left: Typical imperfections in crystal structure—a vacant space; an impurity that either replaces an atom or fills in an interatomic space; and a marginal dislocation (larger illustration). The electrical conductivity of metals is explained by their crystalline structure, which consists of positive ions surrounded by a sea of free electrons that carry the electric current.

Above: Obsidian is an example of an amorphous solid. It does not have an ordered structure but consists of scattered groups of atoms, as shown at right below.

● Electron

 Metallic ion

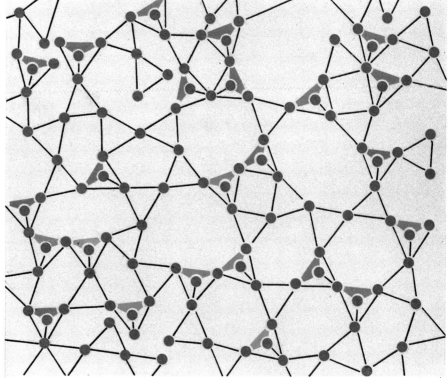

The study of the behavior and properties of solid matter constitute a separate branch of physics, called solid-state physics, as well as a separate branch of chemistry, called solid-state chemistry. These disciplines study crystal patterns, their impurities, and the nature of the forces holding atoms and molecules together.

Liquids

Like a solid, a liquid has a fixed volume. A pint of milk remains a pint whether you pour it into a drinking glass or into a bowl for your cat. The shape of a liquid, however, is not fixed. It will assume the shape of its container, whether a square container, a cylindrical glass, or a hemispherical bowl. A liquid, in short, has no permanent structure. It is a fluid named for the Latin word for "flow."

Molecules in the liquid state have an attraction for each other. This attraction draws the molecules in together nearly as close as they can get—for this reasons, a liquid cannot be easily compressed. Liquids are "sticky"—the molecules tend to cling together in tiny droplets or larger quantities wherever possible. The surface of a liquid acts as if it were a thin skin covering the liquid—a phenomenon known as surface tension.

But the molecules in the liquid state are able to wander in a way molecules in a solid cannot. There is no lattice structure in a liquid; molecules can move past each other and make extended trips around the liquid. Because there is no fixed structure in a liquid, its shape is distorted by forces more readily than the shape of a solid. Gravity is one such force; a liquid quickly spreads out under the force of gravity wherever it can, trying to find the lowest spot. Some liquids flow more slowly than others, and they are said to be more viscous. Viscosity refers to the resistance of a liquid to flow. Motor oil flows more

Left: Viscometer, which measures viscosity of liquids. The time necessary for the liquid to pass through a capillary tube is measured and is compared to the time necessary for water at the same temperature to pass through. Lubricants are graded according to viscosity.

Right: Two liquids separated into layers. Where layers meet, cohesion between molecules creates interfacial pressure, which maintains the separation. This force is similar to surface tension.

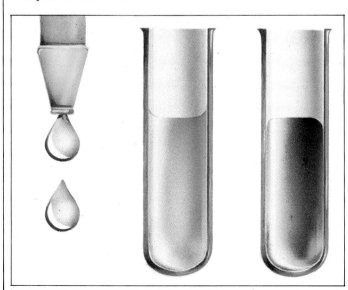

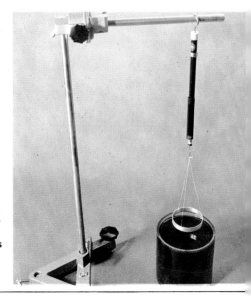

Surface tension reduces to a minimum the surface area of a column of liquid. At the point of contact between a container and liquid, a meniscus forms; concave for liquids that wet the walls of the container, convex for those that do not.

Right: Method for evaluating surface tension. A ring is suspended from a dynamometer and immersed in a liquid. The force necessary to raise the ring and break the surface is measured.

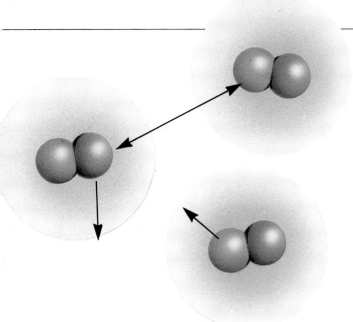

Molecules are attracted to one another by forces that are effective only at short distances. In a gas, intramolecular distances are great; thus, gas molecules have little effect on each other.
Left: Shaded area around molecules indicates the sphere of influence of intermolecular forces. Since it is less than the distance between the molecules, they have no effect on one another.

slowly than water, and its viscosity is therefore higher. In a more viscous liquid, the attraction between molecules is stronger, and the voyages of the molecules are more impeded than those in a less viscous substance.

Because a liquid has a fixed volume and cannot be compressed, it serves as a useful medium of conveying pressure—for instance, in brake lines of an automobile. The study of the behavior of liquids is called hydrodynamics.

Gases

The gaseous state is also fluid. A gas, like a liquid, takes the shape of its container. Unlike a liquid, however, the volume of a gas is not fixed. It will expand to fill any container or until a force begins to hold it back. The body of air surrounding the Earth, for instance, is kept in place by the force of gravity; without it, the atmosphere would diffuse away into space until nothing was left.

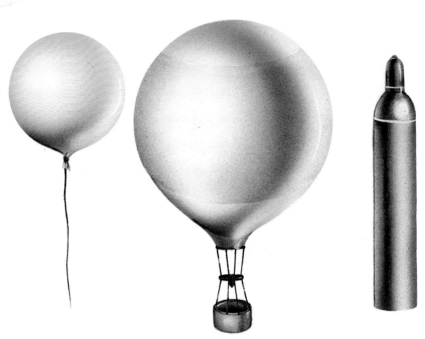

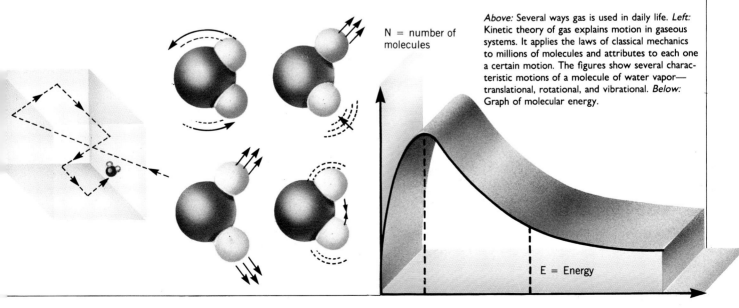

N = number of molecules

Above: Several ways gas is used in daily life. *Left:* Kinetic theory of gas explains motion in gaseous systems. It applies the laws of classical mechanics to millions of molecules and attributes to each one a certain motion. The figures show several characteristic motions of a molecule of water vapor—translational, rotational, and vibrational. *Below:* Graph of molecular energy.

E = Energy

This behavior results from the lack of virtually any bonds between the molecules of a gas. They act independently of each other and are free to wander about in the gas unrestrained. The gaseous state has the least structure of any of the three states. The word "gas" was first used around 1600 by the Flemish chemist Jan Baptista van Helmont. He is said to have taken it from *chaos,* the word the Greeks used to describe the original state of the Universe.

Because the individual molecules of any gas move in a nearly random fashion, the properties of particular gases are less unique than those of more structured liquids or solids. To put it another way, all gases resemble each other more than do liquids or solids. They all obey the same basic laws, such as Boyle's law (the pressure exerted by a gas is inversely proportional to its volume) and Charles' law (volume is proportional to temperature).

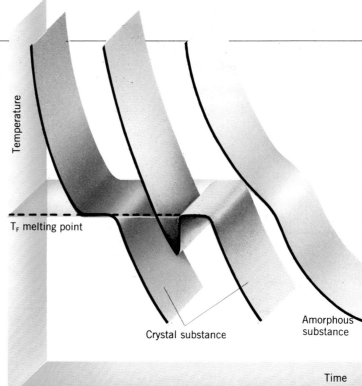

T_F melting point

Crystal substance

Amorphous substance

Time

Left: The 3 curves show changes in temperature over time. In the first, the substance passes from one phase to another; temperature remains constant because the heat of fusion is released. In the second, supercooling occurs, and the substance remains in the liquid phase even though the temperature is below freezing. The third curve is for glass, which does not have a definite melting point.

Below: Kinetic theory uses equations that relate observations made on a grand scale to individual atoms. The diagram shows the number of particles that have a given amount of kinetic energy at a given temperature. This gives the average energy that is proportional to a given temperature.

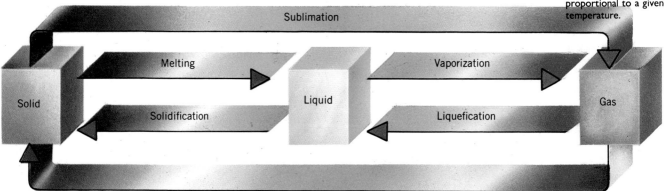

Sublimation

Melting

Vaporization

Solid

Liquid

Gas

Solidification

Liquefication

Mixtures of States

Often two of the three states of matter coexist in the same substance. A colloidal suspension, for instance, is a mixture of tiny solid grains in a liquid. Fine sand suspended in water is an example of a colloidal suspension, as is ink. Smoke consists of a solid (dust particles) suspended in a gas, while froth and foam consist of a gas suspended in a liquid.

Changes of State

The change of state from solid to liquid is called melting; that from liquid to solid is called solidifying or freezing. For pure, crystalline substances, melting and freezing happen at the same temperature. Ice, for instance, melts at 32°F. (0°C.), the temperature at which water freezes.

But merely raising the temperature of ice to this point is not sufficient to melt it. A certain amount of additional heat energy is required to effect the change from the solid to the liquid state—even though

the temperature remains the same. This extra amount of heat required to make the transition, which is absorbed when ice melts and liberated when water freezes, is called latent heat of fusion or just heat of fusion. Any change in state at the melting point involves the loss or gain of a certain amount of heat, and this latent heat is different for each substance.

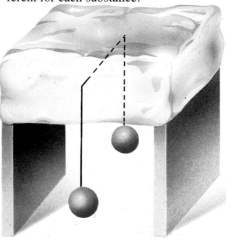

Left: Block of ice under pressure caused by the 2 weights on a string. When the ice melts, the string passes through, and pressure ceases. Then the ice returns to the solid state. *Right:* Graph is divided into 3 zones corresponding to the 3 phases of matter. At point T, called the triple point, all 3 phases exist. A solid at the triple point and at low pressure sublimes if heated.

Impure and noncrystalline substances, however, do not have definite melting points. These substances, including glass, tar, and butter, soften and only gradually become liquid. Not all substances can become liquid; many, like sugar, decompose under the effect of heat. That is, they change chemically rather than physically.

The volume of most substances shrinks somewhat upon solidifying and expands upon melting. Water, however, is an exception. It expands when it freezes, which is why pipes, containers, and engine blocks often burst when water is left in them overnight at cold temperatures.

The change of state from liquid to gas is known as boiling; that from gas to liquid, condensation. Just as it is not sufficient to bring a solid to its melting point to melt it, so it is not sufficient to bring a liquid to its boiling point to turn it into a gas. An additional amount of heat energy, called the heat of vaporization, is required to turn a liquid, such as water at 212°F. (100°C.), for instance, into steam at that same temperature.

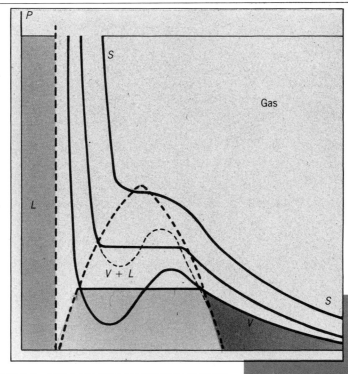

Left: Curves on the graph are called Andrews isotherms. Each one represents the changes in pressure and volume at a constant temperature. Isotherm S (solid) identifies the temperature limits, which in the outlined zone are along an irregular curve because of the presence of both a liquid and gas. To the left there is zone *L* (liquid), in which volume is constant regardless of pressure; to the right, *V* is the vapor phase. Above isotherm *S*, Boyle's law is true.

Below: Sublimation of benzoic acid.

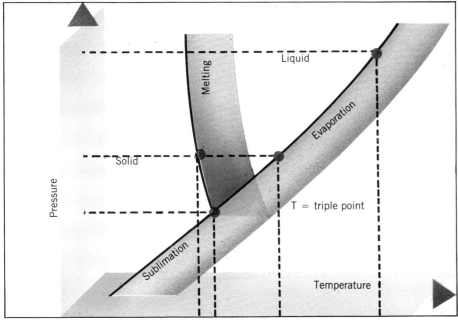

The temperatures at which a substance boils and melts depend upon the pressure they are under. At less than normal atmospheric pressure, for instance, the melting and boiling points are generally lower. On top of Pikes Peak, which is 14,110 feet (4,301 m) above sea level, the atmospheric pressure is lower than it is at sea level, and water boils at only 185°F. (85°C.). An increase in pressure, on the other hand, generally raises the temperatures of the boiling and melting points (water, again, is an exception; its melting point decreases with increased pressure). This is why ice skates work.

Some materials, such as iodine and carbon dioxide, can go directly from solid to gaseous state at normal pressures; this peculiar behavior is known as sublimation. When liquids gradually turn into gases at a temperature less than their boiling point—because of the escape of molecules from the surface—it is called evaporation. Some evaporation occurs from the surface of any liquid at any temperature; it also happens from the surface of solids to a lesser degree.

In this century, scientists have identified what is often called a fourth state of matter. At extremely high temperatures and under high pressures, atoms themselves begin to fall apart into the electrical charges of which they are composed. This is called plasma, and it is seldom found on Earth, which lacks the extreme conditions needed to produce it. Farther out in space, however, these conditions are the norm, and almost all the matter in the Universe is in the plasma state. From the perspective of the Universe at large, our solids, liquids, and gases are rare and unfamiliar states of matter.

See also CRYSTALS AND CRYSTALLOGRAPHY; GAS; HYDRAULICS; SOLID-STATE PHYSICS.

Measles

Measles was first described by the medieval Persian doctor, Rhazes, and has always spread like wildfire under unsanitary conditions. During the American Civil War, for example, 75,000 soldiers caught measles, and about 5,000 died of complications. Today, measles is considered so harmless that often parents let the disease run its course in children without consulting a doctor. That is not necessarily a good idea. Measles is a simple childhood disease, but on occasion, it can have serious complications. Measles is part of the group known as exanthems, or childhood diseases with rashes, along with German measles (rubella) and roseola.

Measles (Rubeola)

Also known as red measles, rubeola is the most long-lasting and severe type of exanthem and is most common among children from 5 to 12 years of age. It is caused by a virus that is believed to travel from the upper respiratory tract through

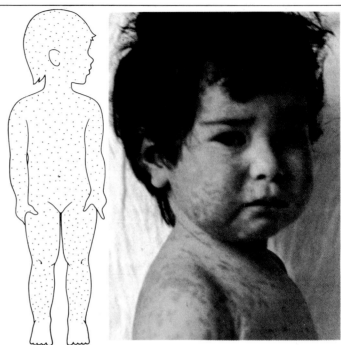

The rash that is the typical symptom of red measles is usually first visible around the ears. It then spreads rapidly over the rest of the body. The rash disappears after a few days without leaving a trace, though damaged tissues of the upper epidermis may later flake away.

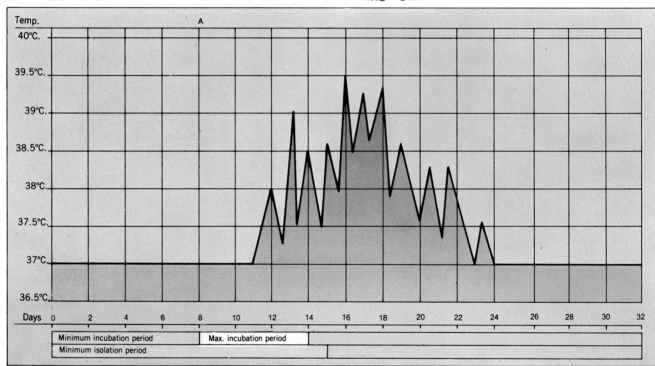

the bloodstream, affecting all the tissues and organs. It takes 1 to 3 weeks for children who have contracted measles to show the rash, with the result that with the help of the coughing that accompanies the disease, children can spread the virus among all their schoolmates before the first case is recognized.

The most noticeable symptoms, besides fever and coughing, are spots on the skin and eye sensitivity to light. Medication is usually not prescribed as treatment. However, a measles vaccine generally given around the child's first birthday is effective in preventing the disease. Until that time, the child is protected by antibodies received from the mother before birth. People who contract measles once usually are immune to the disease, although they may pass the virus on to others. One out of every 15 persons with measles has suffered complications, including bronchitis, pneumonia, or, in rare instances, encephalitis (brain fever). A vaccine for measles now in use has effectively eradicated the disease from the United States. Until this vaccine comes into general use around the world, like the immunization against polio, people will continue to suffer from measles.

Above: Graph traces the course of the fever (in °C.) that generally accompanies red measles. Normal temperature is 98.6°F. (37°C). The bar graph indicates the minimum and maximum number of days of incubation and of isolation to prevent the possibility of contagion.

1960

Below: One of the earliest symptoms of measles is the small red marks appearing on the inside of the cheek, generally opposite the molars. They are called Koplik's spots, after the American pediatrician Henry Koplik, who first noticed them. These spots often disappear even before the measles rash becomes visible on the skin.

Below right: Microphotograph shows cells infected with measles virus illuminated by fluorescent light.

Right: Fever chart for rubella in °C. The minimum and maximum number of days of incubation and of isolation to prevent contagion are shown in the bar graph.

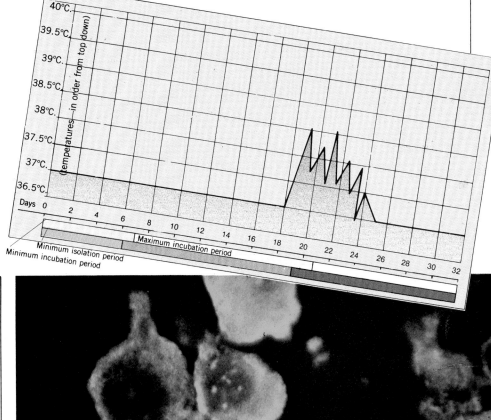

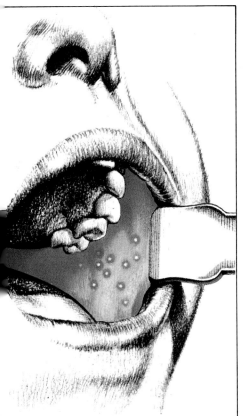

Rubella

For most people, rubella (also known as German measles) is not a serious disease. Also a viral infection, it has a longer incubation period than rubeola, about 16 days; the illness then lasts no more than 3 or 4 days. Symptoms include runny nose, fever, and fine pink spots that appear within a day or two of the other symptoms and fade away after 2 or 3 days. The lymph nodes behind the ears and at the back of the neck are also typically swollen. In adults, a reversible form of arthritis is not uncommon.

When a person contracts rubella, it is important that all women of childbearing age with whom he or she has come in close contact be notified. When rubella strikes a pregnant woman, it can lead to tragedy. Particularly if contracted during the first 3 months of pregnancy, it can cause the baby to be born with a seriously malformed heart, congenital cataracts, or permanent deafness. As a result, a woman seeking a marriage license is often required either to prove she has had the disease or to be vaccinated, and a woman who does contract rubella during the first trimester is fre-quently counseled to consider abortion. It was not until 1968 that a safe rubella vaccine was discovered.

Roseola Infantum

This is the least known of exanthems and is usually a harmless disease of babies. First the child gets a very high fever—about 105°F. (41°C.)—which lasts for 3-4 days. Next, a very fine red rash covers the body; it can last for only a night and never be noticed by the parents, or as long as 48 hours.

Measurement

The ancient teacher Protagoras was famous for his dictum, "Man is the measure of all things." Today, that dictum might be amended to say, "Man is the *measurer* of all things." Measurement plays an essential role in modern technology. Delicate machines such as computers could not be built without precise measured components. A recent branch of technology, which can be called instrumentation, is concerned with the development of new devices that are able to make finer measurements of a growing range of phenomena.

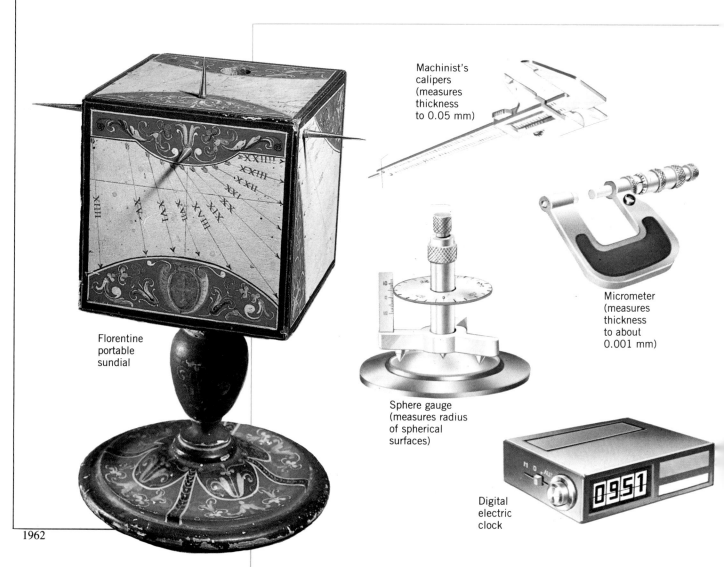

Egyptian scale with weights

Above: Simple bronze scale and the weights with which it was used. The object was found in an Egyptian tomb.
Below: Selection of different types of devices used to measure physical dimensions, weight, time, weather phenomena, and electric current.

Measurement and Comparison

In a sense, measurement is a form of comparison. When we compare two things, we always compare them with respect to a certain property (or properties). Length, for example, is one of several properties that are said to be fundamental in systems of measurement for science. Other properties are amount of mass, duration in time, temperature, flow of electrical current, and intensity of light. From these fundamental properties other properties can be derived. For example, the property of density is defined in terms of mass per volume, and volume is defined in terms of a length cubed (multiplied by itself, then multiplied by itself again).

Let's say we are interested in a given object's length. To measure this property, we compare the object with an object whose length is known; this known object serves as a standard of length. We can then express the length of the given object in terms of the standard. For example, the object might be twice the length of the standard. We can then assign a number and a unit to the given object as the measurement. The unit is the name given to the standard, and the number is the ratio of the length of the given object to the length of the standard. The advantage of quantifying measurements in this way is that they thereby become clearer, more precise, and easier to work with.

Standards of Measurement

The choice of standards for measurement is somewhat arbitrary. Once a standard is chosen, however, three things become important. First, the standard must remain fixed. Second, it must be accessible to anyone who needs to perform measurements. Finally, it should mesh

Florentine portable sundial

Machinist's calipers (measures thickness to 0.05 mm)

Micrometer (measures thickness to about 0.001 mm)

Sphere gauge (measures radius of spherical surfaces)

Digital electric clock

conveniently with standards for measuring other properties. This ensures that there is an orderly relationship among measurements. A set of standards for the fundamental properties (length, mass, time, etc.) determines a system of measurement. The two most prominent systems are the English system of feet, pounds, and seconds, and the metric system of meters, kilograms, and seconds.

The first two requirements above point out the failings of the medieval English standards of measurement. At that time, an inch was defined as the length of three barleycorns placed end to end. It would seem that anyone who needed to measure something in inches could simply take three barleycorns and have the standard. But clearly, not all barleycorns are the same size. Thus, there could be a great difference in length between things measured to be the same number of inches.

In the past, people tried to solve this problem by making durable, unchanging objects to serve as standards. For example, the standard for the kilogram, the measure of mass in the metric system, is a cylinder of platinum-iridium kept in Sèvres, France. But now a new problem arises. This standard is not readily available to people who need to make measurements. Copies of the standard kilogram are made, but they might be off by minute amounts—enough to affect the accuracy of precise calculations.

Modern Standards

Today, scientists are returning to the idea at work behind the barleycorns. That is, they are defining standards in terms of natural phenomena, available to all. Sophisticated devices allow them to choose natural phenomena that are invariant. For example, the second is defined in terms of the vibrations of atoms of cesium. It has been proposed that the meter, which, since 1960, has been determined by wavelengths of light given off by krypton, now be determined by the distance light travels in a vacuum in $\frac{1}{299,792,458}$ of a second. This change would permit measurements of length, and other measurements derived from length, to be made with far greater accuracy than is now possible.

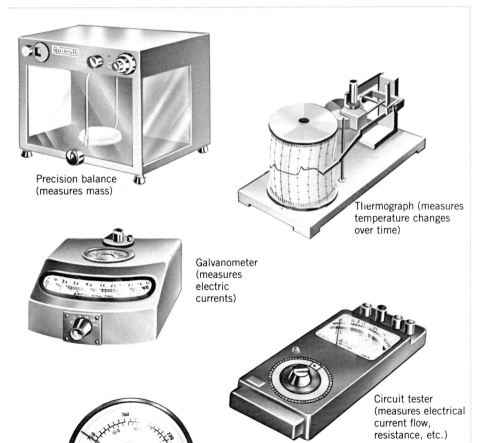

Precision balance (measures mass)

Thermograph (measures temperature changes over time)

Galvanometer (measures electric currents)

Circuit tester (measures electrical current flow, resistance, etc.)

Aneroid barometer (measures atmospheric pressure)

Measurement, Angle

If we are working with geometrical figures on a piece of paper, we can measure the angle between two intersecting lines by using a protractor, an instrument made especially for this purpose. When what we have to measure is not so conveniently small, a whole new set of problems may arise. Sometimes, we may find that the two lines that form the angle we want to measure are more difficult to see than their equivalents on paper. And we may find that some of the points involved are inaccessible. Let us consider some familiar examples that occur in everyday life.

Every time a house is built, or a plot of land is sold or divided into building lots, or a road or a tunnel or a bridge is constructed, measurements have to be taken. If we take all our linear measurements accurately but neglect angular ones, we are likely to build a house in the wrong place, with sloping floors and walls that don't match up at the corners with the floor or the ceiling, but leave gaping holes on one side and extend too far on the other. This may not be a matter of life or death, but with engineering projects like bridge and tunnel building, accuracy is crucial. When a tunnel is dug, it is usually decided in advance where it is going to come out, and often digging starts at both ends, expecting to meet in the middle. Engineers have to be absolutely sure before work begins that they are not going to dig two parallel tunnels that pass each other in the dark and never meet.

There is one instrument that we use to avoid all of these calamities. It is called a transit or theodolite, and it takes very accurate measurements of horizontal and vertical angles. Basically, the transit is a telescope mounted on a tripod. It has a vertical axis around which the telescope rotates horizontally, and a horizontal axis that lets the telescope point up and down. A spirit level is mounted to the telescope to enable the user to establish where the horizontal plane lies. A small, sealed glass tube filled with liquid except for a small air bubble can be laid on its side so that the bubble floats right in the center when the tube is perfectly horizontal. The top side of the tube is usually curved inward slightly to magnify the movement of the bubble when the tube is tilted from horizontal. The vertical axis has a plumb bob hanging from it, so that the instrument can be positioned accurately over the point where the measurement is to be taken. A plumb bob is simply a heavy object—originally a piece of lead, *plumbum* in Latin—hanging from a piece of string and coming to a point at the bottom that indicates a point directly below (or, in the case of tunnels, above) another.

Each of the two axes on which the telescope is mounted runs at right angles (perpendicularly) through a circular plate with gradations from 0° to 360°, just as a protractor is gradated from 0° to 180°. This plate moves independently of the axis and can be clamped to stay in any position. Nested in this plate is a smaller plate that rotates along with the telescope on the axis. If we wish to measure the angle between two lines, we first set up the instrument in the right position by using the plumb bob, then sight through the telescope along one line to a visible point or marker set up for that purpose along the line. We then rotate the outer circular plate till its 0° mark is lined up with the 0 of the inner plate, then clamp it fixed. Moving the telescope to sight along the second line to the second marker, we can read the resulting angle directly. Vertical angles can be read by repeating the process with the other axis and the other pair of plates.

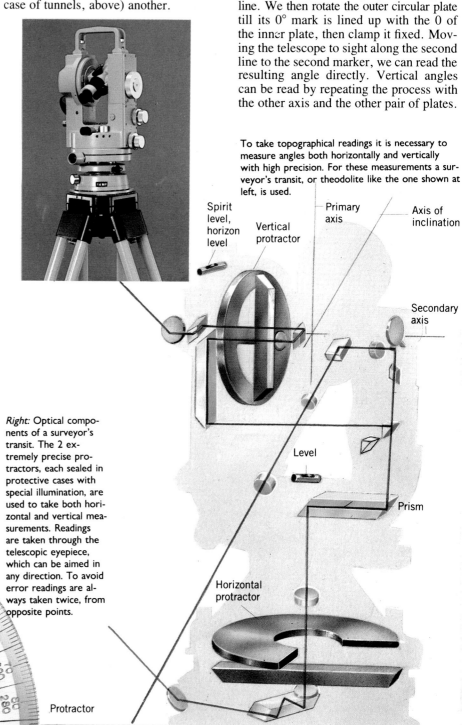

To take topographical readings it is necessary to measure angles both horizontally and vertically with high precision. For these measurements a surveyor's transit, or theodolite like the one shown at left, is used.

Right: Optical components of a surveyor's transit. The 2 extremely precise protractors, each sealed in protective cases with special illumination, are used to take both horizontal and vertical measurements. Readings are taken through the telescopic eyepiece, which can be aimed in any direction. To avoid error readings are always taken twice, from opposite points.

Spirit level, horizon level

Vertical protractor

Primary axis

Axis of inclination

Secondary axis

Level

Prism

Horizontal protractor

Protractor

Vernier Scale

There is one further refinement of this process that is so essential to accurate readings that it is included in all modern theodolites. It involves the use of an invention, made in 1631 by the French mathematician Pierre Vernier, called vernier scales. If we have only a single mark on the inner plate(s) to indicate how far we have rotated the telescope, we will soon find that the telescope is too accurate for the readings we can make from the lines on the outer plate, and if we put in enough fine lines on the outer plate, they will be too close together for us to tell them apart, much less identify them. Ver-

nier decided to set up a second scale in place of the single pointer. The easiest way to understand how this works is to imagine a pair of rulers, one marked off into centimeters and millimeters, the other blank. If we mark off 9/10ths of a centimeter of the blank one and divide it into 10 equal parts instead of nine and mark them 0 to 10, each division will be 9/10 mm long. If we line up the two rulers so that the zeroes are aligned, then move the new scale to the right so that its zero falls between two lines on the standard scale, we can tell its position accurately by looking for a point to its right where two lines most nearly match up. Say the zero is

moved to a position between the 5- and 6-mm marks, and the point on the vernier scale that matches a line on the other scale above it is marked 4. Since each division of the new scale is 1/10th smaller than a centimeter, the zero must be 4/10ths of a millimeter to the right of the 5-mm line, so the ruler has been moved 5.4 mm. Use of this principle in the transit enables us to make much better use of the accuracy of the telescope.

For more information about adjustments that have to be made to readings of elevation to account for the curvature of the earth, *see* SURVEYING.

USE OF A SURVEYOR'S TRANSIT

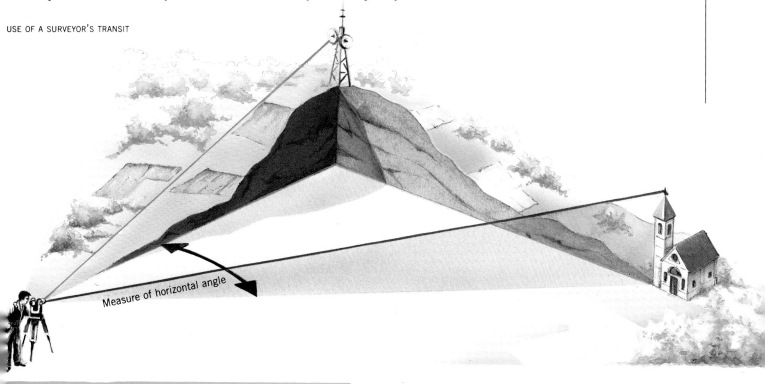

Measure of horizontal angle

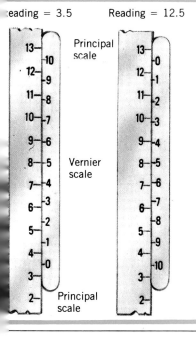

Reading = 3.5   Reading = 12.5

Principal scale

Vernier scale

Principal scale

Use of the vernier scale permits exact calculation of an angle that falls between the smallest gradations of the measuring device. Without the vernier scale, one would have to estimate. The 'zero' of the vernier scale is placed at the desired point on the principal scale (between the 2 measures). The exact fraction to be added is read from the vernier scale at the point where marks on the 2 scales line up.

Computer instrumentation has made necessary the development of equipment that can express angles in binary form without human intervention. An automatic digital protractor contains a glass disk etched with the pattern seen at the right. A photoelectric cell positioned over each of the concentric rings generates an electric current based on the amount of light that passes through the disk. The total electric charge registered corresponds to a precise angle expressed in binary form in the computer memory of the protractor.

PROTRACTOR ETCHED
IN BINARY CODE

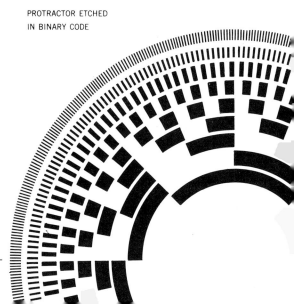

Measurement, Length

Although man's search for a standard unit of length probably began with civilization itself, this seemingly simple matter of convention has yet to be resolved. The present-day conflict between the French metric system, widely used throughout Europe and Asia, and the British Imperial system, used in many of Britain's former colonies, including the United States, merely constitutes the latest verse in a perennial song of dissent.

of platinum-iridium alloy slightly longer than a meter (101.6 cm), which would shrink to the correct length when the bar was at the temperature of melting ice—this being itself a universal temperature standard, the freezing point of water. Though originally conceived as one ten-millionth the distance from the equator to the pole, this basis was officially repudiated in 1889. In the interest of near-absolute accuracy, the meter has in recent

man units of length still exist today, as horses are measured in hands (distance across the four fingers, defined as 4 inches [10 cm] by Henry VIII), and the much more common foot, slightly longer than the Roman *pes*. Various manifestations of the foot, from the Hong Kong *cheh* (14.6 inches; 37 cm) to the Persian *charac* (10.24 inches; 26 cm) can be found in virtually every culture.

The metric (or meter) system appears to be edging out the yard, which is currently represented by the distance between two parallel grooves etched into the center of two gold studs, embedded 1 inch (2.54 cm) from either end of a 38-inch (96.5-cm) bronze bar (thereby spanning the customary 36 inches) immured in the wall of the waiting room of the House of Commons. According to the Parliamentary Weights and Measures Act of 1856, because of expansion and contraction, the exact length of a yard is officially represented at a temperature of 62°F. (16.67°C.). The meter, introduced by a law of the French National Assembly in 1799, was at first represented by the distance between two parallel marks on a bar

years been defined as 1,650,763.73 wavelengths of the orange-red line in the spectrum of the krypton-86 atom under specified conditions.

Ancient Methods of Standardization

Historically, the most common method of establishing a standard unit of length was to associate it with a part of the anatomy. The Roman *digitus*, "finger" (0.73 inches or 1.85 cm), was represented by the distance across the width of the middle finger. Other parts of the body stood for larger Roman units of length. Four *digiti* equaled one *palmus* ("hand"). Four *palmi* equaled one *pes* ("foot"). Five *pes* equaled one *passus* ("pace," approximately 5 feet; 1.5 m). Remnants of Ro-

Above: Museum reproduction of an Egyptian cubit, the standard of measure in antiquity that was roughly 0.52 meters long.

Modern technology requires much more precise measurements than those obtainable with a cubit rod. *Below:* Optical comparator, developed in the early 19th century, measures small distances to an accuracy of about 0.01 mm. The comparator was essentially a ruled rod carrying 2 microscopes that were focused on either end of the object to be measured. The distance was then read on the scale between the microscopes.

Below right: Ruler shows relationship between 2 most familiar measures of distance, inches and centimeters.

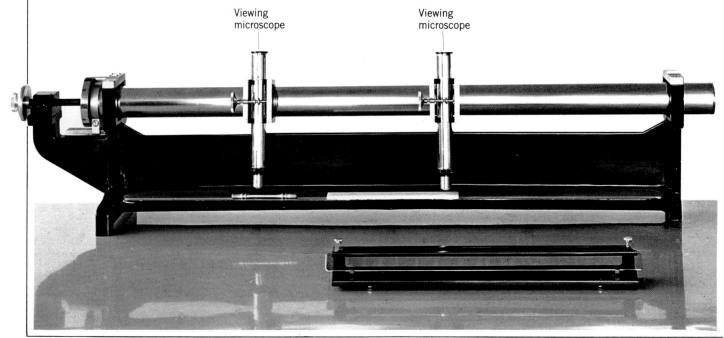

Viewing microscope

Viewing microscope

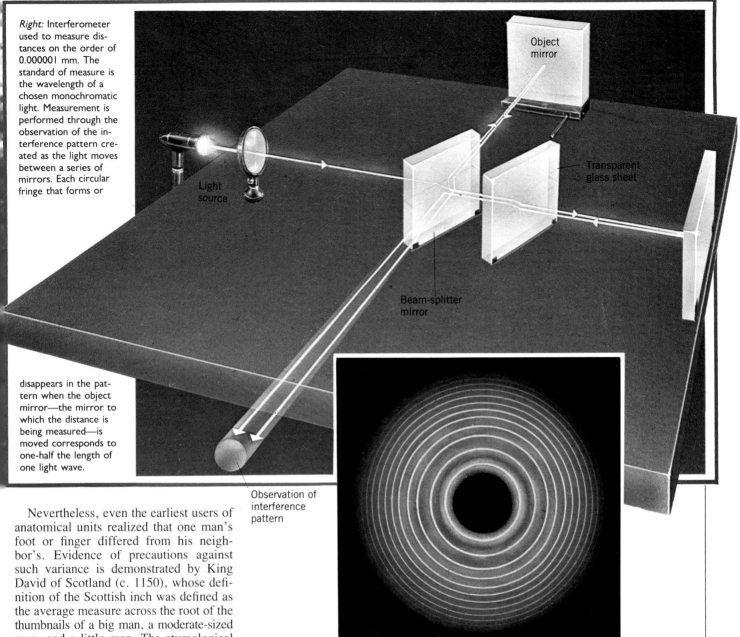

Right: Interferometer used to measure distances on the order of 0.000001 mm. The standard of measure is the wavelength of a chosen monochromatic light. Measurement is performed through the observation of the interference pattern created as the light moves between a series of mirrors. Each circular fringe that forms or

Object mirror

Transparent glass sheet

Light source

Beam-splitter mirror

disappears in the pattern when the object mirror—the mirror to which the distance is being measured—is moved corresponds to one-half the length of one light wave.

Observation of interference pattern

Interference pattern

Nevertheless, even the earliest users of anatomical units realized that one man's foot or finger differed from his neighbor's. Evidence of precautions against such variance is demonstrated by King David of Scotland (c. 1150), whose definition of the Scottish inch was defined as the average measure across the root of the thumbnails of a big man, a moderate-sized man, and a little man. The etymological derivation of "inch" comes from the Old English *unce* or *ynche,* which in turn comes from the Latin *uncia,* meaning "one-twelfth."

History provides countless units of length, but the most ancient and widely used, until recently, was the cubit. Originally identified as the distance from a man's elbow to the farthest fingertip of his extended hand, the cubit existed in many Mediterranean and European cultures, varying in length from the Roman cubit (17.48 inches; 0.44 m) to the Palestinian cubit (25.24 inches; 0.64 m). Evidence from Egyptian excavations testifies to the widespread use of a highly accurate, standardized cubit (20.62 inches;

0.52 m) in ancient Nile civilizations. Today, a similar unit of length, variously called *covid, covado,* and *corido,* is found as far east as India and Siam.

More provincial units, such as the German-derived *rute,* equaled the combined lengths of the left feet of 16 randomly chosen men, placed heel-to-toe, as illustrated in an engraving by the 16th-century artist Master Koebel. The English rod (16.5 feet; 5.03 m), a surveyor's unit, comes from the same word, and should not be confused with a rood, which can either mean a square rod containing

272.25 square feet (25.5011 sq m) or a length of 24 feet (7.3406 m). The longest anatomically derived unit, the fathom (6 feet; 1.8 m), used in reference to aquatic depths, was the distance from fingertip to fingertip of a man's extended arms, which he counted as he paid out weighted line until it reached the bottom. Finally, the yard, which has now come to mean 36 inches (96.5 cm), was most often used by women to measure the lengths of cloth, and was represented by the distance from the nose to the fingertip.

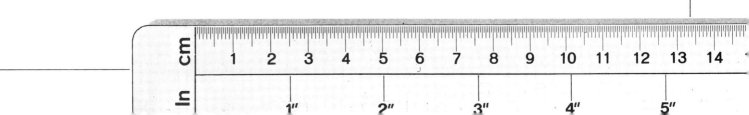

Measuring Instruments, Electric

Electricity is quantified and calibrated in different units of measure. The number of electrons that flow past a given point in a certain amount of time (rate per second) is measured in units called amperes. The unit of measure of electromotive force (emf) that is introduced into an electrical or electronic circuit is called a volt. The amount of resistance (the force that acts to impede the flow of electrons through a given material and determines the conductive or insulating properties of a material) is measured in units called ohms. One ohm of resistance is defined as exactly enough resistance to allow one volt of emf to cause a current of one ampere.

The amount of voltage (force), amperate (rate of flow), resistance (impedance to conductivity), or other quantity that exists in a given device or circuit can be measured by a device called a meter. This determination is indicated by a pointer that moves across a scale calibrated in units of the quantity being measured. Often, one meter will be calibrated to measure two or more electrical quantities.

Most meters have two insulated wires coming out of the main workings, with the conductive ends of each wire exposed. When the exposed tips of the wires are placed at appropriate points in a circuit, the pointer will move across the scale to indicate the correct reading of volts, amps, or ohms. Some meters have conducting terminals (small plates with screws to connect to the line being measured) rather than wire leads.

Why Meters Work

What happens between the two leads or terminals and the pointer moving across the scale? The key to any sort of meter is a phenomenon known as electromagnetism, and for the purpose of understanding the workings of meters we are concerned with two related principles:

First, when an electric current is placed in a magnetic field, the electrons will be pulled in one direction or another (depending upon the direction of current flow). This is owing to the second principle we are concerned with: Electric current flow generates a magnetic field. If such an electric current is placed within another magnetic field, the opposite poles of each of these fields will be attracted to each other. This phenomenon becomes useful if one of the magnetized elements is free to move or pivot, so that the opposite poles are able to seek each other. This necessity dictates the mechanical structure of electrical measuring devices.

How They Work

The prototype of most meters is called a galvanometer, which measures small amounts of amperage. The primary, or constant magnetic field is created with a permanent magnet that is roughly horseshoe-shaped, with the north and south poles on each side of the open end. Between these poles is a stationary iron core that creates a uniformly strong magnetic field in the inside area of the magnet; around this curved area, uniformly spaced numbers can be placed to form the scale of the meter.

The next step is to provide for an electromagnetic field within the permanent magnet. This is done by placing a movable coil of conductive material around the top of the iron core centered between the two poles of the permanent magnetic field. The coil is not actually attached to the core—if it were, it could not move—but it surrounds the core, held in place by pivot attachments. The two leads (or terminals) used to take readings are attached to the moving coil, as is the pointer that moves across the scales.

When the two wire leads are placed at an appropriate point in an electric circuit, they send a small amount of current through the movable coil. This sets up an electromagnetic field with a north and a south pole. The north pole of the coil-generated field will seek the south pole of the permanent magnet, or vice versa, and the coil will turn. The stronger the current, the stronger the magnetic field around the coil and the closer the south pole of

Below: The galvanometer is one of the simplest instruments used to measure electric current. It measures the intensity of direct-current flow through a coil of wire suspended in the field of a permanent magnet. Current moving through the wire causes the coil to develop a magnetic field of its own, which makes it rotate with respect to the magnet, moving an indicator needle.

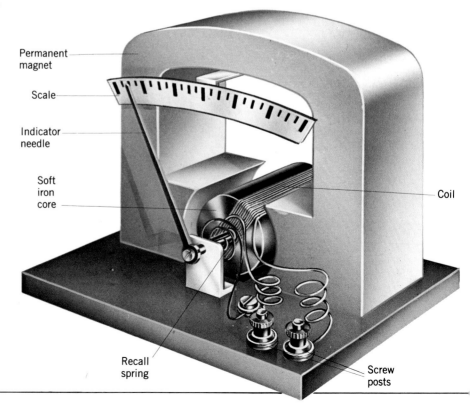

Permanent magnet

Scale

Indicator needle

Soft iron core

Coil

Recall spring

Screw posts

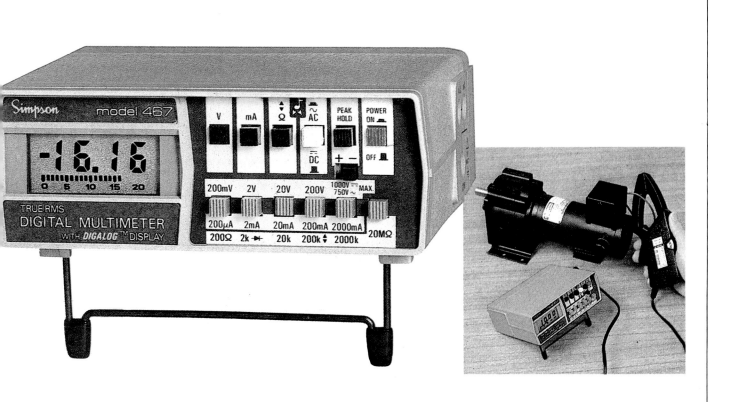

the coil field will be able to move toward the north pole of the permanent field. As the coil moves, the attached pointer will move across the printed scale.

Types of Meters

The galvanometer is useful for reading current that passes in one direction only, that is direct current (DC). To measure alternating current, a device called a rectifier is used in AC meters. The rectifier allows current to pass through during half of each cycle, essentially changing the current from alternating to direct without distorting the voltage, amperage, or resistance values.

The most common meter mechanism in use today is the D'Arsonval-type meter, which consists of a pivoting aluminum frame around which a conductive coil is wound. The frame assembly, with pointer attached, pivots around a stationary cylindrical magnetic core.

A voltmeter is used to measure voltage by placing the two leads in parallel—that is, each lead is placed on a different wire. A voltage reading across two "hot" wires (wires carrying voltage) will equal the sum of the two voltages; a reading across a "hot" and a return line (uncharged neutral wire) will equal the amount of charge in the one line carrying voltage. A reading inadvertently taken across the same wire will be zero. Voltmeters for reading alternating current include rectifier circuits, and most utilize shunts to allow for readings of 1,000 volts or more. As with ammeters, two or more shunt systems can be incorporated into one meter so that scales of several different ranges can be utilized in the same meter.

Unlike the ammeter or voltmeter, the ohmmeter (which measures ohms of resistance) receives power for the measuring process from a source of voltage within the meter, usually a small battery. When the meter is connected to the device or circuit being tested, the current generated by the meter is affected by the resistance of the outside current, and the pointer on the scale will move to a position determined by this added resistance.

Many meters are combination ammeters, voltage meters, and ohmmeters with multiple scales. In the past several years, digital meters have become popular; these meters do not have a dial-and-pointer arrangement, they indicate readings with numbers, like those on digital clocks. *See also* ELECTROMAGNETISM.

Mechanics

The foundations of classical mechanics were laid down as early as the 3rd century B.C., when the Greek mathematician Archimedes derived formulas for describing equilibrium in simple levers and introduced the crucial concept of center of gravity. But it was only with the work of Galileo and, later, of Newton that this entire branch of physics took shape. Classical mechanics (also called Newtonian mechanics) is still used today for the interactions of bodies of relatively large size (larger than atoms), which move at speeds that are slow compared with the speed of light. At the heart of classical mechanics are Newton's three laws of motion.

Newton's Laws of Motion

Newton's laws explain the relationship of bodies at rest or in motion in terms of mass, velocity, acceleration, and force.

First Law. This is known as the law of inertia, and it states that all bodies have an inertial mass that determines that the object will persist in the same state (of rest or constant velocity) in the absence of external forces. If the body is at rest, it will remain at rest; if it is in motion at a constant speed and direction, it will continue at the same speed and direction unless a force from outside either speeds it up, slows it down, or deflects it.

Second Law. Any force applied to a body, whether at rest or in motion, will cause that body to accelerate. The acceleration will be directly proportional to the

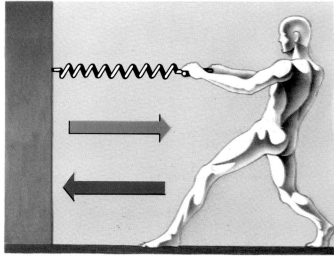

Newton's laws of motion are illustrated on this page.

Left: At top, first law of inertia. Aboard a vehicle moving at a constant velocity, several passengers are standing. When the bus brakes suddenly, the passengers tend to maintain their forward motion because of inertia. At bottom, Newton's second law supplies the correlation among force, mass, and acceleration. When an equal force is applied to 2 objects, the object having less mass has the greater acceleration.

Above: Third law, of action-reaction. When you apply a certain force to a spring attached to a wall, the same amount of force is applied on you by the spring.

Right: Graph at top shows relationship between gravitational force and distance for irregular-shaped objects; lower graph is for a spherical object in which the force of gravity is canceled in the center.

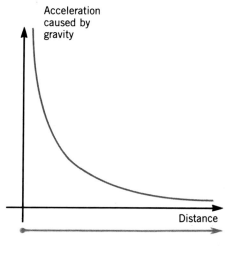

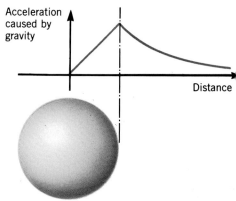

quantity of that force and inversely proportional to the body's mass, in that it requires less force to accelerate a body with a small mass than it does to accelerate a body with a large mass. Acceleration is defined as the change in speed or direction over a given time. It should not be confused with velocity, which consists of the speed and direction at any given instant of time.

Right: Centripetal acceleration causes an object to move in a curve directed toward its center of motion. Because of inertia, a body tends to maintain the same trajectory; also, if it has mass, the body demonstrates centrifugal force, which is the opposite of centripetal acceleration. When centripetal acceleration ceases, the object follows a path that is tangent to the original curved path at the point the acceleration ends. If an object is rotated on the end of a string in a circular path, centripetal force is exerted on the object, centrifugal force on the hand.

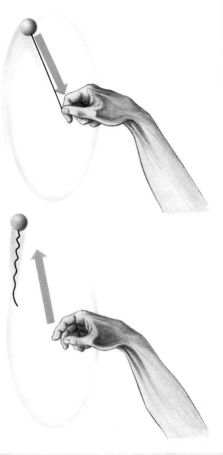

Force is a physical quantity having magnitude and direction; therefore, it is a vector. Two equal forces acting in opposite directions cancel each other, and the object acted upon remains in static equilibrium.

Two forces acting in the same direction give a resultant vector that is the sum of the 2 forces and that acts in the same direction as the component forces.

$$F_3 = F_1 + F_2$$

$$F_3 = \text{diagonal of parallelogram having sides } F_1 \text{ and } F_2$$

When 2 forces act on the same object but in different directions, both magnitude and direction are calculated using the parallelogram method. An example of this is shown below, in which 2 trains move a barge through a canal.

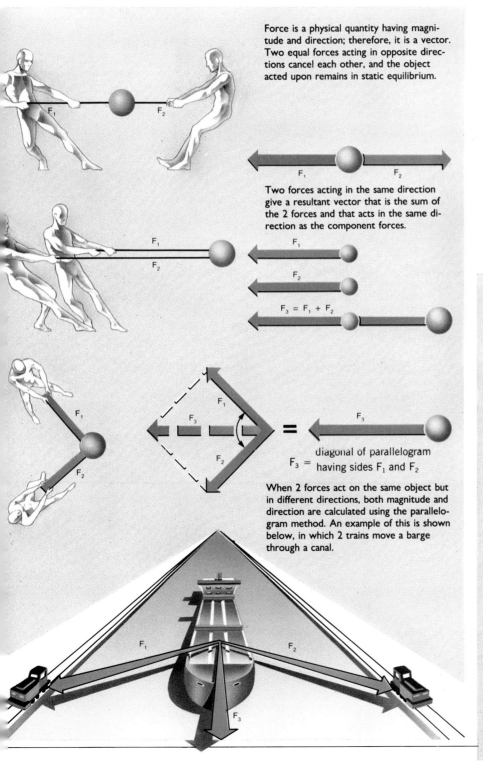

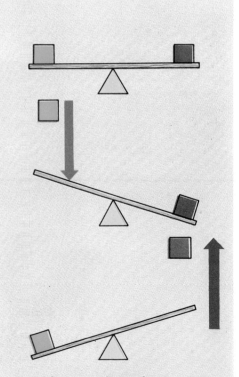

Potential energy can become kinetic energy and vice versa. A falling body transforms potential energy into kinetic energy, which can be transferred to another body.

Third Law. For every action there is an equal and opposite reaction. That is, if you push a table, that table could be said to push you back, for it exerts an inertial force in resistance to the force applied.

Force

The concept of force is central to all these laws. But what is force? Newton tells us that it is the product of mass and acceleration ($F = ma$), which is helpful in any mathematical estimation of its magnitude. In daily life, the forces we meet can be as simple as a push or a pull or even a gust of wind. One force always at work in classical mechanics is the force caused by gravity, which is the natural attraction of physical bodies to one another. The strongest gravitational force we experience is that exerted by the Earth on people and objects on its surface. This force is commonly expressed as an object's weight, which should not be confused with mass (the same mass will have different weights on other planets). Incidentally, gravitational forces are negligible in small bodies like bowling balls, but planetary systems are kept in equilibrium solely by the gravitational attractions among the Sun, planets, moons, and comets.

Frame of Reference

Frame of reference is crucial to all forms of scientific investigation, because it has direct bearing on the measurements of all the quantities we have talked about so far. For instance, the relative motion of a train will seem different from the ground than from the train. It is important to know where you are. Twentieth-century developments have led to branches of physics for which frames of reference have significantly departed from those of Newtonian mechanics. Quantum mechanics, which deals especially with the interactions of small particles like atoms, and relativistic mechanics, which explains the behavior of matter as it approaches the speed of light, view the Universe from perspectives not available to Newton. They show that the findings of classical mechanics are not strictly, but only approximately, correct. Some phenomena that continue ordinarily to be treated by classical mechanics are the movements of cars on a highway, the trajectories of bullets from guns, and the actions of a ball thrown or kicked in a game.

Statics and Dynamics

For all practical purposes, modern uses of classical physics can be divided into statics, which deals with the resolution of forces inherent in systems at rest, and dynamics, which involves the forces in moving bodies.

An example of a simple static system is a book lying on a table. Neither object is moving, but the book is exerting a force (equal to its weight) on the table, and, as Newton's third law tells us, a reactive force is supplied by the table. These forces

Amusement-park equipment can be used to confirm the fundamental laws of mechanics. When this ride begins, the seats are thrown toward the outside along a circular path maintained by the chains. The person in the seat is subject to centripetal acceleration and, since there is mass, is also subject to centripetal force felt along the chains pulling toward the center. The chains are also subject to centrifugal force, depending on the mass of the seat and of its occupant.

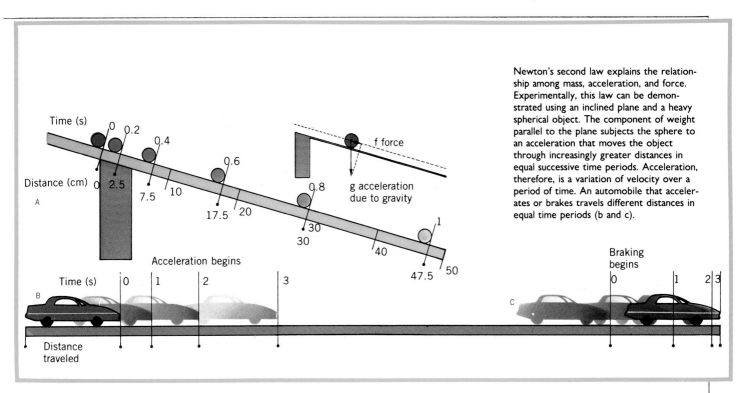

Though stated in abstract terms, the laws of Newtonian mechanics have numerous applications in day-to-day life, as in the amusement-park ride at left or in the concept of acceleration described above.

counteract each other and cancel each other out. That is, the sum of the forces is zero, and so the system is said to be static. More complex static systems are encountered daily by engineers, as they lay out plans for the rigid support beams and girders that form the skeletons of buildings and bridges.

There are numerous examples of dynamical systems, some of which show gravitational forces at work. If you suspend a block from a spring and then allow it to bob up and down, you have created a system in which gravitational forces and the tensile forces of the spring counteract each other, causing changes in the direction and magnitude of the acceleration. These competing accelerations carry the block back and forth past what would be the point of equilibrium in the spring, if the system were static. Ideally, this simple harmonic motion would carry on indefinitely, but in an actual system, motion will eventually cease, thanks to resistance to movement by the air around the block and to friction in the spring material. Two other forms of such simple harmonic mo-

tion are the vibrations of the prongs of a tuning fork and the swing of a pendulum.

Another application of dynamics is found in the motion of a projectile. In the case of a bullet shot from a gun, the explosion sets up a constant horizontal velocity. But there is also a vertical acceleration caused by gravity, which together with the horizontal velocity causes the bullet to assume an arching path for the duration of flight. In any mathematical analysis of either harmonic or projectile motion, Newton's laws must be used.

Momentum and Energy

In all bodies at rest or in motion, some form of energy is present; in moving bodies, this energy is known as kinetic energy. Both forms obey a principle called conservation of energy, which states that energy is not lost in any physical process, although its form, direction, or magnitude may change.

Something of this conservation principle can be grasped if we look at another quantity called momentum. Momentum is simply the product of the mass and velocity of any given body. If you roll a ball that has a mass of 1 kilogram at a rate of 2 meters per second, it will have a momentum of 2 kg/m per second. The interesting point is that this momentum will be transferred from one body to another in accordance with the general law that the total momentum (of both bodies taken together) remains constant. Thus, if the first ball collides with a second, which has a mass of, say, 4 kilograms and which is at rest, the second will move away with a

momentum equal to the first body's momentum before impact, provided the first ball stops on contact. In this case, the second body's speed after impact would be 0.5 meters per second. One reason automobile brakes must be quick and strong is that they must counteract the large amounts of momentum found in a car moving at high speeds.

Another important classical concept is that of gravitational potential energy, which is explained as the amount of work (which equals the force exerted times the distance over which it is exerted) an object would perform if it were to change from a state of rest to a state of motion, as caused by gravity. If you hold a rock above the ground, that rock contains potential energy proportional both to its mass and to its distance above the ground. If you release the rock, potential energy is transformed into kinetic energy, i.e., the energy of motion.

The applications of classical mechanics shown here are necessarily simple. As a branch of physics, it can be enormously complex, utilizing a sophisticated mathematics called the calculus and explaining motions and interactions with hundreds of variables. Regardless of advances in 20th-century physics, Newtonian mechanics retains its importance as an indispensable means of explaining phenomena in the world around us.

Mechanics, Celestial

Humans have always been fascinated and captivated by the regular movements of the stars across the heavens, the waxing and waning of the Moon, the motions of the planets. Primitive peoples everywhere were able to date the passing seasons by the positions of sunrises and sunsets and by the rising of key constellations. The months were marked by the Moon's phases.

The priests of ancient Egypt, Babylonia, and the Mayan Empire recorded the motions of the stars and planets with a high degree of accuracy. They developed calendars. The Mayans, for example, were capable of determining the position of Venus in the sky for centuries into the future. Yet, it cannot be said that they understood any of the basics of celestial mechanics, for none of them ever measured the distance, even in relative terms, from the Earth to any celestial body, such as the Moon, nor had they developed a logical, scientific, or mathematical concept for the movement of those bodies.

Aristarchus of Samos

The true study of celestial mechanics begins in the 3rd century B.C., with Aristarchus of Samos. He determined the relative distances among the Moon, Sun, and Earth by measuring the triangle formed by these three bodies when the Moon was in its half-moon phase. Aristarchus calculated that the Sun was 19 times farther from the Earth than the Moon. The correct figure is 400 times, but his error was in terms of measurement and not in theory. By observing the Earth's shadow on the Moon during a lunar eclipse, he determined that the Moon's diameter was one-third that of the Earth, which is close to the true figure—one-quarter.

Nicholas Copernicus

One of the greatest astronomers of all time, Nicholas Copernicus, was actually an amateur. Unlike the professionals, he was deeply influenced by the writings of several of the ancient Greek astronomers, including Aristarchus, who had believed that the Earth and other planets revolved around the Sun. But more than anything, Copernicus was disturbed by the explanations of the motions of the planets. In his time, their motions were shown in almanacs and astronomical works as being excessively complex. He questioned whether the motions of the planets were in fact all that complex, but only seemed so, because of a basic misconception, the belief that the Sun and planets circled the Earth. Copernicus made up new tables for the motions of the planets and Sun, but basing them on the belief that the Sun was at the center of the Solar System. As he had guessed, the new figures were much simpler and made more sense. They were, furthermore, quite accurate. Not until 1543, when he was on his death bed, did he reveal this work to the world. After looking at his new tables of planetary positions, astronomers began to accept the view that the Sun was indeed at the center of the Solar System.

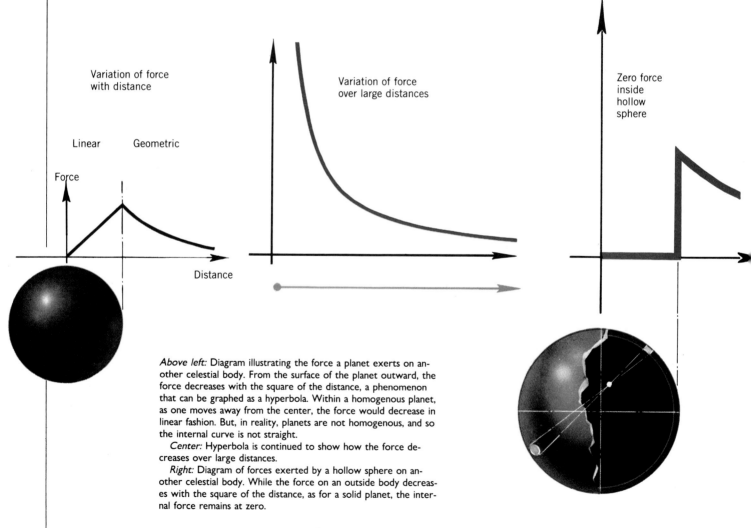

Variation of force with distance

Linear   Geometric

Force

Distance

Variation of force over large distances

Zero force inside hollow sphere

Above left: Diagram illustrating the force a planet exerts on another celestial body. From the surface of the planet outward, the force decreases with the square of the distance, a phenomenon that can be graphed as a hyperbola. Within a homogenous planet, as one moves away from the center, the force would decrease in linear fashion. But, in reality, planets are not homogenous, and so the internal curve is not straight.

Center: Hyperbola is continued to show how the force decreases over large distances.

Right: Diagram of forces exerted by a hollow sphere on another celestial body. While the force on an outside body decreases with the square of the distance, as for a solid planet, the internal force remains at zero.

Johannes Kepler

No one furthered the science of celestial mechanics more than Johannes Kepler. When he began his work, around 1600, there were many questions about celestial mechanics left unanswered. Most astronomers believed that the planets circled the Sun in orbits that were perfect circles. Secondly and more importantly, the relative distances of the planets from each other were unknown. All that was really known was that the orbits of Venus and Mercury were inside the orbit of the Earth, while all the others were outside the Earth's orbit. But how far away? There was hardly a clue.

Kepler's project to determine the shapes of the planets' orbits was an extraordinarily difficult one. He would be required to find the known orbits of planets from the Earth, whose orbit was itself unknown. Kepler began by determining the position of the Sun, Earth, and the planet Mars when Mars was seen by an observer on

Earth to be due south (on the southern meridian) at exactly midnight. He knew that at that precise time the Sun, Earth, and Mars would be aligned. This gave him a baseline from which to work out other calculations and from which to work out various other positions of the orbits of Mars and the Earth. This work required not only his observations of the planets but also those of the Danish astronomer Tycho Brahe, taken over many years.

The mathematical calculations were staggering in their complexity, but Kepler worked them out. After decades of work, he showed that the planets moved around the Sun in elliptical orbits. The Sun was located at one of the foci of the ellipse. He further deduced that planets moved in such a way that an imaginary straight line from the planet to the Sun swept out equal areas in equal amounts of time. He also discovered that the squares of the periodic times the different planets take to describe their orbits are proportional to the cubes

of their mean distance from the Sun. With these discoveries, astronomers not only knew the shapes of the orbits of the planets, but they could also calculate all the relative distances of the different planets from the Sun.

Thanks to Kepler's work, scientists understood how the planets moved, though some basic questions were still unanswered: What moved them? Why did they move at all? What influenced them?

Isaac Newton

Isaac Newton's work on universal gravitation, as he called it, will always be considered as one of the greatest of all scientific achievements. Before Newton solved the problem of gravitation, he faced a basic and interesting question. Could the Moon be falling toward the Earth? Is it falling in the same way an apple falls? Newton reasoned that if it were falling, it would be falling at a much slower rate than an apple, for the Moon is so much

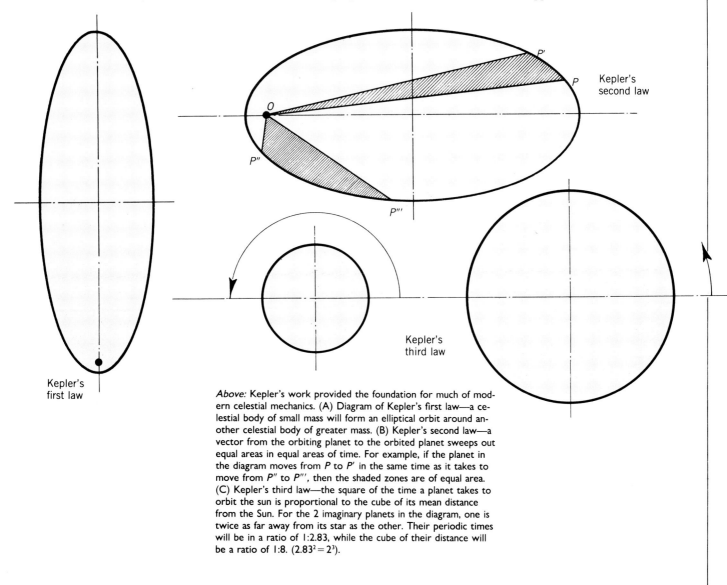

Above: Kepler's work provided the foundation for much of modern celestial mechanics. (A) Diagram of Kepler's first law—a celestial body of small mass will form an elliptical orbit around another celestial body of greater mass. (B) Kepler's second law—a vector from the orbiting planet to the orbited planet sweeps out equal areas in equal areas of time. For example, if the planet in the diagram moves from *P* to *P'* in the same time as it takes to move from *P''* to *P'''*, then the shaded zones are of equal area. (C) Kepler's third law—the square of the time a planet takes to orbit the sun is proportional to the cube of its mean distance from the Sun. For the 2 imaginary planets in the diagram, one is twice as far away from its star as the other. Their periodic times will be in a ratio of 1:2.83, while the cube of their distance will be a ratio of 1:8. $(2.83^2 = 2^3)$.

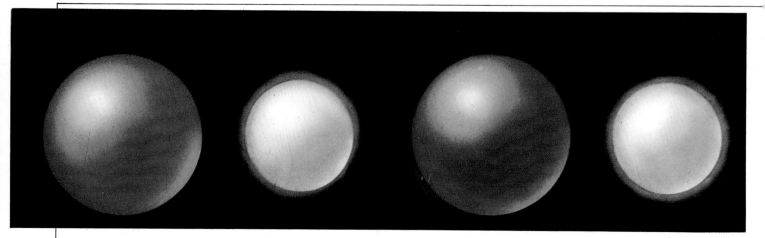

farther from the Earth. Knowing that light diminishes in intensity by the square of the distance from the source, he guessed that gravity would also diminish by the square of the distance. After calculating the falling rate of the Moon and its distance, he saw that its fall toward the Earth was proportional to that of a falling body near the Earth's surface. All the figures checked. He next formulated his famous laws of gravity. Newton never wrote that celestial bodies attract each other. In the *Principia,* he wrote, "I have not been able to discover the cause of those properties of gravity from phenomena, and I frame no hypotheses."

Albert Einstein

With the findings of Albert Einstein in the 20th century, celestial mechanics took a new and unexpected turn. Einstein had at his disposal new mathematical work in non-Euclidian geometry. Several mathematicians, including Herman Minkowski and Georg Riemann, were demonstrating that the geometry of space was influenced by time itself and, moreover, that space was curved. But most mathematicians considered such a space as abstract. It was Einstein's genius that he used such abstract notions for practical purposes. For example, he worked out the orbits of the planets, proposing especially that of Mercury in terms of a curved space, which was non-Euclidean. Though Kepler's and Newton's figures fit the facts, their sources did not correctly predict the orbit of Mercury. They were slightly off, but Einstein's figures seemed to explain the true orbit of Mercury. He discovered that the Sun and planets, being masses, bent the space around them. The more massive they were, the more they bent space itself. We can never actually see this bent space, but it exists.

Einstein's theory of gravity goes back to the 3rd century, when Hero of Alexandria discovered that reflected light trav-

Celestial mechanics now deals with much more than determining the orbits of the planets. *Above:* Diagram illustrates the problem of calculating the mass of an oscillating star. Using celestial mechanics, scientists can determine the heat of the stars and the extent of their expansion and contraction. With this knowledge, scientists can even predict celestial explosions, which result in the formation of supernovas, white dwarfs, and black holes.

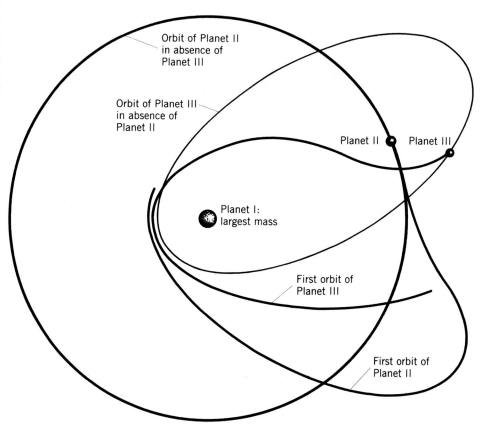

In the nearly 4 centuries in which celestial mechanics has existed, much has been learned about the relationship of 2 orbiting bodies. As yet, however, the laws that govern 3 orbiting bodies have not been discovered. *Above:* The orbits of 2 bodies can be accurately defined and predicted, but when a third body is added, its orbit seems to change constantly, without ever repeating itself.

els by the path that makes distance a minimum. The German mathematician David Hilbert wrote of Einstein's theory, "Gravitation acts so as to make the total curvature of space-time a minimum." Edmund Taylor Whittaker, who wrote about Newton's optics, stated that "gravitation (as stated by Einstein) simply represents a continual effort of the universe to straighten itself out."

The Three Body Problem

In spite of the great progress made in celestial mechanics, several problems remain to be solved. The most challenging for the space age is the three-body problem. Kepler and Newton showed scientists how they could determine the orbit of a planet around the Sun with extreme accuracy. But how do three celestial bodies interact? Oddly enough, this is an unsolved problem. Neither the most brilliant mathematicians nor the most powerful computers have completely solved it. Yet, spacecraft traveling to other planets are actually involved in a three-body problem. Their courses are adjusted in flight so they can travel to a distant planet.

See also RELATIVITY; STAR.

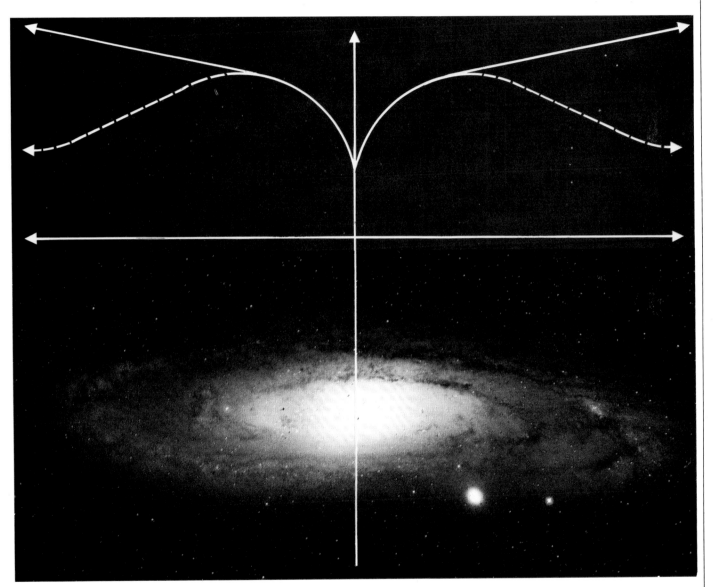

One of the challenges of the future for celestial mechanics is to determine the laws that govern the movement of stellar masses and entire galaxies. Another possibility is the search for black holes in the centers of distant galaxies. By using celestial mechanics, scientists can determine where abnormally great densities lie and then make assumptions about their causes.

Above: Diagram illustrates a problem of galactic dynamics. If a galaxy were to be in perfect equilibrium, its rotational-velocity curve would be a perfect double bell. Since it is not, this suggests that there is in the galaxy matter that sensors do not detect; possibly this matter consists of black holes.

Medical Research

As late as 1920, the prognosis for diabetics was not good. The disease was almost always debilitating and often fatal, for at that time there was no successful treatment for it. One year later, in 1921, with the discovery of insulin, the world changed for sufferers of diabetes. It was suddenly possible, with regular insulin treatments, for even the most severely afflicted to live long and normal lives.

The discovery of insulin by Frederick Banting and Charles Best at the University of Toronto was no chance occurrence; rather, it was the culmination of over 30 years of medical research into the treatment of diabetes.

Types of Research

The two main types of research in medicine are basic and applied. In basic research, there is no particular aim in mind other than the furthering of knowledge in a certain area. Applied research, however, is directed toward a definite goal. An example of the difference between the two is that a basic research project may

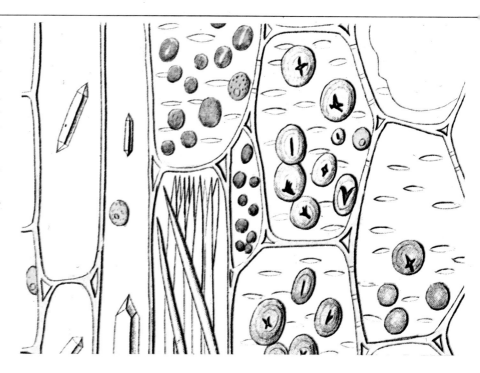

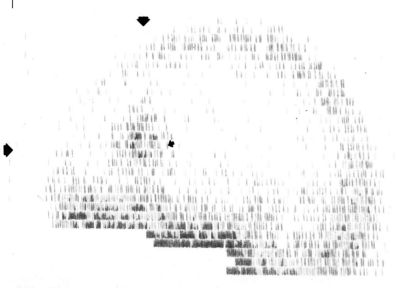

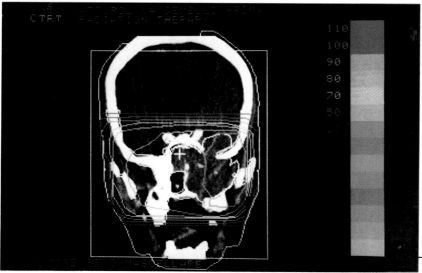

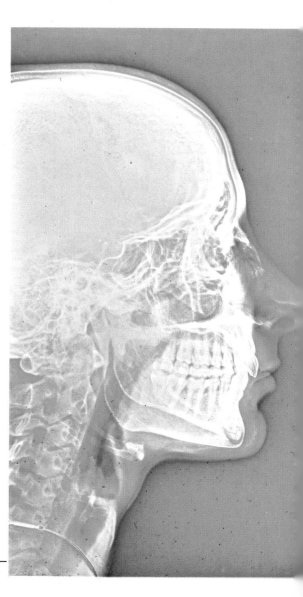

be to further our knowledge of bone structure, while applied research may be undertaken to discover the causes of a certain bone disease—and, possibly, a cure. While applied research is the more common of the two, information uncovered in basic research is often of crucial importance to applied research. As well, the two types may often overlap.

Research may be further subdivided by the ways in which it is undertaken. The two main methods for research are laboratory experimentation and clinical trials. Laboratory experiments, as their name suggests, are scientific investigations carried out in laboratories, often involving animal test subjects. Clinical trials use volunteer human subjects to test the efficiency of such things as new drugs or treatments. In many cases, laboratory experiments must have been conducted before clinical trials can begin.

Laboratory Research

In applied laboratory research, the first step is a recognition that there is a problem to be studied or a question to be solved. After this basic requirement has been met, the research can really begin—generally in a library, to review all the materials currently available on the subject in question. At this stage, the most valued tools are indexes to medical literature, some of which are now computerized, which makes the search for materials even simpler. Once aware of what is currently known in a certain area, the researcher can formulate a hypothesis. The hypothesis should generally be a logical extrapolation from accepted or proven knowledge. It is then the goal of the researcher to see if the hypothesis can be either proven or disproven.

The next stage of research is experimental design. There are many different

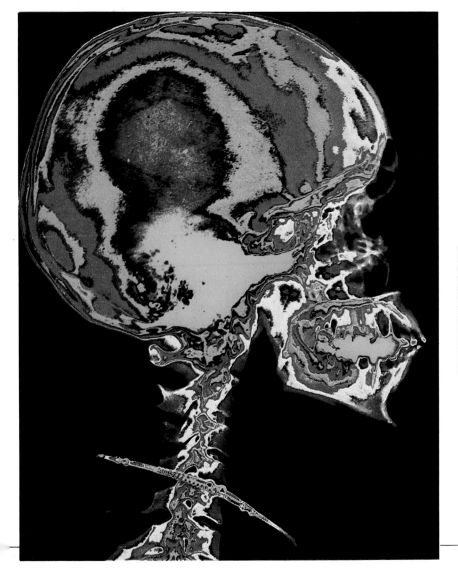

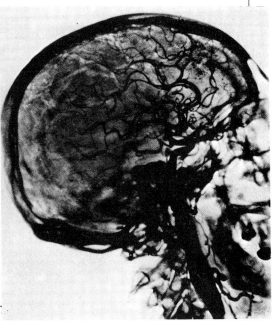

Left: Thermograph displays temperature variations in visible forms.

Below: Conventional X ray. Newer techniques often cannot compete in terms of cost and ease of use with the ordinary X ray, which remains an important tool for both clinical observation and laboratory research.

types of experimental design, but the simplest is the completely randomized design. (Indeed, randomization is an important part of all other designs as well.) A common experiment is to compare groups of subjects that are alike in all respects except one. The like aspects are known as controls, and the unlike aspect is the variable. An example would be the testing of a suspected cancer-causing agent on rats. Rats in Groups A and B may be treated quite similarly (the controls—same food, cages, age, etc.), except that rats in Group A receive doses of the possible carcinogen (the variable), while rats in Group B do not. Any increase in the incidence of cancer among the rats of Group A may indicate that the substance is indeed a carcinogen. It must always be taken into account, though, that individual rats may differ immensely from one another, and so the rats for experimentation are selected at random; as well, the doses of the substance are also administered at random to the rats.

Once an experiment has been designed, it can be set up and put into operation. The process of running an experiment demands highly skilled and specially trained personnel. Often a "dry run" of the experiment is need to iron out any wrinkles in the design before the real experiment is run. Once the researchers begin to receive data from the experiment, it must be readied for statistical analysis, which isolates and validates the important information and which delineates the conclusions that can be drawn from the experiment. To announce the results of the research project, the researchers will release their findings to a medical journal, often first in the form of a letter to the editor, followed up by a longer, in-depth article.

Clinical Research

While it may be shown in a laboratory experiment that substance A cures lumbago in rats, it will not be certain what its effect will be on humans until it is tested on humans. Clinical trials are conducted much like laboratory experiments. First, the aim of the study is defined; second, the study is designed and run; finally, the data is assessed. One of the most common forms of clinical trial is a test to check the effectiveness of a drug or a treatment. Subjects are selected at random from a group of volunteers. In trials of two drugs at one time, each drug may be administered at different times to each subject, or one drug may be given to half of the subjects and the other drug to the remaining subjects, often without the patients knowing which drug they are receiving. In tests

of one drug, one group is given the test drug, and a "dummy" is administered to the other. Often, in trials of this kind, not only the patients but also the physicians are ignorant of who is receiving the drug, who the dummy, virtually eliminating any chance of bias. Not only drugs, but also other forms of treatment, including surgery, may also be tested by clinical trial. The most important rule of all clinical trials is that no patient who consents to be a subject should be worse off after the trial than he or she was before.

Research in History

While experimentation has always played a part in medicine, it was not until the 19th century, with the development of scientific method, that medical research as we know it began. One of the key figures in early medical research was the French physiologist Claude Bernard, whose *Introduction à l'étude de médecine expérimentale* ("Introduction to the Study of Experimental Medicine"), an account of the principles he came upon in his revolutionary work in experimentation, is a classic. Perhaps the two greatest fruits of 19th-century medical research were Louis Pasteur's discoveries in bacteriology and the work done in the United States and, later, in Europe in anesthesiology.

The 20th century has seen the greatest expansion of medical research thus far, as well as its greatest accomplishments. The discoveries of penicillin and other antibiotics, insulin, and vaccines, as well as the surgical developments such as transplantation techniques and microsurgery, are just a few of the more dramatic medical breakthroughs. All these advances have been the result of many years of diligent applied research.

Research Today and Tomorrow

It has become apparent recently that it is hard to define specifically what is and what is not medical research. More and more, the subject has become intertwined with research in biology, chemistry, and physics; indeed, it seems that most modern research is in some way interdisciplinary, employing everything from processes tested and developed in space to tools derived from research in atomic energy. Advanced technology, such as the electron microscope and the CAT scan, has been instrumental in the processes of modern research.

The medical research of the future will have the same goals as research in the past: the search for cures and treatments for diseases and afflictions. A major change will be in the focus of the research. Cur-

rently, cancer and heart disease are receiving considerable attention. As well, there will always be research into improving treatments, such as the recent development of synthetic insulin, which is much cheaper and easier to produce than insulin from animals. If medical research continues to be as successful as it has been in the past, then truly remarkable discoveries are likely to be made.

See also LABORATORY.

Below: The 4 images trace the arrival in the heart of blood carrying a radioactive-isotope tracer. The images themselves are generated by a computer on the basis of sensor readings of radiation levels. The dark-red color corresponds to zones where radioactivity is most intense.

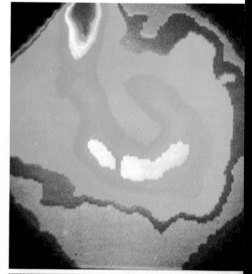

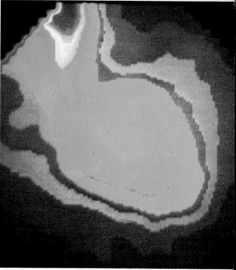

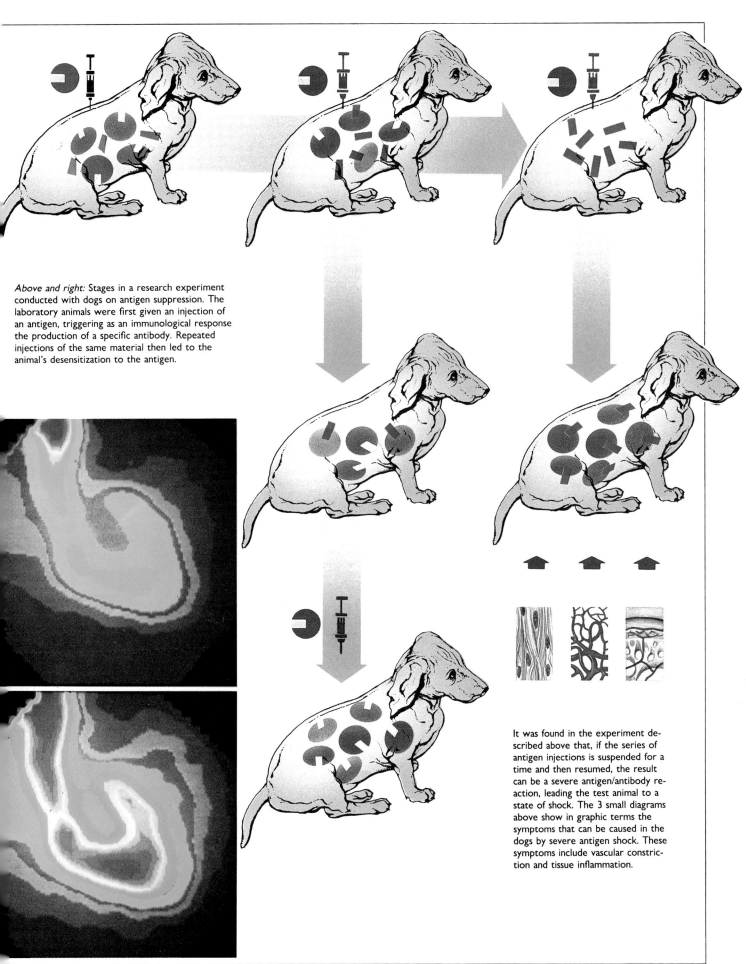

Above and right: Stages in a research experiment conducted with dogs on antigen suppression. The laboratory animals were first given an injection of an antigen, triggering as an immunological response the production of a specific antibody. Repeated injections of the same material then led to the animal's desensitization to the antigen.

It was found in the experiment described above that, if the series of antigen injections is suspended for a time and then resumed, the result can be a severe antigen/antibody re-action, leading the test animal to a state of shock. The 3 small diagrams above show in graphic terms the symptoms that can be caused in the dogs by severe antigen shock. These symptoms include vascular constriction and tissue inflammation.

Medicine

Hundreds of thousands of years ago, when an early human lay shivering with malaria or broke a leg climbing for berries, there was no doubt a healer with special skills and intuition to ease the pain or cure the sickness. Thus, the practice of medicine was born and developed. In prehistoric times, medicine was magic. Illnesses were thought to be caused by evil spirits, and witch doctors drilled holes in patients' skulls to conjure out the disease.

The art and science of medicine have come a long way since then, but modern techniques are just as magical in their own way. Some of the most fantastic include

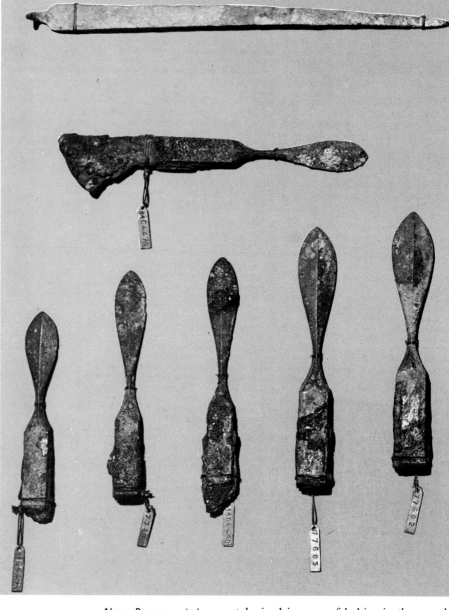

Above: Roman surgical tools. *Left:* Drawing of masked dancer who took part in ceremonies intended to drive evil spirits from the bodies of the sick in the traditional medicine of Lapland.
Above right: Illustrations taken from a medieval manual for obstetricians. They show positions the fetus was thought to assume within the womb. The object in terra-cotta, below, is a model of the liver. It was used for predicting the future on the basis of the shape and appearance of the organ in sacrificial animals in ancient Babylon.

televised images of babies in the womb, artificial arms that move like real ones, organ transplants, plastic hip joints, artificial skin that breathes and stretches, microsurgery to reconnect severed limbs, test-tube babies, and genetic engineering that can actually change the natural function of a cell. Still in the experimental stages are a vaccine against tooth decay and techniques to regrow amputated limbs and heal broken bones with electricity.

All of this technology is at the service of numerous medical professionals, including doctors, nurses, technicians, therapists, and researchers. Health care is big business, especially in the United States, where it is the third-largest industry, following agriculture and construction. In 1950, health-care costs represented 4.5 percent of the U.S. national product, a yearly average of $84 per person. In 1980, it was 9 percent and cost an average of about $900 per person.

Medicine has three main functions: disease prevention, diagnosis (reading the symptoms to identify the disease), and treatment (effecting a cure with drugs, surgery, or other therapy).

Though the art of medicine has been practiced since the dawn of man, it was not until about 50 years ago that physicians gained the ability to cure more than a mere handful of diseases. The time-honored role of the physician was as an intimate counselor to a whole family. He or she treated the soul as well as the body. If there is any objection to the new technology and the specialists required to apply it, it is that the old-fashioned general practitioner may now become obsolete.

Many patients are left alone to face an awesome technology whose complexities they cannot comprehend.

History

The history of medicine reflects the struggle between people's need for spiritual succor and physical healing. The transition from magic (the spiritual side) to science took centuries and is, in fact, still going on today, as faith healers draw on beliefs in supernatural powers. (Many scientists believe it is the patient's own mind that effects a so-called faith cure, through the power of self-hypnosis.) Ancient healers used magical incantations, talismans, and dream therapy. They also examined animal entrails, which they thought paralleled the course of the disease through the patient's body. They often prescribed herbs, some of which are still used today.

Ancient Egyptians, for example, used castor oil, opium, and mercury. Chinese used iron and camphor and developed the still-applied acupuncture system of sticking needles into precisely determined points of the body. Surgeons in ancient India performed some operations, including nose reconstruction (nose amputation was a common punishment for adultery) and removal of gallstones. Babylonians didn't believe in experts. They laid their sick in the streets for passersby to diagnose and prescribe treatment.

Among the Greek physicians was Hippocrates (5th century B.C.), who developed a strong code of medical ethics

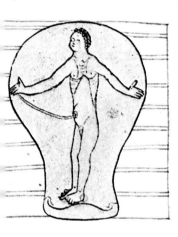   

known as the Hippocratic Oath, which is still administered as part of the graduation ceremony at most medical schools. The Romans advanced the public health with therapeutic baths and craftily engineered sewage and drainage systems. During the Middle Ages, when the Church was so powerful in Europe, people were concerned mostly with spiritual health—scientific medical learning and experimentation were discouraged.

The body remained very much a mystery until the 17th century, when scientists identified the circulatory system and invented the microscope. The 18th century witnessed the development of the

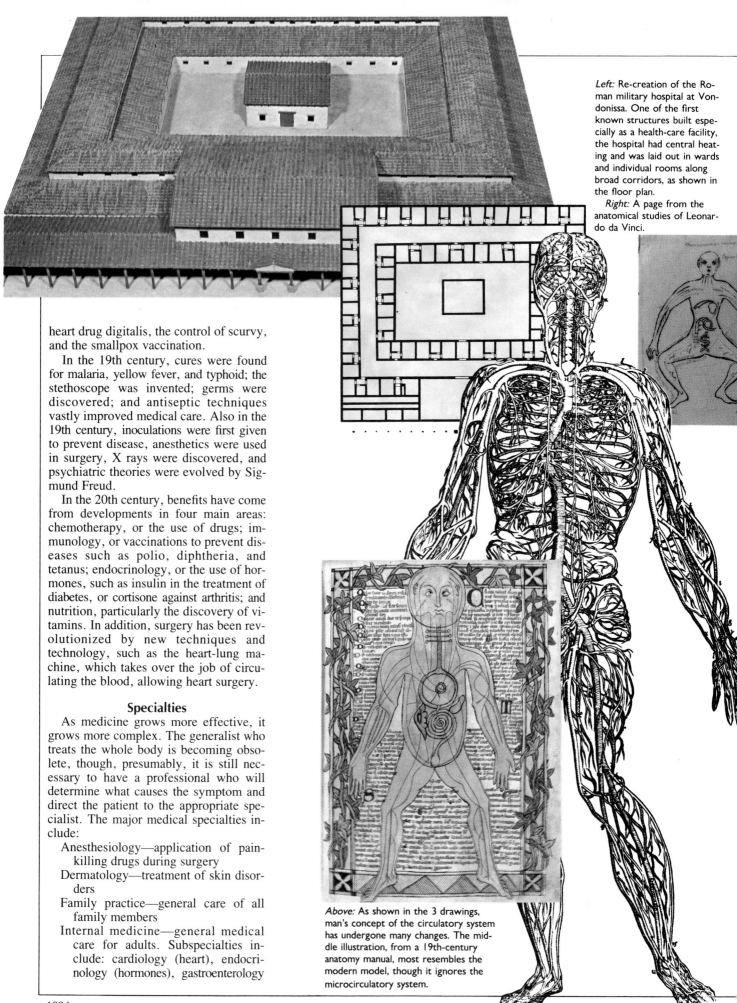

heart drug digitalis, the control of scurvy, and the smallpox vaccination.

In the 19th century, cures were found for malaria, yellow fever, and typhoid; the stethoscope was invented; germs were discovered; and antiseptic techniques vastly improved medical care. Also in the 19th century, inoculations were first given to prevent disease, anesthetics were used in surgery, X rays were discovered, and psychiatric theories were evolved by Sigmund Freud.

In the 20th century, benefits have come from developments in four main areas: chemotherapy, or the use of drugs; immunology, or vaccinations to prevent diseases such as polio, diphtheria, and tetanus; endocrinology, or the use of hormones, such as insulin in the treatment of diabetes, or cortisone against arthritis; and nutrition, particularly the discovery of vitamins. In addition, surgery has been revolutionized by new techniques and technology, such as the heart-lung machine, which takes over the job of circulating the blood, allowing heart surgery.

Specialties

As medicine grows more effective, it grows more complex. The generalist who treats the whole body is becoming obsolete, though, presumably, it is still necessary to have a professional who will determine what causes the symptom and direct the patient to the appropriate specialist. The major medical specialties include:

Anesthesiology—application of pain-killing drugs during surgery

Dermatology—treatment of skin disorders

Family practice—general care of all family members

Internal medicine—general medical care for adults. Subspecialties include: cardiology (heart), endocrinology (hormones), gastroenterology

Above: As shown in the 3 drawings, man's concept of the circulatory system has undergone many changes. The middle illustration, from a 19th-century anatomy manual, most resembles the modern model, though it ignores the microcirculatory system.

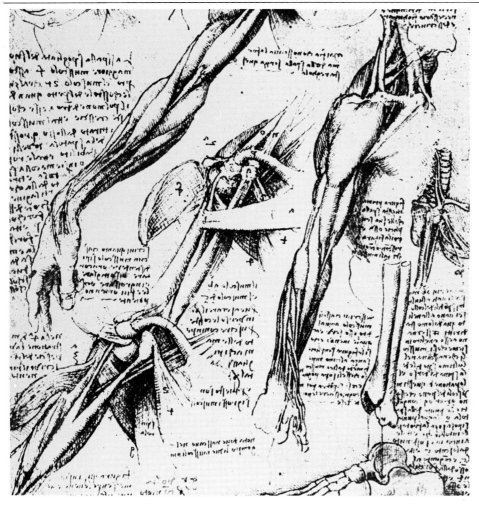

the eyes and prescribe glasses; psychologists treat mental problems; pharmacists fill prescriptions.

Nursing is the largest medical profession. Traditionally the domain of women, it is now attracting more and more men. As physicians become involved in their own specialties, trained nurses are taking over general-care duties. Nurse-practitioners handle routine care, take medical histories, perform examinations, and diagnose and treat simple problems under a doctor's supervision. Nurse-midwives give prenatal care and deliver babies.

Researchers work in laboratories, where they develop all the new drugs and medical technology, often through experimentation with animals.

There are two main types of technicians. Some work with patients; they operate medical instruments, such as radiation therapy machines, to treat cancer patients, or dialysis machines, to filter the blood of kidney patients. Other technicians work in laboratories, analyzing blood and tissue samples to determine the extent of disease. Radiology technicians take X rays of different parts of the body so that a radiologist can diagnose an internal problem.

A master's degree in health administration, public health, or business administration may qualify an applicant for a job as a hospital or health-center administrator or as a public health official.

(stomach and intestines and liver), infectious diseases, nephrology (kidneys), pulmonary (lungs), rheumatology (joints)

Neurology—medical diagnosis and treatment of brain and neuromuscular disorders

Neurosurgery—treatment of diseases of the brain and spinal cord

Obstetrics and gynecology—treatment of the female reproductive system, pregnancy, and childbirth

Ophthalmology—treatment of the eye

Orthopedics—surgical treatment of bone diseases and fractures

Otolaryngology—treatment of ear, nose, and throat diseases

Pathology—study of changes in the body that are caused by diseases

Pediatrics—treatment of children

Plastic surgery—surgical reconstruction, especially of the face, for cosmetic purposes

Preventive medicine—application of measures to prevent disease; includes public-health programs, study of environmental health hazards, diet, and the stresses of modern life

Proctology—treatment of the lower digestive tract and rectum

Psychiatry—treatment of mental diseases

Radiology—diagnostic and therapeutic X rays and other radiations

Thoracic surgery—surgical treatment of heart, lungs, large blood vessels

Careers in Medicine

Men and women who decide on a career in medicine have six basic choices; they can become physicians, other medical professionals, nurses, technicians, researchers, or administrators. Those who choose to be doctors face the most difficult and extensive course of training. Most countries require a 4-year premedical university degree, followed by 3 to 4 years of medical school. Further study includes a year as a hospital intern, treating patients under the supervision of experienced doctors. After the internship, most doctors train for a specialty, with residency in the field they have selected. Residency may take from 3 years for family practice up to 5 years for neurosurgery.

Other medical professionals are qualified to treat special areas of the body. Dentists care for teeth and gums; podiatrists treat foot problems; optometrists examine

Financing Medical Care

Doctors are among the highest paid professionals in most countries. In the United States, they usually go into private practice by themselves or join a group of doctors specializing either in the same field or in complementary fields, thus offering patients a complete treatment center. Most doctors are affiliated with a hospital that permits them to treat patients there or in their offices.

Some countries, such as Russia and China, offer completely socialized medicine—all medical personnel are paid by the government, and all patients are treated free of charge.

In Great Britain, all patients are covered by the National Health Service and entitled to free medical care from a general practitioner, who refers them to a specialist if need be. In most other Western European countries, medicine is at least partially socialized. Most doctors are self-employed, though their fees are set by a government agency. Patients choose their own doctor and are reimbursed for medical care through a plan financed by the social security system. The trend, especially in large metropolitan areas, is toward specialization.

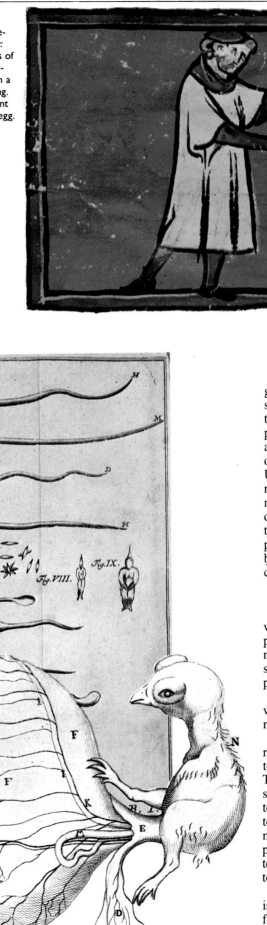

In Africa and parts of Asia, there is a general shortage of trained medical personnel. In northern Nigeria and in Nepal, there is about one doctor for each 100,000 people; in India, one per 6,000; in Britain, one per 1,000; in the United States, one per 800; in Israel and the Soviet Union, one per 450. Poor countries cannot afford better medical care, though in many ways their people need it more than do residents of rich countries. Many of their worst scourges—tuberculosis, syphilis, typhoid, cholera, malaria—could be completely cured with the drugs discovered in the last 60 years.

Diagnosis

In order to help a patient, the medical worker must first identify the disease or problem. Three main clues lead to diagnosis: the patient's case history, the physician's physical examination of the patient, and various medical tests.

The patient provides the case history, which is simply an account of past illnesses and of how he or she now feels.

For the physical examination, a doctor relies on many different diagnostic tools to peer at, probe, and listen to the body. The general practitioner uses six basic instruments: the stethoscope, which is used to listen to heart and lungs; the otoscope, to look into ears and nose; the ophthalmoscope, to look into the eyes; the blood-pressure cuff; the thermometer, to check temperature; and the percussion hammer, to detect internal disorders.

The diagnostic equipment of specialists is often quite elaborate. The obstetrician, for example, can use ultrasound scanning to check the development of a baby in the womb. This technique is now used as an alternative to X rays, which were found to harm unborn babies. Ultrasound sees as a bat does, by bouncing high-frequency (higher than the ear can hear) sound waves off internal organs. The visual image of these organs is then projected on a television screen. Other problems, such as stomach tumors and gallstones (which X rays may miss) may also be diagnosed with ultrasound.

The internist now has a new diagnostic tool, computer scanning, which gives detailed views of the inner structure of an organ by taking X rays of slices of the organ at various depths.

The cardiologist can determine whether blood vessels are open, or whether the heart is working properly, by inserting a slender glass tube into any vein or artery in the body. Dye is then delivered through the tube to the area in question and X-rayed as it passes through the body. They also use echocardiography which, like ultrasound, uses sound waves to see the inside of the heart. Electrocardiography (ECG) registers the electrical activity of the heartbeat.

An internist can see into the stomach, the intestines, or the lungs through a flexible tube inserted into the patient's mouth. The tube is specially designed to let light travel around curve and corners. These tubes are called fiberoptic endoscopes.

When the physician joins investigative forces with the medical laboratory, the results are astounding. Amniocentesis, for example, involves drawing out some of the fluid that surrounds the baby in the womb and then analyzing it to detect birth defects such as Down's syndrome. The same test even reveals the sex of the unborn baby.

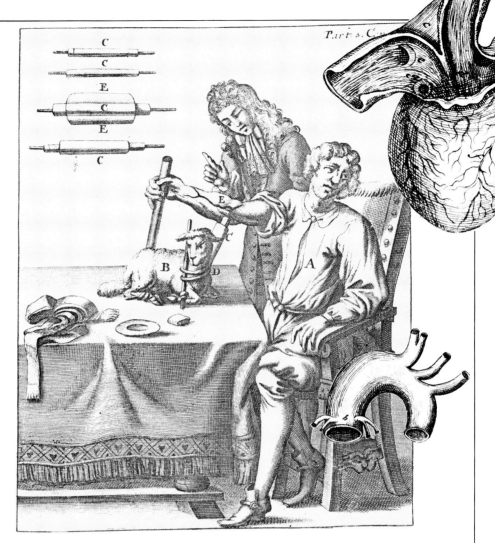

Blood transfusions often had unfortunate results for the patient, until the discovery of blood typing and of the Rh factor in the last century made it a much safer procedure. *Above:* Late-17th-century print showing the experimental transfusion of the blood of a sheep to a human.

Below: Print from an Italian text shows the pustules resulting from an attempt to transplant tissue samples in a patient's arm.

Any body substance—blood, urine, pus, little pieces of tissue—can give a laboratory technician clues about a disease. Blood tests, for example, may determine the existence of many different conditions from anemia to cancer.

Treatment

Once a disease has been identified, the physician decides on treatment, which may include surgery, drugs, or some other form of therapy. For example, if examination reveals heart disease, the physician determines how extensive the damage is. Then a nonsurgical treatment may be prescribed, usually a regimen of low-cholesterol foods and controlled exercise. If arteries are heavily-blocked, however, the doctor may decide to do a heart by-pass operation, removing a vein from the leg and hooking it up to the heart to bypass a diseased or blocked artery.

If the patient is diagnosed as having cancer, the physician may prescribe either surgery or one of a number of nonsurgical treatments. Cancer is still far from being understood. Researchers do know that it is not a single disease; it follows many

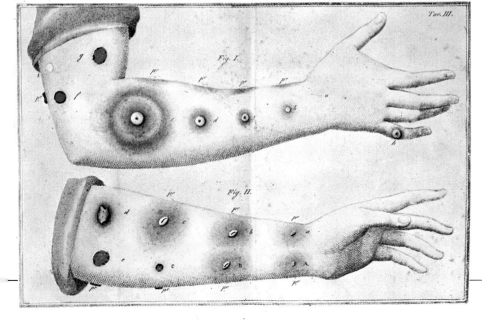

Left: Museum display of some of the laboratory equipment used by Louis Pasteur for his pioneering work in microbiology. *Above and right:* Microscope and slides used by the Italian scientist Camillo Golgi in his studies of the histology of the nervous system. He was given the 1906 Nobel prize for this research.

different routes, may result from many different causes, and responds to different therapies, including various drugs or X-ray therapy. Among the new treatments now on trial are: vitamin A, interferon (a substance that the body produces naturally to fight infection), and heat therapy, which raises the temperature of the body to 107.6°F. (42°C.). Extreme cold has also been used effectively. The newest weapon is the laser, now commonly used to kill precancerous tissue in the womb.

Many diseases are now understood and curable. Notable exceptions—cancer and heart disease, for example—often respond well to treatment. Patients who cannot be completely cured often are able to return to a full life, the disease held in check by drugs, special diets, or other kinds of therapy. Even still mysterious mental diseases such as schizophrenia can sometimes be treated with special diets or massive doses of vitamins; new drugs have enabled some mental patients to leave the institutions in which they were confined.

Prevention

Many doctors and public-health officials believe that the best cure for disease is to prevent it before it starts. Systematic inoculation of children against many diseases such as polio and diphtheria is now standard, at least in industrialized countries. Thanks to the efforts of the World Health Organization (an agency of the United Nations), some diseases, including smallpox, have been virtually wiped off the face of the Earth.

Increased awareness of the health hazards of air, water, soil, and noise pollution has inspired some reforms, though the environment is still in grave danger, according to many experts. Nonindustrialized nations also suffer from problems of the environment, particularly from a lack of clean drinking water and sanitary sewage systems. Some 86 percent of people living in the countryside of developing nations live with inadequate drinking water, and even in towns only 28 percent of the people have satisfactory sewage facilities. These conditions leave people open to such diseases as dysentery, typhoid fever, hepatitis, and cholera. This problem is so important that the United Nations has declared the 1980s the Decade of International Drinking Water Supply and Sanitation.

Preventive-medicine experts believe that daily habits can either make or break health. They recommend that people reduce stress in their lives, drink less alcohol, cut out smoking, and follow a diet that is low in fat, salt, and sugar and high in whole grains, fruits, and vegetables. Regular exercise is also important.

The Future

Medical experts predict wonders for the near and distant future. Wounds may be healed with a spray that covers like a new skin. Artificial hearts may run on batteries. The blind may see through tiny television cameras installed in their eyes. The deaf may hear with electrodes implanted in their ears. Tooth decay may be vanquished with sprays and vaccines. Each person may have an individual diet, determined by a computer analysis of individual needs at that particular time.

Perhaps the most exciting developments are in the new field of genetic engineering. Genes can be likened to computer programs—they tell each cell what to do. Genetic engineering changes that inborn code. For example, if the gene that tells the cells of the pancreas to produce insulin is inserted into a bacterial cell, that bacterium will start producing insulin. This may be a boon to diabetics, whose bodies fail to produce enough insulin naturally. Genetic engineering is now also being used to produce interferon, another substance present in healthy human beings, which is in experimental stages as a treatment for cancer.

Eventually, doctors may be able to take a few healthy cells from a diseased liver, for example, and program them to grow a new liver. The day may come when scientists can tamper with any inborn characteristics, from intelligence to muscle strength, height, and hair color—perhaps even create an ideal person.

Like many of the technological leaps of the 20th century, the revolution in medical care has far outstripped ethical thinking. Genetic engineering may create an ideal, but who decides what that ideal is to be? Doctors can determine whether an unborn baby will be deformed, but who decides whether that baby is to be aborted? Hospital machines keep patients alive by pumping their blood, filtering their urine, even breathing for them, but who decides how long to keep patients on the machines before they are declared dead? Who decides what death is? Is it when breathing stops, when the heart no longer beats, or when the brain ceases to function? Who helps the dying patients and their families? In short, is the humanitarian, caring side of medicine—the side that treats the soul—losing out to the purely scientific side, which treats the body as a mechanic treats an engine?

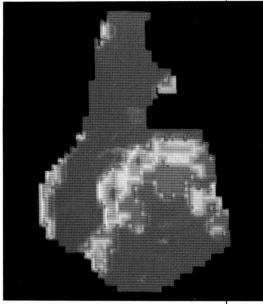

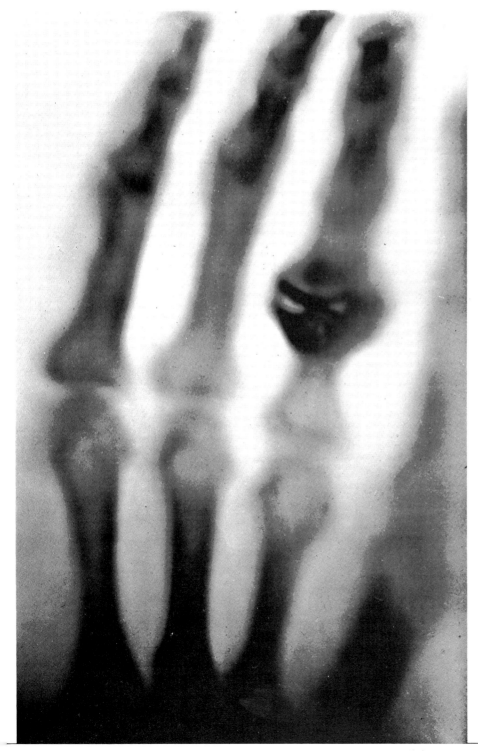

Left: The first X ray ever made. Wilhelm Konrad Roentgen, who discovered the rays, made this study of the bones in his wife's hand on December 22, 1895. *Above:* Computer-generated image displays the results of a heart scan made as a radioactive-isotope tracer was injected into a patient's bloodstream. Zones with the greatest concentration of the radioisotope appear dark red in color.

Some health-care workers are concerned about this question. Hospice organizations, for example, help terminally ill patients to die peaceably at home or in a hospital, by involving the entire family in their care. At the other end of life, many hospitals are now installing birthing centers for parents trained in natural techniques. In these centers, the whole family can participate in the miracle of birth in a warm, homelike room, with all the latest equipment ready behind the scenes to aid mother or baby in case of emergency.

Memory

Many of our actions, from the simplest to the complex, are based on memory, the recollection of past experience. Without memory, we would not know where our clothes are or how to put them on; we would not be able to pass a test in school; in fact, we would not have access to anything we have learned. Forgetting the information needed to perform the acts of daily life can be caused by a failure in any of the three stages of memory: learning, or registering information; storing, or retaining information; remembering, or retrieving information when you need it.

Structure of Memory

When someone first learns a fact, a memory trace is laid down in his mind. (The "memory trace" is not a physical pathway; it is a term used to describe the way your mind operates.) Thinking about the fact that Henry VIII had six wives, or rehearsing the information, helps you learn by strengthening the trace. How well you learn a fact in the first place determines how long you will retain it and how quickly you can retrieve it.

The time between learning a fact and recalling it to your conscious mind is the retention phase. One theory suggests that a memory trace decays from disuse in this phase. If a year passes between the time you studied Henry and the time you take your test, without further rehearsal of the facts, you may not retain the memory. A different theory blames unlearning for failure to retain an idea. In this concept, memory is seen as a series of connections between images or ideas. It is these connections that decay because of neglect.

This concept of connections or association is important in theories of memory process. Association is the memory's way of finding different bits of information by relating them to each other. The memories are "tied together" by associations. Recalling one bit of information may lead to another, as if by following a string from one point to another. These points, or related ideas, can be used as cues to help us recall information. The question "How many wives did Henry have?" may be a cue that leads directly to the answer. But some cues do not correspond to the relevant memory trace because of the way the information is stored; your mind has connected the cue to different bits of information, and you follow the wrong string. The direct question may not cue your memory, whereas the sight of the watch you were wearing while studying about Henry may help you recall the information, since Henry and the watch are associated in your memory with that study session. Retrieving elusive memories is dependent on finding an effective cue.

Recall may also be inhibited by competing memories, or interference. Of course, each bit of information is associated with many others, and there are thus many sets or strings of information. One string or pathway may dominate another, so you cannot follow the cue to the final idea you want. Proactive interference occurs when old memories interfere with new learning. Retroactive interference is the opposite: new learning interferes with the ability to retrieve old memories. Some researchers suggest that interference is responsible for all forgetting; that is, all memories retained can be blocked by conflicting memories learned previously or subsequently. Of course, not all memories block each other; this simplified description belies the tremendous volume and complexity of information and associations your memory can handle.

Long- and Short-Term Memory

Some psychologists divide memory into short-term (STM) and long-term (LTM). Short-term memory contains immediate, still-existing information, present information your senses have just registered; you have immediate access to STM. Long-term memory contains all other informa-

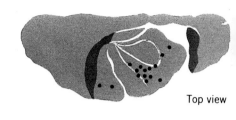

Top view

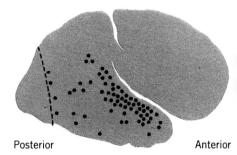

Posterior   Anterior

Right
hemisphere

Bottom
view

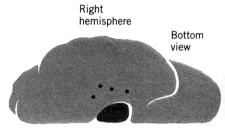

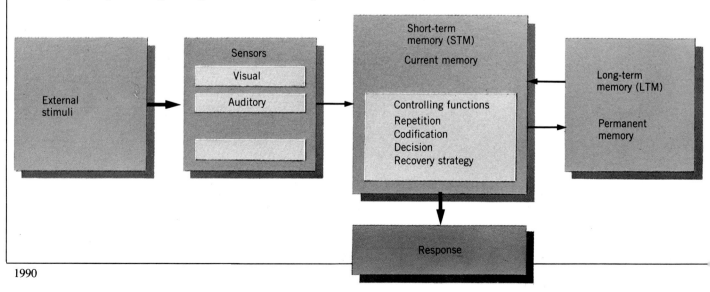

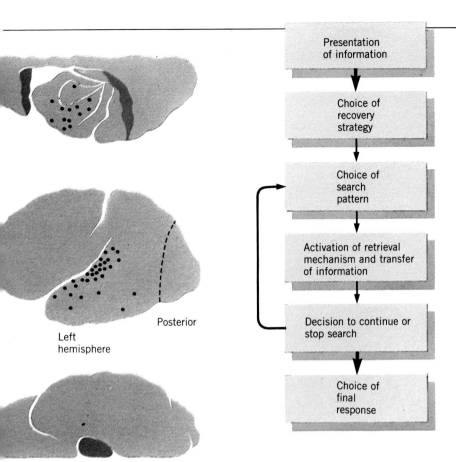

Presentation
of information

↓

Choice of
recovery
strategy

↓

Choice of
search
pattern

↓

Activation of retrieval
mechanism and transfer
of information

↓

Decision to continue or
stop search

↓

Choice of
final
response

Posterior

Left
hemisphere

Far left: Diagram showing memory centers in the brain. *Near left:* Chart shows how the brain searches its memory to locate sought-after information.

Below left: Chart illustrates how the brain's long-term and short-term memory banks interact.

tion stored in your memory, all past impressions. The STM can hold about seven separate items, which are rapidly lost if attention is turned to new information. This explains why, if you are distracted, you may forget a set of directions so quickly after hearing them. The STM can retain information by maintaining attention to it. For example, repeating the phone number keeps it in your awareness, as does visualizing it in the phone book or recalling the operator's voice saying it. As you rehearse the information, you also strengthen the memory trace of it in your LTM. Some psychologists think the STM and LTM are two different mechanisms, pointing out that some patients who sustain injury to the hippocampus, a part of the brain, cannot incorporate new information into the long-term memory but have unimpaired short-term memory functions. Proponents of the two-system theory also cite differences between STM and LTM in capacity and how long they retain information. Others suggest that there is only one "storage system," attributing the STM to very low levels of learning, which creates weak memory traces that decay easily.

Learning and Relearning

Memory, of course, includes more than the rethinking of individual, specific facts. As you learn, you acquire new concepts

and patterns, which are interrelated and associated with each other in your memory. The more you can relate new information to what is already in your memory, the easier it is to learn. This is referred to as meaningful learning. The information is associated with concepts or patterns already in your memory and becomes accessible to cues of other memories related to it. For instance, in Dante's *Inferno,* remembering that the punishments fit the crimes may help you recall which characters suffer what.

The stronger the memory trace, the more likely you will be to retain a memory and be able to retrieve it. Repeated rehearsal to remember information, even after it has been mastered—called overlearning—strengthens the memory. If you continued to practice the names of Henry's wives even after you could recite them easily, you would be likely to remember them longer. Learning results are best when practice sessions are separated by time rather than concentrated into one period. This explains why cramming may help you pass an examination tomorrow, but learning gradually, over a longer period of time, offers you a better chance of retaining the information.

Relearning, or learning information you learned earlier but cannot recall, also seems to aid memory. Relearned material is retained longer and mastered more quickly, with fewer practice sessions, than new information. Thus, if you learned about Henry's wives in September but forgot most of the information by March, you may be able to relearn the information in June in less time than it took to learn it in September, or than it would take if you had not learned it at all.

Diagram shows how fragments of information are forgotten— that is, removed from the memory.

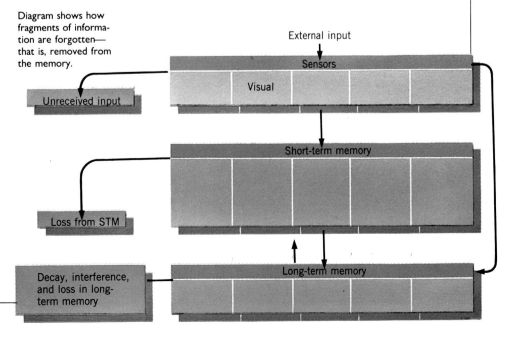

Menstruation

To some, menstruation is tangible evidence that the Moon has an influence on human life—a link between everyday activity and ancient myth. In most societies, the first menstruation signals a young woman's "coming of age," because she is now able to conceive and bear a child. Derived from the Latin *mensis,* meaning month, menstruation signals the onset of the human female's reproductive cycle. It is the sloughing off of blood and debris from the reproductive tract when fertilization does not occur, and it takes place about every 4 weeks or "lunar month."

severe injury to the cells, especially those of the tiny glands in the endometrium. The injury to the cells lining the uterus causes the lining to slough (fall away), which causes the bleeding. The blood does not clot as usual because of the presence of a protein called plasmin in the tissue.

This process occurs in different parts of the endometrium at varying times; blood-filled tissue falls away from the open wounds in the uterine wall, which contract rhythmically to discharge it. After a few days, healing begins automatically as hormone levels change in the blood and a

new lining regenerates. During the menstrual cycle, usually halfway between menstruations (called "periods" in common usage), ovulation occurs. At this time, an egg matures and bursts from the ovary, ready to be fertilized as part of another important human cycle—that of pregnancy and birth.

Symptoms of Menstruation

The first menstruation usually occurs when a young woman is between the ages of 10 and 16 and is called the menarch. She should be prepared for this by her

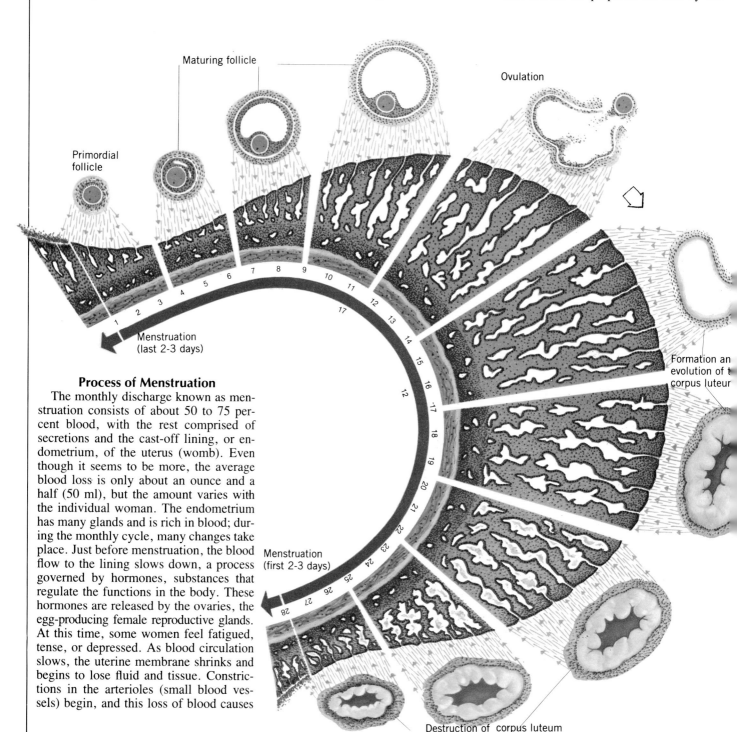

Maturing follicle

Ovulation

Primordial follicle

Menstruation (last 2-3 days)

1 2 3 4 5 6 7 8 9 10 11 12 13 14 15 16 17 12 17 18 19 20 21 22 23 24 25 26 27 28

Formation an evolution of t corpus luteur

Menstruation (first 2-3 days)

Destruction of corpus luteum

Process of Menstruation

The monthly discharge known as menstruation consists of about 50 to 75 percent blood, with the rest comprised of secretions and the cast-off lining, or endometrium, of the uterus (womb). Even though it seems to be more, the average blood loss is only about an ounce and a half (50 ml), but the amount varies with the individual woman. The endometrium has many glands and is rich in blood; during the monthly cycle, many changes take place. Just before menstruation, the blood flow to the lining slows down, a process governed by hormones, substances that regulate the functions in the body. These hormones are released by the ovaries, the egg-producing female reproductive glands. At this time, some women feel fatigued, tense, or depressed. As blood circulation slows, the uterine membrane shrinks and begins to lose fluid and tissue. Constrictions in the arterioles (small blood vessels) begin, and this loss of blood causes

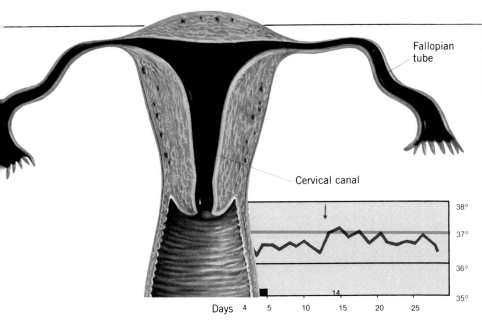

Fallopian tube

Cervical canal

38°
37°
36°
35°

Days 4 5 10 15 20 25

14

Above: Cross section of the uterus. After formation in the ovaries, the egg passes through the Fallopian tubes into the uterus. Graph shows how body temperature changes during the menstrual cycle. The sharp drop in temperature (indicated by the red arrow) signals the point of ovulation.

mother or a female friend or relative, so that she will not be frightened by her first period. For many women, there is little or no discomfort and the usual daily routine is undisturbed. Others experience mild to severe cramping (dysmenorrhea), nausea, and, in extreme cases, vomiting. There are subtle bodily changes at this time—the temperature is lower, the metabolism rate is slower, and bleeding occurs more easily in other parts of the body. The normal female cycle runs from 26 days to 30 days, with the blood flow usually starting slowly, increasing for a day or two, then tapering off. The average length of a period is 4 to 7 days.

The menstruating, or child-bearing, years usually continue until the age of 45 or 50, at which time the climacteric, or menopause, begins. This period may begin earlier or later, depending upon the individual. If a woman's first period occurs early, when she is 9 or 10, it is likely that her hormone levels are high and she will menstruate well into her fifties. If the first period occurs late, however, perhaps at the age of 14 or 15, an earlier menopause is common. Complete cessation of the menses is known as amenorrhea.

Left: Chart of the menstrual cycle. As the egg forms in the ovary, the thickness of the mucous membrane in the uterus increases from 1.5 mm to 6-8 mm. At ovulation the uterus is rich with blood. If the egg is not fertilized, the corpus luteum begins to degenerate, releasing hormones that signal the destruction of the mucous layer. At the 28th day, the mucous layer is sloughed off from the uterus, and menstruation begins.

Right: Changes in the endometrium at various stages in the menstrual cycle. The upper row of tissue samples is shown at low magnification; the lower at higher magnification.

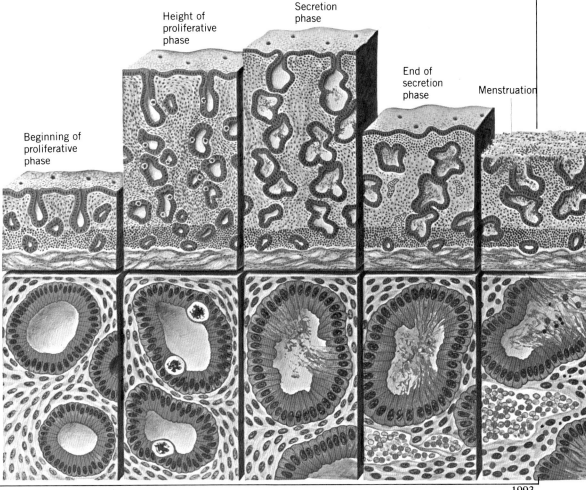

Height of proliferative phase

Secretion phase

End of secretion phase

Menstruation

Beginning of proliferative phase

Mental Retardation

An individual in the developmental period (birth to 18 years) who is found unable to perform activities that are routine for one in his or her age group and who has consistently been shown, on the basis of standardized tests, to have substantially below normal general intelligence, is said to be mentally retarded. The causes of mental retardation may be physical disease, for example, such as Down's syndrome, in which the victim has three instead of the normal two 21st chromosomes; exposure to toxins or radiation, which can destroy brain cells or cause inflammation; or inbreeding. Mental retardation can also have psychosocial causes; a child who is neglected and/or abused consistently from an early age has a higher chance of showing the characteristics of mental retardation than one who is not.

The designation of mental retardation, as used by the World Health Organization, is not meant to be indicative of possible causes (these are determined on the basis of physiological tests and clinical findings); it is merely a label used to describe a person's habits and abilities. The kind of life retarded people can lead and the degree of progress they may make are at least as much a function of the care and treatment they receive as of their level of mental impairment.

Intelligence as a Factor in Diagnosis

If a person is so severely handicapped as to be unable to take standardized intelligence tests (popularly called IQ—intelligence quotient—tests), evidence is very strong that that individual is severely, or profoundly, retarded. Beyond this, the score of a testable person may be a good indication of the extent to which he is retarded. A score of two or more standard deviations below the average for a person's age group is usually considered to indicate the possibility of mild retardation; the possibility of moderate retardation is indicated by a larger deviation from the norm; as a rule, severe and profoundly retarded persons are unable to take IQ tests. It must be emphasized that the results of an IQ test alone are insufficient for a determination of mental retardation.

Behavior as a Factor in Diagnosis

Though behavior can be more difficult to assess than an intelligence quotient arrived at mathematically, clinicians have nonetheless established a range of normal behaviors for each age on the basis of developmental tasks. During infancy and early childhood, a normal child will learn to feed himself, recognize those who are close to him, respond to them in a predictable way, and begin to communicate with words and phrases. Impaired sensory

Right: Mental retardation may be caused by biological, psychological, or sociocultural factors, or a combination of all of them.

and/or motor development is an important sign of possible mental retardation. During childhood and early adolescence (ages 5 to 12), a normal child will begin to show reasoning capabilities and the social skills necessary to be part of a group. A normal person at the peak of adolescence and beyond will be able to assume responsibility for his time, money, social actions, and the environment in which he lives.

In an effort to use behavior as a gauge in determining mental retardation and its extent, researchers have delineated cer-

Below: Test images used by doctors to check for possible mental retardation in children of age 4. Careful testing is necessary to distinguish different kinds of learning handicap. Many factors, including metabolic imbalances, deafness, and poor vision, may cause behavior that is easily mistaken for mental retardation.

BIOLOGICAL FACTORS
STRUCTURAL OR FUNCTIONAL DEFICIENCY OF NERVOUS SYSTEM
INNATE METABOLIC IMBALANCES   MOTOR DEFICIENCIES
PERCEPTIVE DEFICIENCIES
SENSORY DEFICIENCIES:
VISUAL
AUDITORY
MOTOR
LANGUAGE DIFFICULTY
CONVULSIONS
COMBINATION OF ABOVE FACTORS

SOCIOCULTURAL FACTORS
NUTRITIONAL DEFICIENCIES   LOW SOCIO-ECONOMIC LEVEL
POOR LIVING CONDITIONS   POOR ENVIRONMENT
MINORITY-GROUP STATUS   PREJUDICE
POOR EDUCATION
POOR WORK OPPORTUNITIES
LACK OF MEDICAL TREATMENT
LACK OF SOCIAL SERVICES
COMBINATION OF ABOVE FACTORS

BIO-PSYCHO-SOCIAL ADAPTATION

PSYCHOLOGICAL FACTORS
SENSORY DEPRIVATION
RELATIONSHIP WITH MOTHER:
INSUFFICIENT
DISTURBED
INTERRUPTED
ADJUSTMENT DIFFICULTIES   ANXIETY
COGNITIVE DEFICIENCY   ISOLATION
COMBINATION OF ABOVE FACTORS

tain "signal behaviors" for each age group. A 3-year-old, for example, who eats only soft foods with a spoon, drinks from a cup with considerable spilling and mess, tries with mixed success to wash himself, yet is aware when he needs to go to the toilet—behavior usually associated with younger children—would be classified as mildly retarded, if his IQ tests scores were also below normal. A 6-year-old with more or less the same behavior would be deemed moderately retarded, and a child 12 or older would be considered profoundly retarded, again, if IQ tests or the inability to take such tests bore this out.

Making Prognoses for the Mentally Retarded

The determination that a person is mentally retarded, especially if the retardation is not profound or severe, need not doom him to a life of utter dependence on his family or a life without education, accomplishment, and employment. Indeed, with the proper training and education, a mildly or moderately retarded adult can hold a job, if the majority of his responsibilities can be performed by rote and he is capable of being contributing member of family and/or community.

See also INTELLIGENCE QUOTIENT (IQ).

Right: Mazes used to check for mental retardation in 9-and 10-year-old children. *Below:* Chart indicating the capabilities of babies, children, and adults with varying degrees of mental retardation.

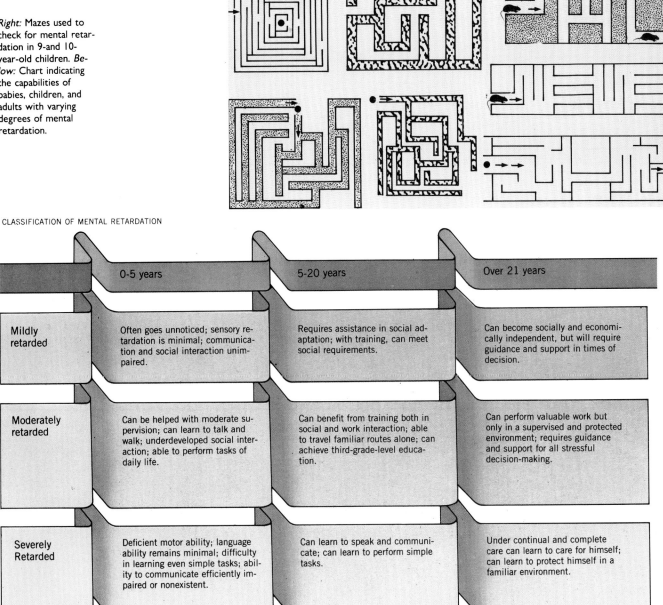

CLASSIFICATION OF MENTAL RETARDATION

	0-5 years	5-20 years	Over 21 years
Mildly retarded	Often goes unnoticed; sensory retardation is minimal; communication and social interaction unimpaired.	Requires assistance in social adaptation; with training, can meet social requirements.	Can become socially and economically independent, but will require guidance and support in times of decision.
Moderately retarded	Can be helped with moderate supervision; can learn to talk and walk; underdeveloped social interaction; able to perform tasks of daily life.	Can benefit from training both in social and work interaction; able to travel familiar routes alone; can achieve third-grade-level education.	Can perform valuable work but only in a supervised and protected environment; requires guidance and support for all stressful decision-making.
Severely Retarded	Deficient motor ability; language ability remains minimal; difficulty in learning even simple tasks; ability to communicate efficiently impaired or nonexistent.	Can learn to speak and communicate; can learn to perform simple tasks.	Under continual and complete care can learn to care for himself; can learn to protect himself in a familiar environment.
Profoundly Retarded	Almost total lack of motor and sensory ability; in need of continual care.	Shows some motor development; can learn to help himself in minimal tasks.	Can learn to help himself at minimal tasks; in need of continual assistance.

Merchant Ships

Merchant ships have been around for about 8,000 years, and for the first 7,950 years or so, the prototypical ship was a vessel that could carry anything, from potatoes to people, from railroad trains to rutabagas, from grain to gravy boats. Today, to an increasing degree, the ship is being built to match the cargo. Only the tramp steamer remains what it always was: a jack-of-all-trades plowing the seas on the lookout for cargoes of opportunity.

The idea of carrying supplies by water is certainly more than 8,000 years old, probably going back to the day a man first saw a log, or a raft of logs, drifting down some river and realized that putting hides or meat or his mate on board would be far easier than carrying them himself.

The oldest vessels that can be documented, however, were not made of logs but of reeds. They show up in Egyptian art dating from 6000 B.C., and they figure in myths and legends from an even earlier time in the eastern Mediterranean. Such ships were built of bundles of reeds lashed together and held in shape by a rope tied fore and aft, which held the bow and stern in an upward-curved position. This set the basic style of bow and stern for vessels of the Western world for centuries to come.

The Versatile Junk

The Chinese form of ship, by contrast, evolved directly from the dugout canoe. When something larger was needed, the shipbuilders took two canoes, tied them together using planks to form a floor, then built up the sides and bow and stern to create the ancestor of one of the most sturdy and efficient vessels ever made, the Chinese junk. To add strength, the junk was compartmented into 12 or more internal boxes, foreshadowing the internal bulkheads built into modern ships today.

The reed boat evolved because of the lack of timber in Egypt, but elsewhere along the Mediterranean, wood was the favored building material. Around 2000 B.C., the Minoans of Crete were the leaders in building commercial vessels, but the Phoenicians, who lived along the coast of what today are Israel and Lebanon, were the greatest voyagers. They traded as far north as Britain and even sailed along the

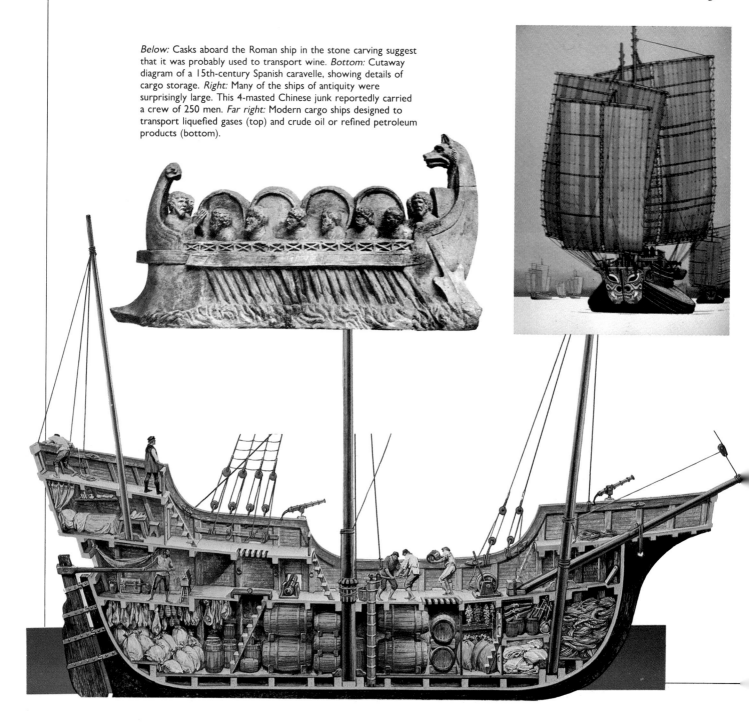

Below: Casks aboard the Roman ship in the stone carving suggest that it was probably used to transport wine. *Bottom:* Cutaway diagram of a 15th-century Spanish caravelle, showing details of cargo storage. *Right:* Many of the ships of antiquity were surprisingly large. This 4-masted Chinese junk reportedly carried a crew of 250 men. *Far right:* Modern cargo ships designed to transport liquefied gases (top) and crude oil or refined petroleum products (bottom).

coast of Africa, possibly rounding the Cape of Good Hope.

Wind power was a decisive factor in the evolution of commercial vessels, with the prize going to those who learned how to sail into the wind. This was achieved in medieval times by a northern vessel, the knorr, which around 1400 A.D. became a standard European type, blunt-bowed, broad for carrying capacity and deep for stability. When a rudder was added at the stern, replacing the steering oar, and a spar was built onto the bow to extend the sail area, the knorr became the cog, setting the pattern for ship design in Europe for the next 400 years.

From Cog to Nef

Eventually, the cog was interbred with a Mediterranean type of vessel known as the nef, which was rigged with lateen sails—a large triangular sail on a single spar that could be used for running before the wind or, hauled around lengthwise, for sailing into the wind. Thus was born the carrack, a three-masted ship that appeared on the scene just in time to make full use of a new invention, the magnetic compass, which, among other things, helped steer Columbus to the New World.

By this time, merchant ships had grown to nearly 100 feet (30 m) in length and become very efficient cargo carriers. They sailed the oceans of the world, with trade to the Orient becoming increasingly important. It was the China trade that led to the most beautiful and fastest sailing ships of all, the China clippers, which in the early and middle 19th century reached the pinnacle of sailing prowess, setting records for round trips to the Orient around Cape Horn.

Tea had become the favorite drink of England, and speed in delivering the annual crop became a vital factor among competing merchant fleets. The clipper, evolved from an American design common in Maryland's Chesapeake Bay, was the answer. Long and slender, V-shaped at the bow and U-shaped aft, these ships dominated the final years of the Great Age of Sail. They racked up speeds no one had even imagined. Right from the start, the *Rainbow* set the style: 6 months and 14 days from Europe to Hong Kong and back. The voyage was no fluke. Later ships covered an average of 400 miles (650 km) in 24 hours. The British took up this design and added composite structures, with ribs of iron and planks of maple and other hardwoods.

The Steamship

The clipper's supremacy on the seas was cut short by the steamship, a development in shipbuilding that would revolutionize

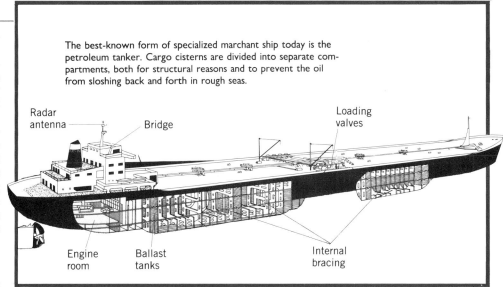

The best-known form of specialized marchant ship today is the petroleum tanker. Cargo cisterns are divided into separate compartments, both for structural reasons and to prevent the oil from sloshing back and forth in rough seas.

Radar antenna — Bridge — Loading valves — Engine room — Ballast tanks — Internal bracing

Pressure tank for liquefied gas

Lateral cargo cistern

seaborne trade. The steamers were not only entirely independent of the wind, they could also be built in sizes that far surpassed the dreams that sailing-ship designers might have had.

The pattern was set by the end of the century, when the British steamer *Oceanic* was launched, 704 feet (215 m) long. As the 20th century began, German shipbuilders took over the lead. Speed was their aim at first. The *Deutschland* sped across the Atlantic Ocean at an average of 23 knots. Then came size. The 54,000-ton *Vaterland*, launched in 1913, was 904 feet (276 m) long.

Two engineering developments in the realm of propulsion made ships of this fantastic size possible. The first was the invention of the steam turbine. In 1897, Charles A. Parsons, an English turbine pioneer, built a ship of his own design, the *Turbinia*, that attained the astonishing speed of 34½ knots. And in Germany, Rudolf Diesel was perfecting an internal-combustion engine fueled by the same low-grade oil used to fire boilers. Eventually, this engine, named after its inventor, would drive even the steam turbine from the seas.

The *Vaterland* became one of the most famous ships in history. She was built for the passenger trade between Europe and America and could accommodate 4,000 persons in four classes. She was in New York in 1917 when the United States entered World War I. Seized as a prize of war in April of that year, she was converted to the world's largest troopship.

At the end of the war, the *Vaterland* was claimed as reparations by the U.S. government and turned over to William Francis Gibbs, the famous naval architect, for a complete refurbishing. Under the name *Leviathan*, she ruled the seas for many years, the largest and fastest (27½ knots), ship afloat.

The *Leviathan*, like others in the passenger trade that followed her, was a glamour ship. The world's commerce, however, was being moved by hundreds of obscure vessels about one-eighth her

Low labor costs and subsidies from their governments have made the merchant fleets of Eastern European countries sharp competitors for international cargo traffic. *Left:* Russian container ship in a port.

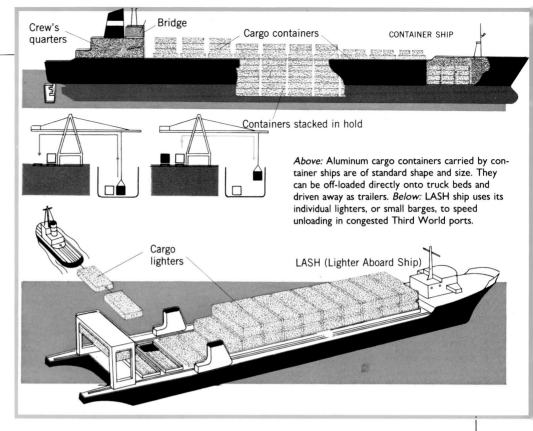

Crew's quarters · Bridge · Cargo containers · CONTAINER SHIP

Containers stacked in hold

Above: Aluminum cargo containers carried by container ships are of standard shape and size. They can be off-loaded directly onto truck beds and driven away as trailers. *Below:* LASH ship uses its individual lighters, or small barges, to speed unloading in congested Third World ports.

Cargo lighters

LASH (Lighter Aboard Ship)

One reason for the decline of mixed-cargo ships is that they are costly to load and unload, increasing turnaround time in port and boosting labor costs. Two answers to the problem, both means of mechanizing cargo handling, are shown in box.

size and less than half her speed, which plodded from port to port, carrying coal, oil, grain, lumber, and all the rest of the world's goods.

Requirements of War

By the time World War II broke out, many of these ships were powered by diesel engines. Under the pressure of war, hundreds more were built to meet emergency needs. As wars so often do, this one spawned some revolutionary ideas.

One of these was the LST, for Landing Ship Tank, developed from a British design. Entrenched on an island, England saw the need for a ship that could carry wheeled vehicles and off-load them quickly when she reached her destination. The LST filled that requirement with a bow door from which it let down a ramp, allowing the vehicles to drive directly onto a beach. Inside the LST were ramps and turntables on which trucks, tanks, and artillery could be loaded and driven from one deck to another.

When the United States got into the war, American shipbuilders developed the Liberty ship, 441 feet (134 m) long, displacing 10,490 tons, with oil-fired reciprocating steam engines—a simple, sturdy design. The industrialist Henry J. Kaiser devised a method of building that cut construction time to 10 days, with 4 more for fitting out and delivery. By the war's end, 2,610 Liberty ships had been built. In all, American shipyards turned out 5,874 merchant vessels totaling 57,205,407 deadweight tons, which was more than one-third of the total of all merchant ships in the world at the start of the war.

Postwar Advances

Of the ships built, many were special designs for special purposes, and of these, some important types survived to undergo new developments in the postwar era. The LST, for instance, evolved into the "roll-on-roll-off"(RO-RO) ship of today, which has doors in the stern as well as in the bow and may also have side doors. A

similar innovation is called the LASH—Lighter Aboard Ship. The vessel carries a huge crane that actually lifts loaded lighters (barges) from the water and stows them away as cargo. At her destination, the vessel off-loads the lighters into the water, thus avoiding the need for a harbor suited to her draft and size, a major consideration in many undeveloped ports.

One of the most important developments has been the "container ship," which has all but revolutionized the shipment of cargoes by sea. A container ship is built to transport boxes of standard size, 20 by 8 by 8 feet (6 × 2.5 × 2.5 m), that arrive at dockside already loaded. Such prepackaged shipments came into use during the war to save time and stevedoring costs. Their virtue is that they can be taken by rail or truck from some inland point directly to dockside, then immediately loaded into the ship. They can be off-loaded directly onto a truck or train and sent off to any destination. Since the boxes are never opened, pilferage is reduced to a minimum, and stevedoring costs are all but eliminated.

Supertankers

Tankers, a highly specialized form of merchant ship, have been in use since the turn of the century, but they have vastly increased in size since World War II. Today's supertankers have attained undreamed-of dimensions, up to 326,000 deadweight tons and 1,132 feet (345 m) in length. Following the maxim that the longer a ship, the less power (proportionally) required to move it, these vessels are

highly economical to run. Their drawbacks are that their great length makes them vulnerable to breaking up in heavy seas and also makes them difficult to maneuver. Because of the huge amounts of oil they carry, they also represent an environmental hazard. But their economy makes them so attractive that they are likely to grow even larger in the future. Tankers of a million tons or more are being planned, probably to be loaded and unloaded at offshore stations equipped with mooring buoys, pumps, and pipelines to transport the oil.

Another type of tanker is especially equipped to carry frozen natural gas at −260° F. (−162° C.), transporting it in insulated aluminum tanks. In prospect are tankers that can carry mixed cargoes, such as crushed iron ore or coal mixed with water to make it transportable by pipeline in the form of a slurry. The American tanker *Manhattan* was fitted out as an icebreaker to test the feasibility of carrying Alaskan oil directly from its Arctic source. Such a vessel, however, is expensive to build, since it requires a specially reinforced design to allow it to move through the ice, breaking it by sheer weight. The hull must also be reinforced to withstand the constant pounding against the ice, and the propellers require special protection. The propellers must also have removable blades that can be replaced at sea should they be broken or damaged by the ice.

Mercury (Element)

One day in 1956, someone in the Japanese fishing village of Minimata noticed that nearly all the cats had died. The animals had displayed bizarre, delirious behavior that occasionally culminated in their leaping into the sea. Townspeople, too, were beginning to suffer a strange and horrible illness, eventually affecting thousands, whose symptoms included convulsions, emotional instability, paralysis, and brain damage, often leading to death. Autopsies of victims of the Minimata disease, as it came to be known, revealed that a strange substance had attacked and damaged their brains, rendering them spongelike. It also affected unborn human fetuses, and many babies were born deformed and retarded, although carried by apparently healthy mothers.

The affliction proved not to be a disease at all, but a widespread case of poisoning. The poison had contaminated the sea upon which the townspeople depended for sustenance. It came from the local chemical industry, which dumped its wastes into Minimata Bay. One ingredient of these wastes, mercury, found its way into the fish and shellfish of the bay. These, in turn, formed an important part of the diets of the cats—and of the townspeople, as well.

Mercury poisoning has been known for a long time and is an occupational hazard of many industries. The expression "mad as a hatter" arose in the 19th century from the frequent poisonings of hat-factory employees exposed to mercury used in the treatment of wool for felt hats. Despite the dangers of its use, mercury has a peculiar set of physical and chemical properties that make it an extremely useful material for a wide variety of purposes.

Left: Native mercury in association with cinnabar ore. The metal is occasionally found naturally in its pure state.

Below: Photographs show a drop of mercury placed on a copper plate and on a glass slide. Mercury will not wet glass but, after a time, will form an amalgam with copper.

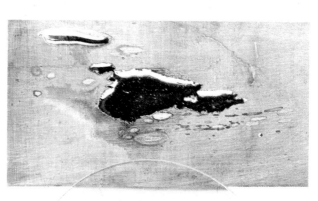

NAME	Mercury
SYMBOL	Hg
ETYMOLOGY OF SYMBOL	from its Latin name, *hydrargyrum*, 'silver water'
ATOMIC NO.	80
ATOMIC WT.	200.59
NATURAL STATE	mostly in combination form in mercury ores; occasionally found in liquid state
DISCOVERY	already well known in antiquity
PRODUCTION	by roasting of sulfate ores or by heating sulfate with iron or lime
FZG. PT.	−38.87°C.
BLG. PT.	356.58°C.
SPECIFIC WT.	13.593
PROPERTIES AND USES	silvery metal; liquid at room temperature; forms amalgams with other metals; used in many kinds of measuring devices; some mercury compounds have pharmaceutical uses

The Liquid Metal

The physical properties of mercury are unlike those of any other metal. It is a dense, silvery-white liquid, the only metal that is a liquid at room temperature. The alchemists called it quicksilver. Its chemical symbol, Hg, is an abbreviation of its Latin name, *hydrargyrum,* or "silver water." It has a high surface tension, which means that it tends to cling to itself and form little balls rather than spread itself out when placed on a flat surface. Though a liquid, it doesn't tend to make

Below: Brightly colored mercury compounds in solution in the test tubes: (a) mercurous iodide, (b) mercurous iodide with traces of metallic mercury, (c) mercuric iodide, (d) mercuric ammonium nitrate, (e) mercuric ammonium chloride.

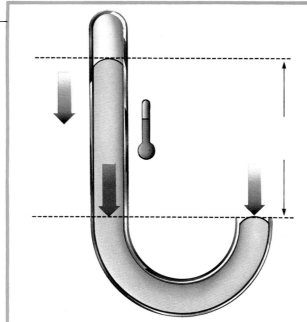

MERCURY BAROMETER
Mercury barometers measure atmospheric pressure according to the distance that the pressure will push a column of mercury up a glass tube. For precision use, allowance must be made for the effect of temperature changes on the volume of the mercury, for the altitude, and for variations in local gravity.

a surface "wet." Like all metals, it expands slightly when heated; unlike many, its rate of expansion is uniform.

Its chemical properties are equally unique. It is relatively inert but will dissolve many common metals (iron and nickel are among the exceptions), forming a mixture called an amalgam. Mercury compounds are catalysts for many chemical reactions—that is, they instigate the reaction—even though the mercury compound itself does not take part.

Applications

Because it does not wet glass and expands evenly with increased temperature, mercury is used in thermometers and other scientific equipment. Its density makes it suitable for barometers. Mercury also conducts electricity and is used in electrical equipment such as batteries and mercury vapor lamps. Mercury batteries can be made very small and are therefore useful where space conservation is a critical factor, as in hearing aids and space vehicles. Sun lamps often use mercury lamps which emit ultraviolet light.

Mercury's ability to dissolve many metals makes it useful for certain industrial processes; for example, mercury amalgamation is one method of recovering gold and silver. Because of its role as a catalyst, its compounds are also used in many large-scale industrial preparations.

Mercury compounds were once widely used in manufacturing pesticides and fungicides. The dangers of mercury poisoning have underscored the importance of removing mercury from anything that might be discharged into the environment.

Mercury (Planet)

Imagine standing at the equator and watching a very peculiar sunrise. First, the Sun would look about three times bigger than it usually does as it climbs above the horizon. Then it would climb slowly overhead, stop at its zenith, and begin to go backward. Soon afterward, it would reverse direction once again and continue on to the far horizon. This loop-the-loop Sun journey would appear from the planet Mercury, where one Mercurial day (the time it takes for one complete revolution around the planet's axis) equals about 59 of ours. It is unlikely that any human will ever witness this strange sight, however, because under the broiling rays of Mercury's noontime Sun, the temperature climbs to about 800°F. (about 425°C.). Indeed, no planetary surface in the solar system is as environmentally forbidding as Mercury's.

Characteristics of Mercury

Mercury is a dense, airless, lifeless, Sun-baked planet, the smallest in the Solar System and one of the most unusual. The planet's density of 5.2 suggests a core of iron-nickel, perhaps with a thin mantle of silicate, much like Earth, which has a density of 5.5. It has a diameter of 3,025 miles (4,868 km), not much larger than the Moon, whose surface, pitted with impact craters, it closely resembles.

It is also the closest planet to the Sun. On average, 36 million miles (58 million km) separate the two bodies, although Mercury's elliptical orbit brings it within 28.5 million miles (46 million km) at perihelion (the point of closest approach to the Sun). The planet travels in a highly eccentric (or elongated) elliptical orbit around the Sun. From the Earth, Mercury can occasionally be seen as an orange

Above: The internal structure of Mercury is thought to consist of an unusually large molten core of nearly pure liquid iron. This hypothesis is based on the need to explain how a planet as small as Mercury can have a density similar to that of the Earth. *Below:* Photograph of the planet's surface, showing the scars left by the impact of meteors and meteorites.

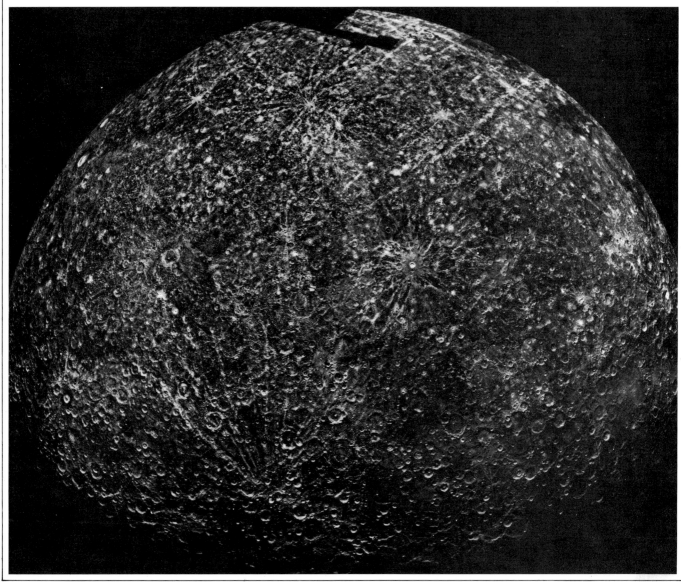

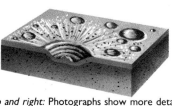

Top and right: Photographs show more details of the surface scarring on Mercury caused by meteor impact. *Above:* Sequence illustrates mechanisms responsible for creation of 'ray' patterns around many of the larger craters. Shock waves are set up as a meteor strikes the planet, and there is a secondary impact of loose blast materials falling back to the surface.

speck on the horizon just before sunrise or just after sunset.

Spin-Orbit Coupling

Visual perception of Mercury, even with a telescope, has always been so poor that the nature of the planet's rotation and orbit escaped definitive explanation for centuries. It was long believed that Mercury rotated about its own axis once every 88 days, the time it took to complete a single orbit around the Sun (traveling at an average speed of 30 miles, or 48 km, per second). This so-called synchronous rotation would have meant that the same face of the planet was always turned toward the Sun. This mistaken interpretation persisted until 1965, when data supplied by radio astronomers (studying the radio waves emanating from the planet) supported a different, though no less interesting, theory.

Radar pulses were ultimately decisive in determining that Mercury rotated once every 58.65 days (compared with one rotation every 24 hours on Earth). It thus turns out that Mercury rotates on its axis precisely three times for every two orbits around the Sun. That phenomenon, called spin-orbit coupling, apparently indicates that a stable state has been reached in the gravitational and orbital interaction between Mercury and the Sun.

Surface Features

The U.S.-launched Mariner 10 spacecraft, which passed within several hundred miles of Mercury during flybys in 1974 and 1975, provided detailed photographs of Mercury's surface. Dark and igneous in origin, Mercury's terrain is pockmarked with craters—some as large as 105 miles (170 km) in diameter. The surface is exposed to intense solar winds (charged particles, mostly protons and electrons, traveling at supersonic speeds from the Sun) and extremes of temperature. From a daytime high of about 800°F. (about 425°C.), the temperature drops to −279°F. (−173°C.) at night.

The craters are possibly 3,000 to 4,000 million years old and appear to be in perfect condition, an indication that Mercury has been without an atmosphere (and its eroding action of wind and weather) for at least a similar amount of time. There is also evidence of early volcanic activity, which spread vast, sealike plains of lava across the surface.

Transits of Mercury

Since Mercury lies between the Earth and the Sun, it is difficult to observe directly because of solar glare. About 13 times each century, however, Mercury's orbital path carries it right across the surface of the Sun—a bit like a tiny black marble rolling across a big yellow beach ball from the perspective of Earth. These passages, called transits, next occur on November 12, 1986, and November 5, 1993, and can be observed from Earth. Against the surface of the Sun, the planet—like a sunspot—is sharply defined and can be discerned with strong binoculars. (Important warning: filters or other protective devices must be used when observing the Sun.)

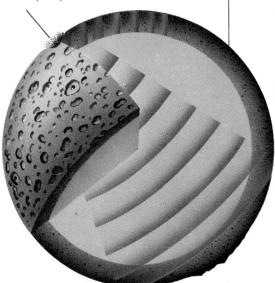

Below: When very large meteors strike the surface of Mercury, the impact is such that shock waves pass from one side of the planet to the other. They are reflected back and forth, causing Mercury to 'ring like a gong' for long periods afterward. Astronomers have measured impact vibrations in the planet's interior caused by meteor strikes perhaps centuries old.

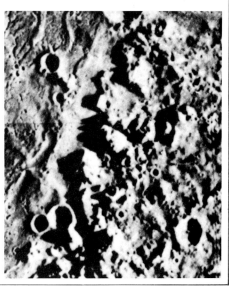

Mesozoic Era

If we took a camping trip 100 million years back in time, to the middle of the Mesozoic era, we might not believe at first that we had left our present era at all. The plains and forests would look familiar; we'd recognize pine trees, ferns, and grasses; and the same insects—flies, bees, wasps—would buzz around our ears. However, a flying reptile swooping down on us, or our first sight, at a safe distance, of a towering Tyrannosaurus would quickly convince us that we were visiting a prehistoric world.

The age of dinosaurs, the Mesozoic, encompasses a geological era that began around 200 million years ago and lasted for about 160 million years. The name "Mesozoic," from the Greek for "middle life," was first proposed in 1841 on the basis of the known fossil record in Great Britain. Subsequently, the Mesozoic era was divided into three periods, of which the Triassic (lasting about 35 million years) is the oldest, the Jurassic (55 million years) the middle, and the Cretaceous (70 million years) the most recent.

Animal Life

On the basis of fossil remains, the Mesozoic can rightly be called the era of reptiles, beginning with frogs, toads, and other amphibians in the Triassic. The enormous herbivorous (plant-eating) dinosaurs—for example, the whale-sized brontosaurs and the armor-plated stegosaurs—first emerged in the Jurassic, as did the archaeopteryx, a primitive bird that had reptilian teeth and feathers. The carnivorous (meat-eating) tyrannosaurs and the flying reptiles (pterodactyls) date from the Cretaceous, as does the oldest known salamander. Reptile families from the Mesozoic that survive today include snakes, turtles, and alligators. Fish such as sturgeon and sharks and insects such as grasshoppers and ants also originated in the Mesozoic. The first mammals probably came from some reptilian ancestor in the Triassic, but they remained subordinate until the close of the era, when the dinosaurs suddenly died out. The extinction of the dinosaurs remains one of the great mysteries of animal evolution.

The conifers (needle trees) of the Mesozoic are mostly preserved in the form of petrified forests, but the gingkos or maidenhair trees, which have leaves, have survived down to our times. Perhaps the most remarkable development of flora was the emergence of angiosperms—flowers. As the oceans rose, many plants were trapped in the sediments that formed on the floor of shallow marine basins and in time turned into vast coal and ironstone deposits. Their extensive presence in

Below: Reconstruction of the vegetation that covered the Earth during the Mesozoic era. At the center of the drawing is a *Cycadeoidea,* a beautiful plant characteristic of the period. Perfectly preserved fossils of *Cycadeoidea* have been found. *Right:* Schematic diagram showing the relationship among the various dinosaurs that inhabited the Earth during the Mesozoic era.

PLEUROMEIA

VOLTZIA

CALAMITES

CYCADEOIDEA

The Mesozoic era represents a transition phase in the development of the Earth, both in its physical structure and in the life forms that populated it. The beginning of the Mesozoic was marked by the end of the wrinkling of the Earth's crust. The end of the era came after a resumption of major disruptions, resulting in the formation of the Appalachian, Andes, and Himalayan mountains. The Mesozoic saw the proliferation of the great dinosaurs and then their unexplained decline. In plant life, flowers appeared for the first time, and plants developed their distinct reproductive organs, stamens and pistils. In the oceans, the whales reached their full size, and at the same time the spiral-shelled periwinkles developed.

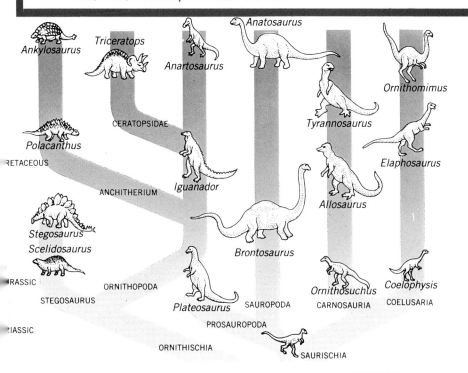

northern regions, such as Canada, indicates that the worldwide climate was milder and more humid than today; there were no polar ice caps during the Mesozoic. The marine limestone and sandstone formations from the Mesozoic also contain large beds of manganese and phosphorites, which are mined.

Paleogeography

Geologists have speculated that in the early Mesozoic there were initially two major continental areas (shields), which they have called Laurasia, including most of North America and Asia, and Gondwanaland, encompassing South America, Africa, and Australia in the Southern Hemisphere. They were divided by the Tethys Ocean, which extended from the Caribbean, through the Mediterranean and Middle East, to Indonesia and New Zealand. Apparently, the oceans were most restricted at the beginning of the Triassic; but they gradually covered greater portions of the landmasses, advancing and receding repeatedly during the whole era. They reached their greatest extension in the Cretaceous, when they created a spectacular sea corridor in the middle of North America from the Arctic to the Gulf of Mexico.

During the Triassic and early Jurassic periods, there was little volcanic activity and mountain-building, but in the later Mesozoic, great upheavals took place on many parts of the continents, forming the Appalachians, the Andes, and the eastern Asian mountain systems. The latest cycle of continental drift started sometime during the Mesozoic, creating the beginnings of the Atlantic and Indian oceans.
See also CONTINENTAL DRIFT.

Above: Fossilized remains of Archaeopteryx, the world's first bird (actually, a flying reptile with primitive feathers).
Right: 100-million-year-old fossil dragon fly.

Metabolism

All living things need energy to survive, and it is a fundamental law of nature that energy can neither be created nor destroyed—merely transformed. In green plants, for example, the energy of the Sun's rays is captured in the green pigment known as chlorophyll. This trapped energy, transformed from radiant to chemical form, then allows the plant to manufacture food (a carbohydrate) out of chemical raw materials (water and carbon dioxide) in the process of photosynthesis.

Like all other forms of metabolism in living matter, photosynthesis converts energy into forms usable by an organism, then expends that energy to power the fundamental, life-sustaining chemical reactions that occur in each cell. Just as fire and oxygen liberate energy from a log in the form of heat, body chemistry uses oxygen and other substances to liberate energy from food. Rather than floating up

essential biochemical structures (such as the complex macromolecules of proteins).

The chemical processes of metabolism perform several key functions. They provide the energy necessary for work—not only the mechanical work that involves the use of muscles, but also the chemical work required to build complicated molecules likes DNA, RNA, and proteins. Metabolic reactions also convert food into forms that can be stored until needed, providing cells with a kind of wood pile of combustible material. In warm-blooded animals, metabolic reactions convert energy-rich compounds into the heat that keeps body temperature at a steady level.

Adenosine Triphosphate

The basic unit in metabolism is a molecule called adenosine triphosphate, or ATP. It consists of two phosphate groups attached to an easily converted compound

plants; every molecule of ATP derives, directly or indirectly, from the Sun.

Whenever one or two phosphate groups are removed from the ATP molecule, energy is released. Whenever one or two phosphate groups are added to AMP, energy is preserved (or latent) in the bond, ready to be used in other reactions. The addition and deletion of phosphate groups, like the flicking of an on-off switch, is what happens in metabolic processes.

During catabolism (the breaking-down phase of metabolism), energy is captured from organic material and transformed into ATP. During anabolism (the constructive phase of metabolism), ATP is consumed in the building process. It requires the energy of ATP, for example, to pry open the chemical structure of amino acids so that they can be joined into small sequences (known as polypeptide chains) or long sequences (proteins), which are then used by the body for a variety of purposes.

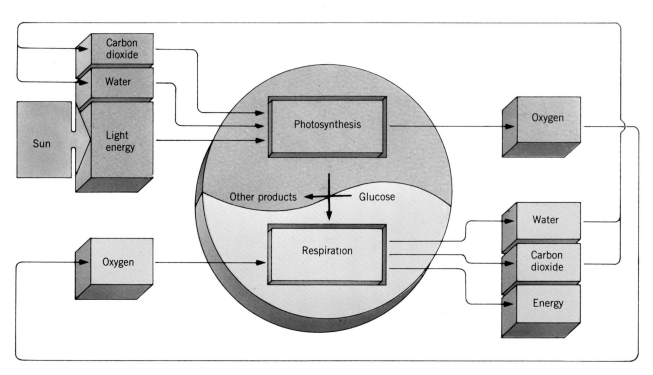

into thin air like heat, however, this metabolic energy is used in the creation of everything from enzymes to genes.

Basic Processes

Metabolism, whether in butterflies or human beings, is characterized by two basic sets of reactions. One set, known collectively as catabolism, breaks down (or degrades) organic material such as food and renders it into usable chemical components. The other set, known collectively as anabolism or biosynthesis, takes these chemical components and joins them, like so many building blocks, into

called adenosine monophosphate, or AMP. The key to energy use is the addition or deletion of these phosphate groups. Adding one phosphate group to the basic unit, AMP, creates a two-phosphate molecule called adenosine diphosphate, or ADP; the addition of yet another phosphate group creates ATP, a three-phosphate molecule. The points where the phosphate groups attach (known as the chemical bonds) are incredibly rich in energy, and thus the molecule with the most bonds, ATP, possesses the greatest energy. ATP is the chemical substance formed in the chlorophyll chambers of

Metabolism consists of a series of chemical processes that occur in living tissue cells and that determine the formation, breakdown, and functioning of an organism. *Above:* Relationship between photosynthesis in green plants and respiration in animals. Green plants use the Sun's light to synthesize glucose from water and carbon dioxide while releasing oxygen. Animals, however, use the energy stored in glucose and release water and carbon dioxide while using oxygen.

The principal nutrients are polysaccharides, lipids, and proteins. The enzymatic breakdown of these substances provides living cells with the chemical compounds necessary to provide energy and synthesize their own compounds. Catabolism of lipids, polysaccharides, and proteins occurs through a long chain of biochemical reactions, which can be divided into 3 phases. In the first phase, large molecules are broken down into smaller ones: lipids are broken down into fatty acids and glycerin; polysaccharides, into glucose; and proteins, into amino acids. In the second phase, these smaller units are further broken down into a 3-carbon compound called acetyl coenzyme A. This process releases energy. In the third phase, this compound is further broken down into carbon dioxide and water. This process provides most of the energy.

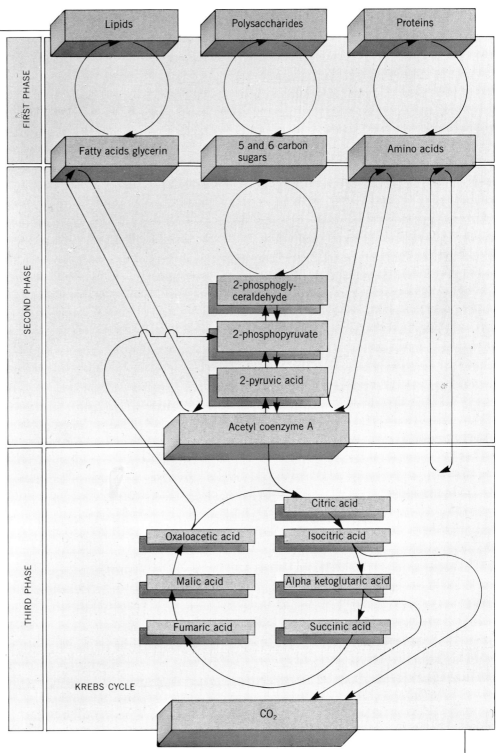

From Digestion to Degradation

The foods we eat provide the raw materials for human metabolism. The main sources are carbohydrates, fats, and proteins. The breakdown of carbohydrates and fats yields ATP. The breakdown of proteins provides the building blocks for new or replacement proteins (only half of the 20 amino acids commonly used in protein synthesis can be chemically manufactured in the body by metabolic means; the rest must be obtained in the diet). The diet is also the source of vitamins, which are essential in the production of many enzymes. Each type of food is broken down by a particular set of reactions, and each reaction is facilitated by an enzyme that "holds" the reactants together to speed up the process. The set of reactions, taken as a whole, is called a metabolic pathway—a chemical highway, as it were, that travels toward a particular chemical destination. Although it is beyond the scope of this article to outline each metabolic pathway, an attempt will be made to describe particular processes, where they occur in the body, and why.

Metabolism begins in the stomach and intestines. If we eat a potato, for example, we receive a supply of starch. Starch is a complex sugar—too complex for metabolic purposes. So digestive enzymes in the intestines attack these large molecules and break them down into glucose, a simple sugar. The glucose molecule is small enough to pass through the wall of the intestines and enter the bloodstream. The blood delivers the sugar to liver cells and other tissues such as the muscles.

Glycolysis

Inside muscle cells—specifically in the mitochondria (the tiny, organlike power plants of animal cells)—is the site of one of the most important metabolic pathways, glycolysis. This is a long series of chemical reactions that converts each molecule of glucose into two molecules of ATP. This is particularly necessary in the muscles (although it occurs elsewhere), because ATP is used up in facilitating the contraction of muscle fibers and must be rapidly replenished after even short bursts of activity.

In an abbreviated and simplified version, glycolysis works like this. The glucose molecule is converted to fructose, a related sugar, with a phosphate group on each end. This process, known as phosphorylation, is costly in energy terms—it uses up two molecules of ATP for each molecule of glucose. But the new sugar molecule, symmetrical in structure, can be chemically cut into two equal subparts by an enzyme (a process called cleavage).

These smaller molecules, known as triose phosphate compounds, each yield one molecule of ATP during a subsequent reaction with a coenzyme (a substance that works in conjunction with an enzyme). Several steps later, two more molecules of ATP are derived from a reaction that produces a substance called pyruvate. The net gain from the metabolism of one glucose molecule to pyruvate is two of ATP. The ATP molecules are usually stored in the mitochondria until needed. The pyruvate can then be broken down further for more energy.

The Tricarboxylic Cycle

The ATP is free to be used in energy-consuming reactions elsewhere in the cell. The pyruvate, however, can continue to be metabolized within the mitochondria, producing a coenzyme called acetyl coenzyme A. This complicated compound is the starting point of a cyclical metabolic pathway known as the tricarboxylic (TCA), or Krebs, cycle. It can be compared to a traffic circle, or roundabout, in the sense that it follows a circular path (it begins and ends with oxaloacetic acid, which combines with acetyl coenzyme A to form citric acid), and compounds produced along the way (known as intermediates) can peel off into different metabolic pathways, as if taking an exit. Hydrogen molecules are released at various stages and enter another pathway to produce even more ATP.

For every glucose molecule that is metabolized to the final end products of carbon dioxide (CO_2) and water (H_2O), 38 ATP molecules are formed. In addition to carbohydrates like glucose, fatty acids can also be broken down to acetyl coenzyme A, yielding both ATP and raw materials for the TCA cycle. So when the body is starving and living off stored fat, fatty acids enter the Krebs cycle to keep up the production of ATP.

The Urea Cycle

The breakdown of protein, which contains nitrogen, produces the toxic by-product NH_3—ammonia. Since ammonia is lethal to cells, a metabolic pathway called the urea cycle is necessary in liver cells to convert this poison into an acceptable waste product. Ammonia combines with carbon dioxide and ATP to form an

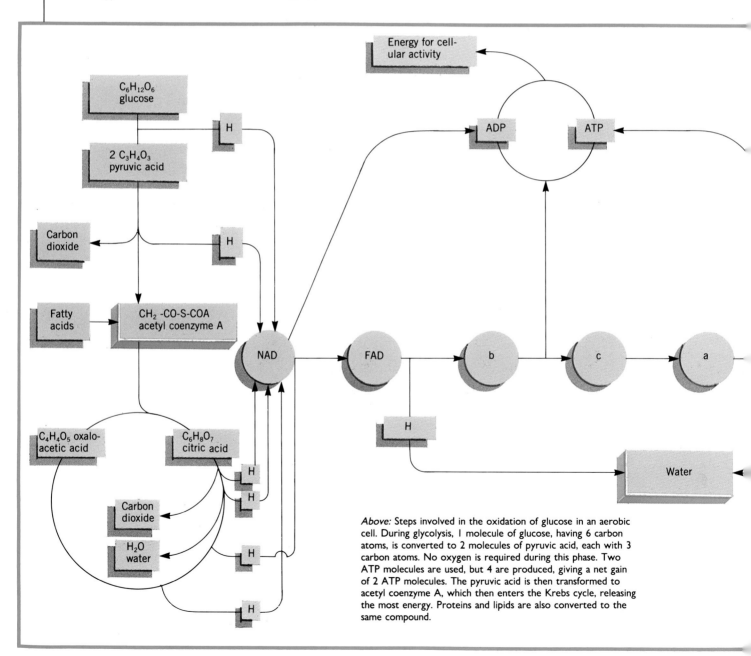

Above: Steps involved in the oxidation of glucose in an aerobic cell. During glycolysis, 1 molecule of glucose, having 6 carbon atoms, is converted to 2 molecules of pyruvic acid, each with 3 carbon atoms. No oxygen is required during this phase. Two ATP molecules are used, but 4 are produced, giving a net gain of 2 ATP molecules. The pyruvic acid is then transformed to acetyl coenzyme A, which then enters the Krebs cycle, releasing the most energy. Proteins and lipids are also converted to the same compound.

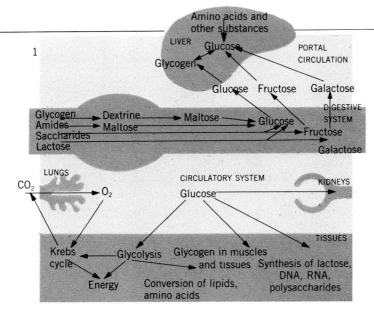

1

Amino acids and other substances

LIVER

Glucose

Glycogen

PORTAL CIRCULATION

Glucose — Fructose — Galactose

DIGESTIVE SYSTEM

Glycogen → Dextrine → Maltose → Glucose
Amides → Maltose
Saccharides → Fructose
Lactose → Galactose

LUNGS

CO_2 ← → O_2

CIRCULATORY SYSTEM

Glucose → KIDNEYS

TISSUES

Krebs cycle ← Glycolysis → Glycogen in muscles and tissues

Energy — Conversion of lipids, amino acids — Synthesis of lactose, DNA, RNA, polysaccharides

---

2

Krebs cycle → Energy

Beta oxidation

LIVER

Ketone bodies

Lipids

Fatty acids and glycerin

Triglycerides → Fatty acids — Glycerin

CO_2 ← → O_2

Fatty acids and glycerin

Krebs cycle ← Beta oxidation

Stored lipids — Fatty bodies

Energy

3

NH_3 + keto acids → Urea — LIVER

Glucose

Fatty acids

Amino acids

Proteins → Peptides → Peptides → Amino acids

LUNGS

CIRCULATORY SYSTEM

KIDNEYS

Amino acids

Protein synthesis — Protein catabolism — Synthesis of essential nonprotein nitrogenous compounds

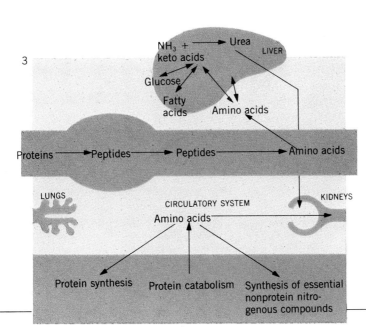

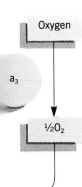

Oxygen

a_3

$\frac{1}{2}O_2$

Left: Major steps in the human metabolism of (1) carbohydrates, (2) lipids, and (3) proteins. Carbohydrates, which are complex compounds, are broken down to simple sugars such as glucose, fructose, and galactose and then carried to the liver via the circulatory system. Here they are converted to glucose, which is the point of departure for the metabolic breakdown of carbohydrates. Glucose is oxidized in various tissues to provide energy, is used in the synthesis of other compounds, or is polymerized to form glycogen, which is stored in the liver.

Lipids, in the form of triglycerides or fats, are broken down to glycerin and fatty acids by an enzyme, lipase, then pass through the intestinal walls with the the help of bile salts produced by the liver. Through the lymphatic system, they reach the circulatory system and the liver, which breaks them down and distributes them throughout the body via the circulatory system. They can be used to provide energy by entering the Krebs cycle or for the synthesis of lipids to be used as a stored energy reserve.

Proteins are broken down in the gastrointestinal tract to amino acids, which are then carried by the portal vein to the liver. Here they are used to synthesize new proteins or are broken down to keto acids and ammonia. The ammonia is converted to urea and excreted as urine; the keto acids can be used to synthesize glucose or fatty acids, which in turn can be broken down to release energy. Proteins are mainly used for the formation of new tissue.

intermediate compound, which in turn combines enzymatically with the amino acid ornithine to form citrulline.

The exact chemistry here is not so important as the fact that, several steps later, the compound arginine is broken down into two substances: urea, which can be safely excreted as waste, and the amino acid ornithine, which can plug back into the cycle to keep things going. This reaction, like many other metabolic processes, recycles compounds that can be used to keep the pathway functioning.

Metabolic Intersections

The various metabolic pathways of the body are a little like freeways. Although they are a fast mode of chemical travel, specific compounds can enter and exit at various stages along the way, and the pathways themselves intersect at key points. This means that a "junction" substance such as pyruvate, which represents one step in the degradation of glucose, also is a starting point for biosynthesis.

By means of these intersections, the body is always channeling chemical traffic through various pathways to get the most out of the metabolic processes. And once it gets the two main ingredients, energy and raw materials, the body can build anything—an infant out of a fertilized egg, an adult out of a child. Both these miracles of growth are, in fact, the most spectacular examples of human metabolism.

Metal Detector

Buried treasure—the words conjure up a romantic vision of pirate booty hidden on remote islands. For today's treasure hunters the reality is more mundane, yet equally alluring. The variety of available "finds" on just one beach may be endless: watches, rings, coins, bullets, and, of course, worthless items such as tinfoil, bottle caps, and rusty nails. Once considered no more practical than dowsing, or using a forked twig to locate water, hunting for treasure has come into its own with

netic fields are so constructed as to exactly cancel each other out. The monitor, scanning the magnetic field, therefore reads zero. When one of the coils is brought near a metal object—which will produce an electrical charge that distorts the magnetic field emanating from that coil—the exact cancellation is altered. This discrepancy registers on the monitor, and the metal is detected. In practical use, these units are limited by their own sensitivity. They react to subtle variations in

the Earth's magnetic field, therefore are only functional over a very small area.

2. *Field search units* are balanced coil systems designed to accomplish a specific purpose. Consisting of a wire loop directing a magnetic field over a large area, these machines examine the variations in the magnetic flux of that area. When used at archaeological digs, these units can determine the extent and even the shape of man-made relics and ruins buried beneath the ground.

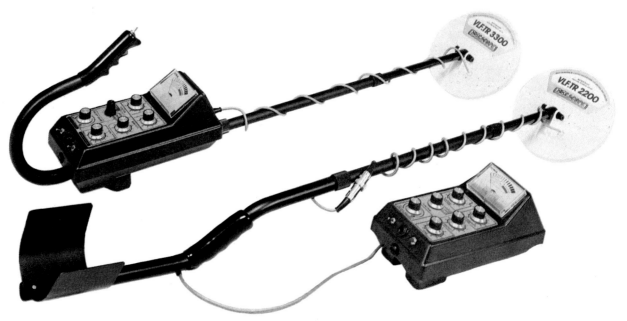

Above: Metal detectors for amateur treasure hunting. These instruments make use of integrated ADC (analytical discrimination control) circuits to distinguish between interesting finds and useless rubbish like metal foil or bottle caps. *Below:* Illustration of how the magnetic field generated by the detector head interacts with metallic objects buried at varying depths.

the metal detector, a sophisticated electronic instrument capable of helping its user zero in on important finds. Detectors are also useful whenever it is necessary to determine the native metal content of certain mineral deposits; for instance, in prospecting for gold.

Types of Detectors

Metal detectors differ greatly in price and quality. Basically, they consist of a hand-held box of electronics gear with a rod that extends downward to a sensitive head, or "coil," which hovers just above the ground and sends back signals that become audible by means of earphones or visible by means of a dial. Generally, detectors are of three types:

1. *Balanced search-coil units* consist of two balanced coils producing magnetic fields of equal intensity. The two coils are connected in opposition; that is, the mag-

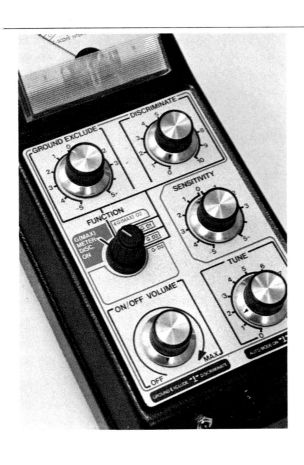

Left: control module for a metal detector equipped with discrimination circuits. The ADC circuits in these detectors perform an electronic analysis of the object detected and can not only distinguish between different kinds of metals but also exclude false 'parasite' signals generated by soils with a heavy salt or mineral content. *Below:* Treasure hunting with lightweight metal detectors.

3. *Pulse magnetization units* are a kind of radar unit in that they depend upon the transmission and subsequent detection of a magnetic impulse after reflection, or echo. A strong magnetic pulse is sent out by the search coil in its transmitter mode. The coil then immediately switches to the receiver mode. If the pulse strikes a metal object, it induces a magnetic field, which is then received and registered by the coil. Because electromagnetic radiation moves at a finite speed (like all radiation, at the speed of light), the location of the object can be determined by analyzing the elapsed time between the transmitted and received signals.

Some types of metal detectors are known as discriminating and can distinguish between junk (cans, foil, nails, etc.) and metals such as gold, silver, and brass. Several detectors are designed for use underwater. Detector heads, or scanners, are encased in heavy-duty plastic and are generally resistant to scrapes and scratches. It is important to keep them as close to the ground as possible, even lightly touching it, if the terrain permits. For maximum coverage, they should be swung slowly from side to side in an overlapping swath.

Metallurgy

Imagine what it is like inside a jet engine. Highly reactive gases are expelled under tremendous pressure and at extreme temperatures. Obviously, the materials used to construct these machines must be incredibly tough. Many components of jet engines are made of a class of metals called superalloys, whose main ingredients are nickel and chromium. These superalloys, however, are found nowhere in nature—they are manufactured especially for "specialized tastes." The manufacture of superalloys is one aspect of metallurgy. In general, metallurgy (from the Greek word for "metalworking") is the broad system of scientific theories and procedures by which we take ore from a mine and work it into a finished metal.

that only the desired minerals will adhere to air bubbles. When air is bubbled through a mixture of ore and water, the minerals will rise to the top to form a froth that can be easily scooped off.

Some nickel-bearing ores are treated by this "flotation" method. In some cases, more complicated processes—involving magnetic separation of chemical baths—are used instead.

Extraction

After minerals have been separated from the gangue, metals must be extracted from the minerals. There are three main classes of extractive techniques, with great variation in each class to solve problems posed by different metals and by the different

Flow chart describes steps in production of steel beginning with extraction of iron ore. Steel is, properly speaking, actually an alloy of iron with carbon. Many other metallic trace elements are also alloyed with steel to give it special characteristics, including resistance to corrosion and high tensile strength.

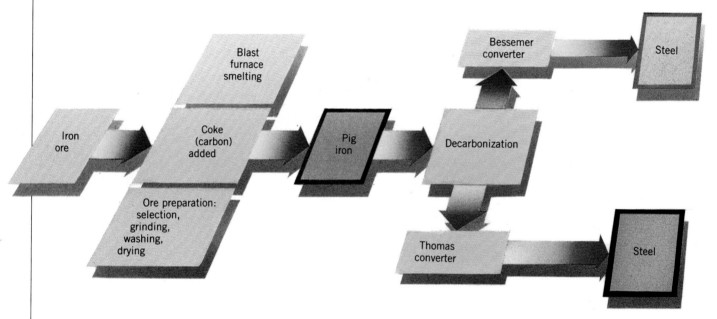

Mineral Dressing

Pure metals are almost never found in nature. Instead, they are usually found in complex compounds with other elements. These compounds, or minerals, constitute the enormous variety of ores found in deep rock formations. The goal of mining is to gather ores. In order to get metal from an ore, the mineral must be separated from the non-metal-bearing material, or gangue. This is called mineral dressing.

The first step in mineral dressing usually involves crushing the ore. Crushing prepares the ore for the separation and concentrating of the mineral, a process called beneficiation.

Where the particles of mineral and gangue have different densities, they can be separated by gravity. The ore is put in water—sometimes flowing, sometimes still—and the different particles settle at different levels in a large volume of water. The ore can also be treated chemically so

chemical compositions of minerals bearing the same metal.

The commonest class of extractive techniques involves the use of heat; these are called pyrometallurgical processes. Pyrometallurgy is much more than simply melting minerals down. In many cases, minerals are first "roasted" to induce certain chemical reactions. This is true of nickel, for example, which is often found combined with iron and sulfur. In roasting, the iron and sulfur are oxidized, which facilitates their removal from the ore. When the roasted material is then smelted (i.e., melted), much of the iron oxide contained by the ore forms a glass-like, nonmetallic by-product called slag, which can be skimmed off. The remaining material—called a matte—is then Bessemerized. This is a process, developed for steelmaking, in which air is forced through molten matte in order to purify it further. In the case of nickel, the

matte that remains usually contains sulfides of both nickel and copper. These can be separated by crushing and flotation, and the nickel sulfides purified by the second kind of extractive technique.

The second type of extraction process is electrometallurgical. This makes use of the fact that electric currents can decompose metallic compounds and cause metals to be deposited on an electrode (the electrical conductor immersed in the solution containing the given materials). With nickel, one electrode is made from the nickel sulfide, the other from purified nickel. In the refining process, the nickel sulfide is broken down, and its nickel is deposited on the nickel electrode.

The third class of extractive techniques makes use of chemical baths and is called hydrometallurgy. Ammonia, for example, is used to leach nickel ores, ultimately yielding very pure nickel powder.

Alloys

Once a metal has been purified, it is ready to be used. Few pure metals are suitable for almost any purpose, however, since they are too brittle, or lack specific qualities such as resistance to high temperatures. Thus, they are combined with small amounts of other materials, usually other metals, to create alloys. The addition of alloying agents to base metals, as they are called, alters the properties of the base metals in a predictable way. Thus, base metals can be strengthened, made more resistant to corrosion, or made easier to work by alloying.

Alloying is one of the most important branches of metallurgy. Metallurgists are constantly experimenting with new combinations of metals to create materials that meet ever more demanding specifications. Nickel-based superalloys are among the greatest achievements in this field. Whereas most alloys include three or four metals, superalloys include up to 10, in carefully controlled proportions.

Metalworking

Once an alloy has been created that is suited to a given job, it must be fashioned into the proper shape. The technique used to shape a metal is very important, because certain techniques have the effect of strengthening the finished product.

There are two basic metalworking processes. The first is casting, in which the standard procedure is to pour molten metal into a mold. When the metal solidifies, the mold is removed, leaving the metal cast in the desired shape. Casting can also be done with powdered metals. The powder is forced into a mold, which is then heated. The powder does not melt; rather, it fuses in a process called sintering.

The second basic metalworking process shapes metals by mechanical means, making products that are said to be "wrought." For example, metals can be hammered on an anvil, squeezed between rollers, stamped with dies, and drawn out through holes.

Metals can be wrought when they are hot or cold. When cold, a metal has a well-defined crystalline internal structure, but when hot, its crystal structure becomes

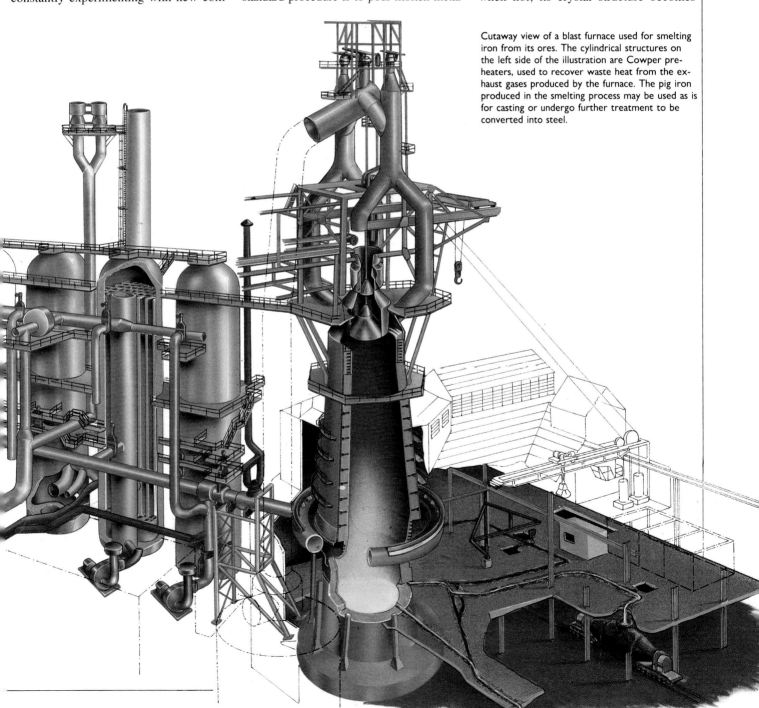

Cutaway view of a blast furnace used for smelting iron from its ores. The cylindrical structures on the left side of the illustration are Cowper pre-heaters, used to recover waste heat from the exhaust gases produced by the furnace. The pig iron produced in the smelting process may be used as is for casting or undergo further treatment to be converted into steel.

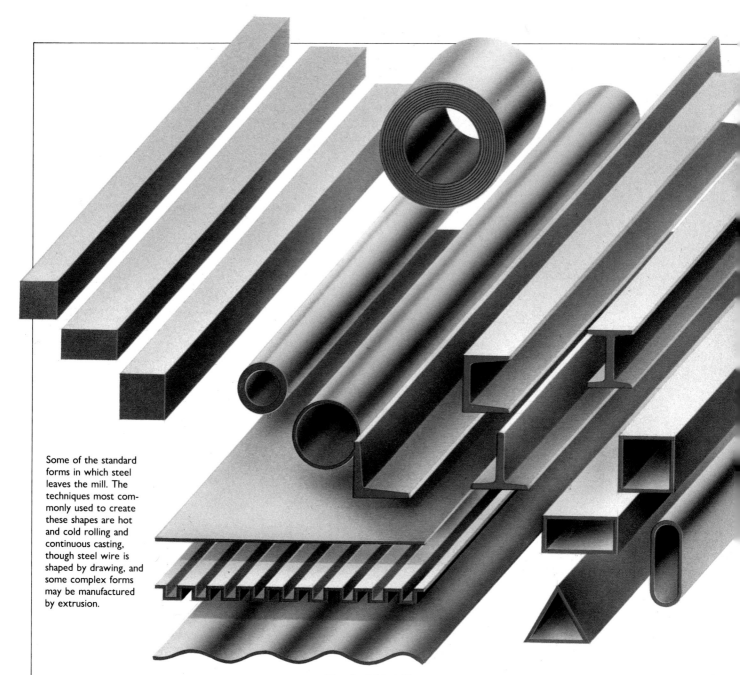

Some of the standard forms in which steel leaves the mill. The techniques most commonly used to create these shapes are hot and cold rolling and continuous casting, though steel wire is shaped by drawing, and some complex forms may be manufactured by extrusion.

more varied, easily deformed, and at the melting point is lost altogether. This microstructural deformability at higher temperatures makes the metal easier to work, and new crystals can grow as it cools. When a cold metal is wrought, its crystals are broken up and rearranged. In both cases, the alteration of the crystal structure gives the metal greater strength.

Because heating a metal to certain temperatures for determinable periods of time can alter its crystal structure, lending it greater strength upon cooling, many metal products are given treatments of carefully controlled heating and cooling. This is especially the case with alloys, whose different ingredients create a complex inner structure quite sensitive to heat. Superalloys in particular are given very precise heat treatments to guarantee their strength.

Physical Metallurgy

The fact that cold-working strengthens a metal has been known for millennia, but the reason came to be understood only about 1890. It was at that time that scientists began to gain knowledge of the crystalline inner structure of metals. Indeed, all metallurgical processes can be explained in terms of this microstructure, the study of which is called physical metallurgy.

Physical metallurgy draws on chemistry, physics, and thermodynamics, among other branches of science. In concentrating on the crystal structure of metals, it makes particular use of two techniques. One involves the use of phase diagrams, the graphs that show, for different combinations of metals, what crystal structure will predominate at what temperatures. Phase diagrams are crucial for an understanding of the properties of alloys at dif-

ferent temperatures. The second technique is called metallography—the direct observation of metallic crystal structures by naked eye, microscopes, or X-ray techniques. Samples are highly polished or etched with acid to reveal the crystal structure, then studied under special lighting conditions that bring out the geometry of crystals. Different crystal phases can also alter the resistance of a given metal to corrosion, vary its vibration properties, and drastically affect the length of time over which it will withstand particular kinds of stresses. This "fatigue life" is crucial in the production not only of such highly loaded metal structures as superalloy turbine blades but also steel I-beam structures, welded steel plates with which ships are built, and riveted aluminum sheets of aircraft.

Some of the basic techniques of metallurgy. From top left, clockwise: ladle for a continuous casting mill; steel bars produced by
hot rolling; preparation of sand casting molds for iron pipe
fittings; pouring of ingots of cast iron.

Metals

Metals are so important that we often define historical periods according to the predominant metals people used. There were, for example, the Bronze Age, the Iron Age, and the Steel Age. And, prior to the metal ages, there was the Stone Age—a culture so primitive that it lacked metals. These definitions have some value, for, in general, the wider use of more refined metals such as steel and aluminum has an enormous impact upon the way people live.

Pure metals have certain physical characteristics. In their pure state, they are usually shiny. Most can either be pulled into wires or flattened into foil such as gold leaf or tin foil, or both. Furthermore, metals are usually good conductors of heat and electricity. Unfortunately, no absolute line can be drawn between metals and nonmetals, for some metals show both metallic and nonmetallic qualities.

Chemists define metals as those elements, such as sodium, iron, tin, and silver, that have a tendency to form positive ions. This means that in chemicals that have some metal components, the metal atoms are generally positively charged and the nonmetals are negatively charged. In sodium chloride ($NaCl$), for instance, which is common table salt, the chlorine atoms are negatively charged, but the metal sodium has a positive charge.

About 75 percent of all known elements are metals, according to this chemical classification. Several elements are, chemically speaking, borderline cases. That is, they have as many metallic as nonmetallic characteristics. Arsenic, silicon, and antimony are among the examples of such metalloids.

Above: Metals are not always hard, resistant, and shiny. One example is butter-soft sodium, illustrated at right. The layer of rust covering the block of iron, at left, attests to the metal's affinity for oxygen.

Right: Round drop of tin on the aluminum plate keeps its form because a layer of oxide on the aluminum blocks the tin from wetting it.

Occurrence of Metals in the Earth

The Earth's inner core is made up mostly of iron; between that and the iron found in other parts of the Earth, iron is by far our most common metal. The crust of the Earth, which varies in depth from 3 to 20 miles (5-32 km), *contains all the known metals.* The most common are listed in order of their abundance in the crust: aluminum, iron, calcium, sodium, potassium, and magnesium.

Ores

Metals are found in natural substances called ores. These ores contain metal-bearing minerals and vary a great deal in the percentage of metal they contain.

Native ores may contain the pure metals of gold, silver, copper, mercury, bismuth, arsenic, and antimony. In compounds called oxides, the metals are combined with oxygen. Typical oxides are those of iron, aluminum, manganese, tin, and chromium. Sulfides are metals combined with sulfur, and include copper, lead, zinc, silver, nickel, cobalt, arsenic, antimony, and mercury. There are iron sulfides, too, but those ores are used more to obtain the sulfur than the iron. Carbonates are compounds containing carbon and oxygen. Sodium carbonate is Na_2CO_3. Lead, zinc, iron, copper, calcium, strontium, barium, and magnesium are all found in carbonates. Chlorides are chemicals that contain both metal and chloride ions. Sodium, potassium, magnesium, calcium, and silver are obtained from chlorides. Sulfates are compounds containing a metal and sulfur and oxygen. Sodium sulfate is Na_2SO_4. Calcium, strontium, barium, and lead are metals found as sulfates.

Metals are obtained from the ores by metallurgical processes. This usually entails concentrating the valuable metal-containing minerals from waste rock. Then the compounds are smelted, that is,

chemically treated and often heated in order to extract the metals. In the final step, the metals are refined.

Alloys

Rarely are metals used in their pure state. The metals we see around us are almost always alloys, which are either mixtures of various metals or mixtures of metals and nonmetals such as carbon. Metals often mix very well with other metals. Bronze, for example, is an alloy of copper and tin. Gold jewelry is not made of pure gold but of gold mixed with other metals, usually copper. An alloy in general is not a chemical compound, but a uniform, solid mixture of metals. That is, as two or more metals in an alloy crystallize, the atoms can fit together with each other in tightly packed, alternate fashion. There are literally thousands of alloys of various metals.

The Use of Alloys

Metals are generally made into alloys so that their hardness, strength, and resistance to rust may be improved. There are many other reasons for making alloys.

Bronze—copper and tin—was the first major alloy used by mankind. Swords made of bronze were found to be less brittle than those made of copper. A tin sword would have been so soft as to be useless. But together, they formed a durable metal that could hold a cutting edge. Bronze can also be cast more easily than pure copper.

The ability of metals to undergo deformation without fracturing is called plasticity. *Above:* Sample of lead originally had the form of a cube, but a few hammer blows reduced it to a thin sheet. *Right:* Copper is a less plastic metal, and so its deformation requires much greater energy.

CONDUCTIVITY OF SEVERAL METALS AT 0°C.	
METAL	CONDUCTIVITY (SIEMENS/M)
Silver	66×10^6
Copper	64.5×10^6
Gold	49×10^6
Aluminum	40×10^6
Magnesium	25.4×10^6
Sodium	23.4×10^6
Tungsten	20.4×10^6
Potassium	16×10^6
Lithium	11.8×10^6
Cesium	11.5×10^6
Iron	5.2×10^6

Left: Photographs illustrate another important property of metals, thermal conductivity. The metal rods shown were each coated with paraffin, then immersed in boiling water. The higher the level of thermal conductivity, the greater the melting of the paraffin above the water line.

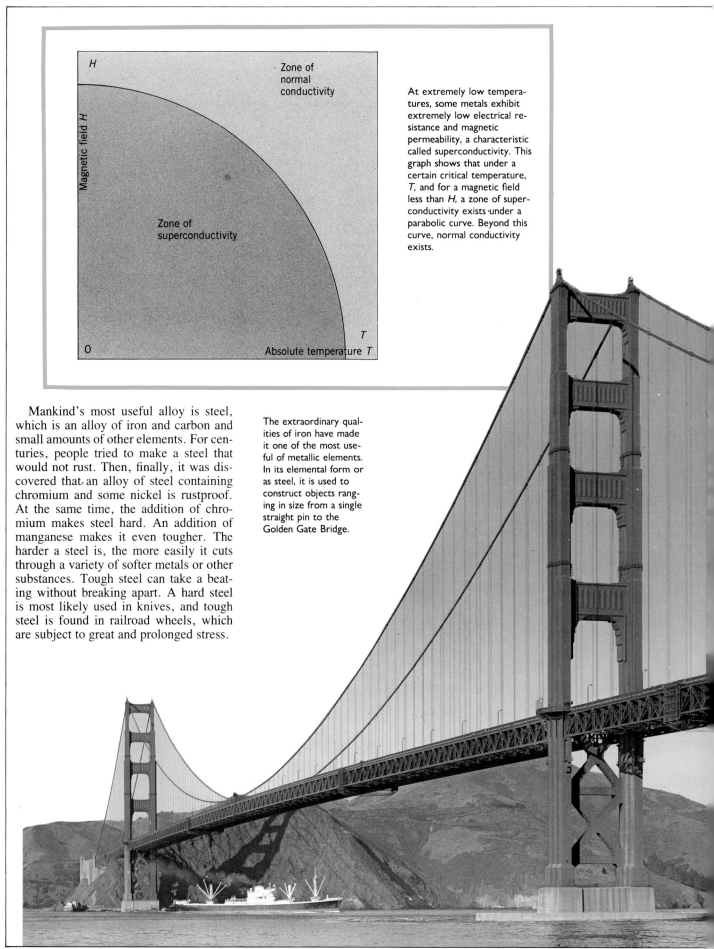

H

Zone of
normal
conductivity

Magnetic field H

Zone of
superconductivity

0

T

Absolute temperature T

At extremely low temperatures, some metals exhibit extremely low electrical resistance and magnetic permeability, a characteristic called superconductivity. This graph shows that under a certain critical temperature, T, and for a magnetic field less than H, a zone of superconductivity exists under a parabolic curve. Beyond this curve, normal conductivity exists.

Mankind's most useful alloy is steel, which is an alloy of iron and carbon and small amounts of other elements. For centuries, people tried to make a steel that would not rust. Then, finally, it was discovered that an alloy of steel containing chromium and some nickel is rustproof. At the same time, the addition of chromium makes steel hard. An addition of manganese makes it even tougher. The harder a steel is, the more easily it cuts through a variety of softer metals or other substances. Tough steel can take a beating without breaking apart. A hard steel is most likely used in knives, and tough steel is found in railroad wheels, which are subject to great and prolonged stress.

The extraordinary qualities of iron have made it one of the most useful of metallic elements. In its elemental form or as steel, it is used to construct objects ranging in size from a single straight pin to the Golden Gate Bridge.

In the airplane industry, there is a great demand for lightweight metals for use in the frames of airplanes and many other parts of aircraft, including engines, seat frames, and so on. While magnesium is one of the lightest metals, it is not very strong. To give it enough strength so that it can be used in airplanes, it must be alloyed with other metals, such as aluminum or zinc.

An alloy of mercury is called an amalgam. Amalgams are generally semisoft or liquid. They are used, for example, in dental work to fill a cavity. The semisoft amalgam is pushed into a cavity and in turn hardens and fills the tooth.

Left and below: Aluminum, like iron, is a structural metal of great importance. This sequence of photographs shows stages in the forging of massive aluminum structural elements.

Metalworking

Few artists have inspired as much awe as the French sculptor Rodin. It has been suggested that the sense of his elemental power stemmed from the fact that he worked with molten metals. Rodin's famous bronze casts are outstanding achievements in the art of metalworking, but of course, metalworking is not solely an artistic pursuit. At the center of modern industry are the techniques of shaping metals into usable forms.

Basic Metalworking Techniques

The basic techniques of metalworking can be divided into two categories. The first is casting, when molten metal is poured or injected into a mold. When the metal solidifies, the mold is removed, leaving the metal cast, as it is called, in the desired shape. There are several different casting methods, which vary according to whether the mold can be used repeatedly or only once.

The most widely used casting method is sand casting. Here, an object that has the shape of the final product (allowing for product shrinkage) is pressed into a moist, sandy material. This object—called a pattern—is removed, and the sandy material hardens to form a mold. When a mold is to be made that must completely surround the final product, the mold is divided into two halves, which are contained in the top and bottom halves of a special box. When the halves of the box are put together, the complete mold is fully contained within it. In this case, however, the pattern must impress channels into the sandy material, so that molten metal can reach the empty mold within the box. After the metal solidifies, it is taken from the mold, and any excess metal is removed to make the finished casting. Sand casting is used very widely to make products ranging in weight from a few ounces to hundreds of tons.

The second category of basic metalworking techniques includes those where solid metal is mechanically forced into a desired shape. Metals worked in this way are said to have been wrought, or forged. The simplest (and oldest) way of shaping metal is beating it with a hammer. More complicated processes of this sort include stamping pieces of metal with dies, squeezing sheets of metal between rollers to make them thinner, and drawing or forcing metal through small holes to make wire or tubing. Metals can be wrought when they are at room temperature, or they can be heated to make them more malleable. The physical manipulation of metals often has the additional effect of making them stronger but less ductile.

Metalworking in Industry

Both basic techniques of metalworking are applied throughout industry. The familiar I-beams used for construction are made by passing hot bars of steel between rollers that have special grooves cut into them. A common alloy of iron known as gray iron is used for casting such products as engine blocks and other machine parts.

An interesting metalworking technique is sometimes used to make small machine parts that require a high degree of precision. This technique involves powdered metals. Powder made from given metals is forced into a mold and then heated. The material doesn't melt; instead, in a pro-

A. Rolling

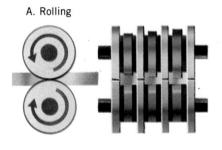

B. Forging

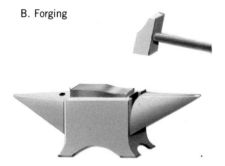

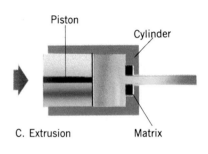

Piston · Cylinder
C. Extrusion · Matrix

D. Drawing

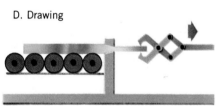

E. Stamping

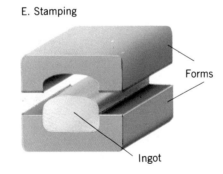

Forms

Ingot

Diagrams illustrate the principal metalworking processes. Rolling is the process used to make the familiar I-beams. The hot, but not liquid metal is passed through a series of shaping rollers. In forging, the metal is heated and worked into the desired shape on an anvil. Iron worked in this way is called wrought iron. In extrusion, heat-softened metal is forced through a narrow opening by pressure to produce wires and tubes. In drawing, heated metal is drawn out through a narrow opening. In stamping, the heated, but not liquid metal is pressed between forms. In casting, the liquid metal is poured into a mold.

F. Casting

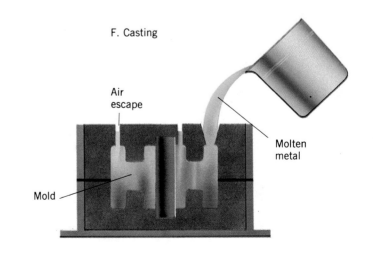

Air escape

Molten metal

Mold

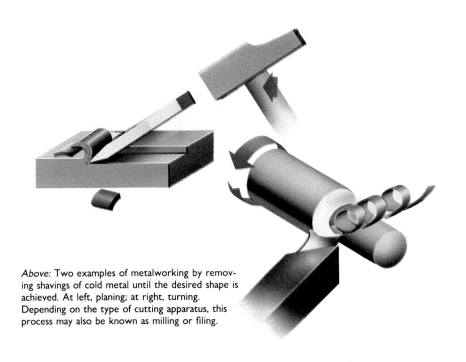

Above: Two examples of metalworking by removing shavings of cold metal until the desired shape is achieved. At left, planing; at right, turning. Depending on the type of cutting apparatus, this process may also be known as milling or filing.

cess called sintering, the metal particles bind together to make a solid mass in the desired shape.

Metalworking in Art

Today, many monumental artworks are made using metalworking techniques taken from industry. Certain factories work exclusively with artists to produce enormous steel sculptures. Artists and craftsmen of the past have left us a tremendous variety of ways to work with metal on a smaller scale. Sculptors from Egypt to classical Greece and Rome, and through the time of Rodin, have used various techniques to cast statues. Since antiquity, jewelers have hammered metal into different shapes, adding designs with punches or by incising lines, which may or may not be filled with some other material. One of the most remarkable metalworking techniques is gilding. Gold is beaten out into leaves perhaps a quarter-millionth of an inch (0.00001 cm) thick, and then delicately applied to the surface of less valuable materials, giving them a golden surface.

Two products of the metalworking process. *Above:* Newly produced and still red-hot extruded wire. *Right:* Rolling machine producing sheet steel.

Metamorphic Rock

Stone, so frequently employed by sculptors, builders, and writers to symbolize immutability, nonetheless changes under certain conditions. Some rocks change so much, in terms of structure and chemical composition, that the material of which they were originally formed is almost unrecognizable. Rocks that have undergone such drastic changes are called metamorphic rocks, from the Latin, meaning "transformed."

How Metamorphic Rocks Are Formed

Metamorphic rocks were formed through the effects of heat, pressure, and chemical activity. Some metamorphic rocks were heated deep beneath the Earth's surface until they became viscous (not quite liquid) and then flowed during mountain building; they were further modified by intense pressure. Other rocks that originated far below the Earth's surface (as much as 6 miles or 10 km) simply absorbed (and were softened by) the Earth's interior heat.

Pressure, such as that produced when continents move or mountains rise, is often enough to metamorphose rocks. These pressures can, for example, realign the crystal structures in the minerals that make up the rock until the crystals change, forming new minerals. Micas are often made this way.

Chemical changes in rocks occur in several ways. Hot water, steam, or various gases may drive the oxygen out of rocks; or circulating fluids and gases containing dissolved chemicals may fill rock pores with the new chemicals (this is how metal ores are formed).

Metamorphic rocks are frequently more obviously crystalline than other rocks and, on their surfaces, have bands of alternating colors and textures. These bands—owing to the pressure that helps to form metamorphic rock—often become bent, welded, and even looped.

Metamorphic Rocks Compared to Other Rocks

Ever since the Earth was formed, magmas have existed in its depths. On occasion, these magmas have reached the surface of the Earth and erupt as volcanic lava. At other times, the magmas cooled and eventually solidified beneath the Earth's surface. A rock that was liquefied (rather than softened) and then cooled is called an igneous rock. Of these, the most common are granites and basalts.

Frequently, igneous rocks were reheated and transformed physically and chemically until they became metamorphic rocks. Schist, for example, is meta-

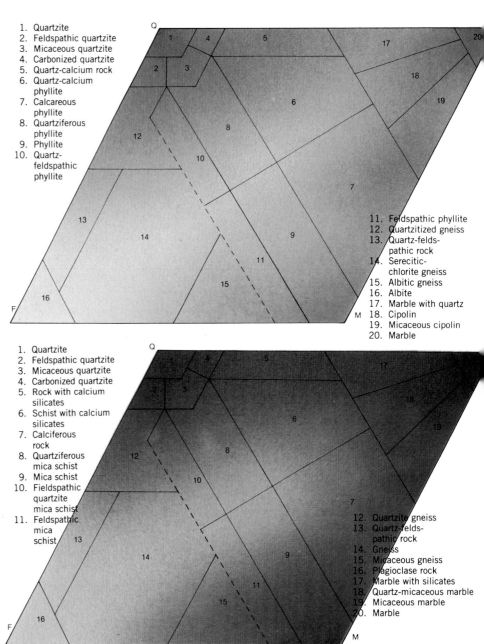

1. Quartzite
2. Feldspathic quartzite
3. Micaceous quartzite
4. Carbonized quartzite
5. Quartz-calcium rock
6. Quartz-calcium phyllite
7. Calcareous phyllite
8. Quartziferous phyllite
9. Phyllite
10. Quartz-feldspathic phyllite
11. Feldspathic phyllite
12. Quartzitized gneiss
13. Quartz-feldspathic rock
14. Serecitic-chlorite gneiss
15. Albitic gneiss
16. Albite
17. Marble with quartz
18. Cipolin
19. Micaceous cipolin
20. Marble

1. Quartzite
2. Feldspathic quartzite
3. Micaceous quartzite
4. Carbonized quartzite
5. Rock with calcium silicates
6. Schist with calcium silicates
7. Calciferous rock
8. Quartziferous mica schist
9. Mica schist
10. Fieldspathic quartzite mica schist
11. Feldspathic mica schist
12. Quartzite gneiss
13. Quartz-feldspathic rock
14. Gneiss
15. Micaceous gneiss
16. Plagioclase rock
17. Marble with silicates
18. Quartz-micaceous marble
19. Micaceous marble
20. Marble

Metamorphic rock is classified according to its mineral content. Illustration at top refers to rocks that have been metamorphosed in the green schist facies—at temperatures of under 500°C. and maximum pressure of 5,000 atmospheres. The lower diagram is a representation of amphiobolite facies, formed at 500-650°C. and pressure of 4,500 to 7,000 atmospheres. The original mineral components in the two facies are identical, but the different pressure and temperature conditions produce different final states.

morphosed from basalt. Schist, unlike basalt, contains mica.

When a mountain, hill, or other land form is eroded by rivers or by glaciers, rock fragments such as gravel, sand, and mud are carried away and deposited elsewhere. When, because of pressure and chemical activity, the sediments have hardened, they are called sedimentary rocks. They, too, can become metamorphic rocks. Quartzite is a metamorphosed sandstone. It has a slightly glassy look and is the toughest of all rocks.

Some sediments are made up of organic materials that turn into rocks or hard rocklike substances, such as limestone and coal. Metamorphosed limestone is marble, and metamorphosed coal is anthracite. Because hot water, steam, and gases carry metals into rocks undergoing metamorphosis, these rocks often become ores of valuable metals such as zinc, copper, and lead. Many important mines have ores in metamorphic rocks.

Left: Marble quarry and, below, a thin section of schistose crystalline limestone, with traces of metamorphosed carbon.

Below right: Ecologite from Norway in a standard photograph and a microscopic cross section. This type of rock is called a ferromagnesian metamorph.

Above: Another example of ferromagnesian rock. At top, the raw rock; at bottom, a microscopic photograph of its crystalline structure.

Left: Rodignite from the Piedmont area of Italy, an example of metasomatic rock. *Below:* Thermometamorphic rock, which is recrystallized under high heat but without high pressure.

Metamorphosis

At the start of winter, certain species of mature caterpillars hunt out a sheltered place. Once there, a caterpillar hangs its head down and rests very quietly, while wondrous things begin to happen inside its body. The body itself shortens and fattens, and its hard outside skeleton, or exoskeleton, splits right off. A tough brown casing, the chrysalis, forms around the body. After winter ends, the case splits open, and a whole new creature emerges—a magnificent butterfly.

This is an example of metamorphosis, the miraculous transformation in form or structure of an animal in its postembryonic development. It is common in insects and in some amphibians and crustaceans. For many animals, metamorphosis means a change not only in physical form but in habitat and diet as well. For example, a caterpillar chews leaves, but when it turns into a butterfly, its mouth structure is adapted solely to sucking flower nectar. Baby dragonflies are aquatic, while their adult counterparts are strictly flying insects. Some animals, such as crustaceans, go through metamorphosis without any apparent change in either their looks, habits, or habitat. Their metamorphosis consists of simply shedding, or molting, their nonexpandable skeletons each time they grow bigger.

Left: Adult form of a tubular annelid polychete, attached to a bivalve. *Below:* The larval state, a trochophore.

Stages of Metamorphosis

Most insects undergo several distinct stages from egg to adult. Grasshoppers, aphids, and termites, like crustaceans, go through a gradual metamorphosis. This means that their physical forms remain basically the same throughout life, except that they grow bigger and, in many cases, develop wings. There are three stages of gradual metamorphosis: egg, nymph (called a naiad if it is aquatic in early life),

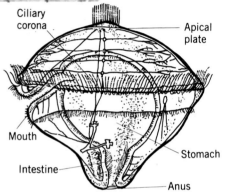

Ciliary corona — Apical plate — Mouth — Intestine — Stomach — Anus

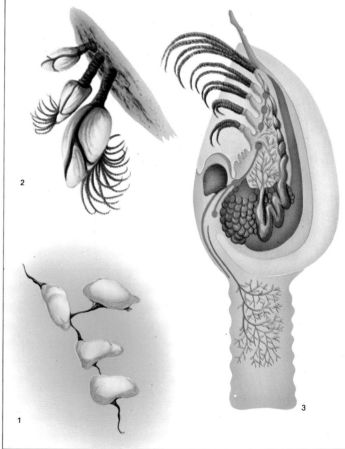

Above: Cirripedes (barnacles) in the larval state. *Right:* Stages in the metamorphosis of a barnacle of the genus *Lepas.* Once the egg hatches, the first stage is that of the nauplius. When this begins to develop a shell, it becomes a cyprid. The cyprid cements itself to a fixed object, and metamorphosis begins (1). The barnacle then develops a footstalk and tendrils (2), eventually becoming an adult barnacle (3).

and adult. The nymph hatches from the egg; it is wingless and without reproductive organs, but otherwise, it looks like a miniature adult. During the nymph stage, the insect grows out of its exoskeleton, shedding this outer layer completely. The insect may molt in this manner five or more times. Finally, when the nymph develops wings, it passes into adulthood.

Insects that go through a total physical transformation, such as moths and beetles, are said to experience complete metamorphosis. They move through four developmental stages: egg, larva, pupa, and adult. The eggs hatch into larvae, immature life forms resembling worms. Caterpillars, maggots, and grubs are the larvae of butterflies, flies, and beetles, respectively. The larvae are wingless, lack compound eyes, and often possess more legs than their adult counterparts, and different mouth parts, too. Larvae tend to consume larger quantities of food, grow rapidly, and molt. Each molted larva enters an inactive pupa stage, in which it develops a hardened cuticle or casing around its body. From all outer appearances, the pupa seems dead, but inside, the tissues of the larva are changing into those of the adult that will soon emerge.

What Makes Metamorphosis Happen

Biologists have recently discovered that metamorphosis may be controlled by hormones, chemicals secreted by glands or organs into the blood. In experiments with cecropia moths, scientists have found that a brain hormone appears to be triggered into action (possibly by winter's cold weather), setting off the pupal phase and its subsequent transformations. When the pupa's brain was removed, it did not mature into an adult. When the brain from another pupa was inserted into the debrained one, it metamorphosed.

Metamorphosis is one of the best examples of nature's magic; it also represents a brilliant biological adaptation. Because animals that undergo metamorphosis do not often eat the same sorts of food as infants and adults, there is never any competition between the young and the old. Since they are not competing for nourishment, both forms have a much better chance of survival.

Right: Development of a butterfly. Sequence of photos shows the various states of the complete metamorphosis. (1) egg, (2) larva emerging from egg, (3) first-stage larva, (4) third-stage larva, (5) molting fourth-stage larva, (6) mature larva, (7) mature larva forming chrysalis, (8) newly formed chrysalis, (9) adult emerging from chrysalis, (10) adult butterfly.

Meteor

On November 25, 1833, a correspondent for the *Connecticut Observer* wrote: "We pronounce the raining of fire which we saw on Wednesday morning . . . a merciful sign of the great and dreadful day when the Sixth seal shall be opened." He was describing the great meteor shower of that month by referring to the Bible, *Revelations* 6:13: "And the stars of heaven fell unto the earth, even as a fig tree casteth her untimely figs, when she is shaken of a mighty wind." By all accounts, the shower seen over large areas of the United States was awesome, striking fear into many. The sky seemed to rain down stars and fire for hours.

No one was hurt. There is no record of even one meteor falling to the Earth. The entire shower seems to have burned up in the upper reaches of the atmosphere.

Shooting Stars and Meteors

Meteors are often called shooting stars, even though they are not stars at all. Some that get close to us are indeed brighter than the brightest stars; they are called fireballs or bolides. A few appear exceptionally bright, being more brilliant than the full Moon. Often they are seen to flare and leave behind glowing trails of incandescent dust, which may remain for several seconds, even minutes. A fireball seen during the day has a dark trail of dust behind it.

Meteors contain ice and small pieces of rock and sand. They usually burn up at heights of 55 to 65 miles (90-105 km) in the atmosphere, They burn up because they are traveling through space at such high speeds, usually about 20 to 35 miles (32-56 km) per second. When they slam into the atmosphere, even where it is thin, the friction of the air simply burns most of them away.

In spite of their great speed, no meteors have been known to travel fast enough to escape the gravity of the Solar System. This fact leads scientists to believe that all meteors originate in the Solar System and are trapped within it.

A very small number of meteors do get through the atmosphere and crash on the surface of the Earth. When they do, the rocky parts are called meteorites. Of course, the dust from burning meteors eventually filters down through the atmosphere. At least 200,000 tons of meteor dust are added to the Earth every year.

Since most of the meteors burn up, laboratory investigation is impossible. But spectra of their light as they burn up shows what kind of ice they contain. The rocky meteorites are of two types: either stony (rich in silica) or ferruginous (composed almost entirely of iron).

There is evidence connecting meteors with comets. Both travel in the same type of orbit; the orbits of some meteors are actually identical with the orbits of old comets that have decayed. As comets fall apart, dust and particles become widely scattered in their orbit. If the Earth passes through such an orbit, it may move through the particles, which appear in the sky as meteor showers.

Some meteors date from the time when the Solar System was just a large cloud of dust and gases. This cloud eventually collapsed because of its own gravity. As it did, the Sun, planets, and satellites formed, and dust in the form of meteors and meteorites fell on to them. The Moon, Mars, and Mercury, for example, are all pockmarked with craters formed by meteorites that fell there when the Solar System was young. The planets' gravitational pull has swept up most of the dust, but much remains. Some meteors are the remains of that original dust cloud, which is at least 4,600 million years old.

Observing Meteors

Most meteors are seen one at a time and by pure chance. These single meteors are called sporadics. It is estimated that about 10 trillion (10^{12}) meteors encounter the Earth every year. A person watching the clear sky from sunset to dawn is almost assured of seeing at least one.

Every year, there are some small meteor showers that fall at regular times. The best known are the Quadrantids, which appear from January 2nd to 5th, when about 110 meteors per hour may be seen; the next best are the Perseids, of July 27th to August 16th, when about 65 meteors per hour may be seen; the Geminids of December 7th to 15th are almost as good, with about 55 meteors per hour.

Below: Individual meteor showers seem to originate or 'radiate' from one part of the sky. The chart indicates the radiant point for the Perseid meteors, which are at their peak around August 12 each year.

Bottom: Diagram at left illustrates tendency of meteors falling just before dawn to appear both brighter and to be falling faster. At right, a meteor shower radiant in the night sky.

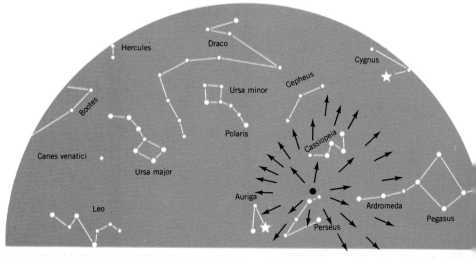

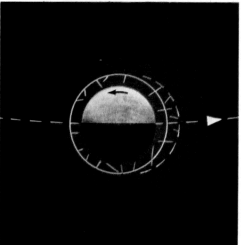

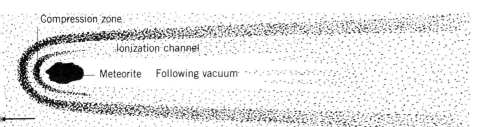

Compression zone
Ionization channel
Meteorite   Following vacuum

PRINCIPAL PERIODIC METEOR SHOWERS			
Date	Name	Radiant constellation	Meteorites per hour
January 2-3	Quadrantids	Bootes	35
April 20-22	Lyrids	Between Lyra and Hercules	
May 1-4 (heaviest, May 4)	Eta Aquarids	Aquarius	12
July 25-30 (heaviest, July 28)	Delta Aquarids	Delta Aquarius	
August 1-17 (heaviest, Aug. 12)	Perseids	Perseus	50
October 9	Draconids	Draco	Variable
October 16-22 (heaviest, Oct. 21)	Orionids	Between Orion and Gemini	20
October 15-22 (heaviest, Oct. 19)	Leonids	Leo	20
November 17-23	Andromedids	Andromeda	
December 9-13 (heaviest, Dec. 12)	Geminids	Gemini	40

Above: Comets and meteors tend to have similar long elliptical orbits around the Solar System. In fact, it is possible that in many cases meteors are residue left behind by a comet. This would explain why meteors tend to come in showers.

Left: Table of the more predictable and most visible meteor showers. The radiant constellation is the zone from which the meteors tend to come.

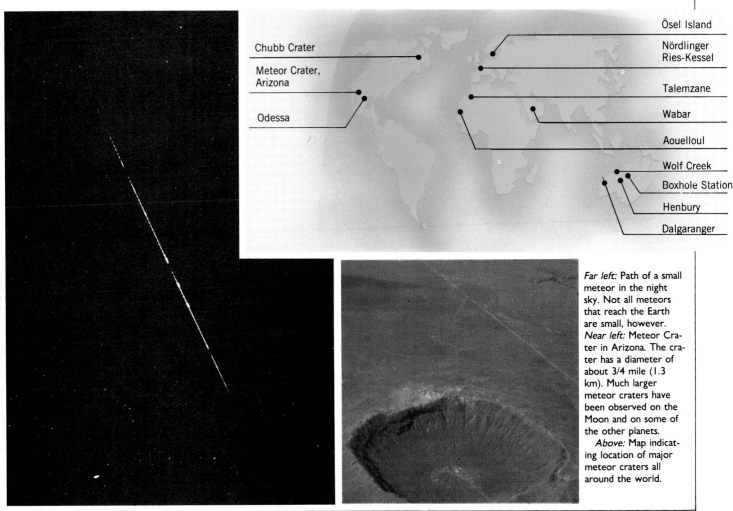

Chubb Crater
Meteor Crater, Arizona
Odessa
Ösel Island
Nördlinger Ries-Kessel
Talemzane
Wabar
Aouelloul
Wolf Creek
Boxhole Station
Henbury
Dalgaranger

Far left: Path of a small meteor in the night sky. Not all meteors that reach the Earth are small, however.
Near left: Meteor Crater in Arizona. The crater has a diameter of about 3/4 mile (1.3 km). Much larger meteor craters have been observed on the Moon and on some of the other planets.
Above: Map indicating location of major meteor craters all around the world.

Meteorology

Many primitive peoples have personified the elements. The ancient Greeks, for example, imagined wind gods who playfully and often maliciously interfered in the Earth's climate.

Today, we know that the various phases of the weather have to do with a complex system of atmospheric and land conditions rather than with the whims of the gods. Weather is the result of an interaction of natural forces—precipitations, humidity, temperature, pressure, cloudiness, wind, etc. Furthermore, these various factors are all involved in an enormous movement of air masses, a great river of air whirling, surging, and eddying all around the Earth.

Meteorology is the study of the physics and chemistry of the atmosphere—the way that temperature, humidity, and wind formations interact. A more comprehensive understanding of these large-scale pressure and circulation patterns helps mete-

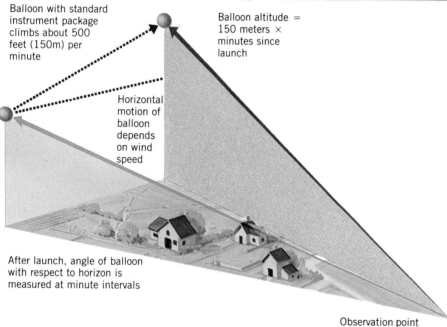

Balloon with standard instrument package climbs about 500 feet (150m) per minute

Balloon altitude = 150 meters × minutes since launch

Horizontal motion of balloon depends on wind speed

After launch, angle of balloon with respect to horizon is measured at minute intervals

Observation point

orologists construct weather maps, which are necessary for accurate short-range as well as long-range weather forecasting.

Detailed, painstaking, continuous, and coordinated scientific study and observations have helped provide an understanding of the physical laws governing weather, while laying to rest centuries of folklore and superstition. Since the start of the 20th century, millions of measurements have been made by balloons, aircraft, ground-based weather stations, and, in the last two decades, satellites. It has been the task of meteorologists to piece together the parts of this vast, enormously complex, and perpetually moving mosaic of weather to create a picture of weather conditions all over the world.

The Weather Machine in Motion

What these meteorologists have discovered is that the ebb and flow of our daily weather is closely bound up with patterns of large-scale air movement over the Earth. The weather "machine" is set in motion by the interplay between masses of air from the polar regions coming into contact with subtropical winds.

The heated air over the equatorial regions rises and flows poleward in both hemispheres. When the warm and cold air masses meet, the weather is likely to change rapidly and dramatically—from warm to cold or from rainy to clear. Hence, the study of boundaries, or fronts, between air masses is of great importance.

Top: Radar station used for the study of atmospheric physics.

Radar and satellite observations give a broad overview of weather phenomena. *Above right:* On a smaller scale, weather balloons like the one being launched from a U.S. Navy ship in the photograph yield detailed information about the atmospheric dynamics of a more restricted area. *Above left:* Weather balloon sightings are used to measure wind speed and direction at different altitudes.

The clash of the two currents, with their different levels of temperature and humidity, creates a condition of atmospheric instability. Great eddies and vortices of wind intermittently form and break off into whirling masses of air within the general circulation. Meteorologists call wind systems cyclones and anitcyclones. These air

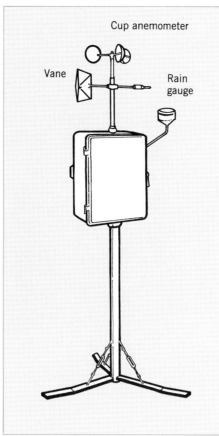

Cup anemometer

Vane

Rain gauge

Left: Outdoor weather station equipped with instruments to register changes in air temperature and relative humidity, barometric pressure, soil temperature, and evaporation. Portable weather station is shown in diagram mounted with an anemometer for measuring wind speed and direction and with a gauge for measuring rainfall.

particles are transmitted from the Sun to the Earth, the atmosphere, and back to space. Also of critical importance is the Coriolis force, which is the specific directional influence of the Earth's rotation on the global circulation of the winds.

Technological Breakthroughs

Two technological developments in the 20th century are helping meteorologists better understand the workings of the weather system. There are now dozens of weather satellites surveying the Earth's atmosphere, so that we can follow weather systems as they are born, grow, and evolve. A mass of new information on both regional and large-scale weather patterns has come out of this upper-atmosphere reconnaissance. Meanwhile, high-speed computers assimilate the vast amounts of data from a huge network of weather-reporting satellites and stations to help in the construction of more comprehensive weather maps. Thus, weather prediction has become much more scientific and precise. Nevertheless, even with the available knowledge and technology, it does not yet rule out the appearance of unpredictable "freak" storms and other weather patterns.

masses move in large clockwise and counterclockwise whorls, covering an area some 500 to 1,000 miles (800-1,600 km) in diameter.

Cyclones comprise an area of low atmospheric pressure, characterized by inwardly spiraling winds. They are usually harbingers of bad weather—clouds, rainstorms, blizzards, etc.—and are the familiar "lows" on the weather map. The stormy weather associated with cyclonic air masses may affect an area of more than a million square miles (2.6 million sq km). (Tornados are sometimes misleadingly referred to as cyclones, but a tornado is a much smaller weather system that does not involve large-scale wind formations, although its winds move in a regularly rotating fashion.) Anticyclones are areas of high atmospheric pressure characterized by outwardly spiraling winds. The anticyclones, the weather map's "highs," are usually associated with calm, stable, generally warm weather. These winds are deflected by the Earth's rotation, so that, instead of blowing north or south, they become prevailing westerlies or easterlies.

The formation of these fronts and air masses, as well as of more strictly local weather systems, is greatly modified by the interactions among land, water surfaces, and the atmosphere—in particular, the amount of heat and moisture ex-

changed among these three constituents of our weather system.

Other factors that meteorologists must study include the influence of the Sun—more specifically, the process by which electromagnetic waves and subatomic

Below: Evaporation gauge consisting simply of an open pan of water of known volume and surface area measures evaporation in the arid climate of Tucson, Arizona.

Methane

Methane, a colorless and odorless gas, is the main component of natural gas, in some cases amounting to 99 percent of the product as it comes from the well. It is also known as fire damp in coal mines, where its presence has to be monitored—although not itself poisonous, it can asphyxiate miners and can also cause explosions when mixed in proportions (ranging from about 5 to 14 percent) with air. It is also known as marsh gas when produced as a result of the decomposition of vegetable matter underwater by the action of bacteria. In the form of marsh gas, it is estimated that a single African lake (Lake Kivu) may contain as much as 200,000 million cubic feet (5,600 million cu m) of methane. In China, methane used for fuel has been collected on a modest scale from similar sources for a number of years.

In more industrially developed countries, such as the United States, extensive pipelines exist to transport natural gas from the source to the consumer. It can be stored and transported in liquid form, which reduces its volume to 1/600th of its gaseous volume.

Besides being obtainable directly from wells, methane can also be produced on a

Methane is an important compound because it is the basic starting unit for the synthesis of numerous industrial derivatives and also because it is the simplest hydrocarbon, upon which all others are based. *Above:* Molecular structure of methane.

Methane CH₄	Gaseous hydrocarbon. Boils at −161.4°C. Density: 0.054 at 20.0°C. (air = 1)
In nature	Natural gas, mine gas (fire damp), combustion of fuels
Chemical Preparation	Reaction between carbon sulfide and hydrogen sulfide catalyzed by copper
	Redaction of CO_2 by hydrogen in the presence of nickel at 250-400°C.
	Decomposition of metallic carbons in water
	Decomposition of methyl magnesium iodide in water
Important industrial derivatives	Acetylene, ethylene, lamp black, methanol, formaldehyde, carbon sulfide, chloromethane, hydrocyanic acid

Above: Principal characteristics and properties of methane. It is sometimes called 'marsh gas' because it can be formed by bacteria during underwater plant decay. Methane is the building block for alkanes. It is found in natural gas and in mines in the form of explosive vapor called fire damp. Various methods for synthesizing methane exist, of which the hydrogenation of CO_2 is the most used.

Above: At left, methane pipeline being laid; at right, part of a tunnel under the Alps through which passes a methane pipeline running from Holland to Italy. *Below:* Plant used for the production of methane derivatives.

large scale by various industrial processes. Soft, or bituminous, coal is burned by a process called destructive distillation to produce coal gas. Methane is a major constituent of coal gas. And a form of sewage treatment called the activated-sludge method also produces a methane-rich gas.

Methane is used in the chemical industry to produce other useful products, such as wood alcohol (methanol), formaldehyde, chloroform, and carbon tetrachloride. It is also used in the manufacture of the refrigerants and aerosol propellants known as Freons. Moreover, engines (including automobile engines) can be made to run on liquid natural gas, which is cheaper than gasoline and, when burned under the proper conditions, produces no pollutants.

Chemistry

Methane is the first and simplest of a series of very useful compounds of carbon and hydrogen called the alkanes or paraffin hydrocarbons. Methane consists of a single carbon atom bonded to four hydrogen atoms. It is represented by the formula CH_4, as shown schematically by the diagram

$$
\begin{array}{ccc}
H & & H \\
& C & \\
H & & H
\end{array}
$$

The two hydrogen atoms to the left of the carbon atom are in one plane, and the other two are in a plane at right angles to it. That is, if the first two are in the same plane as this page, the other two project at nearly right angles to the page.

The other members of the alkane series, each with one more carbon atom and two more hydrogen atoms than the one preceding it, are ethane, propane, butane, pentane, hexane, heptane, octane, and so on, with subsequent names derived from the Greek word for the number of carbon atoms in the molecules. A closely related series, the alkenes, is identical to the alkanes, except that one pair of carbon atoms in the molecule is joined by a double bond; the molecule consequently contains two fewer hydrogen atoms. The naming procedures follow the same principle as for the alkanes; that is, starting with the two-carbon-atom molecule, they are ethene, propene, butene, etc. They also have the more familiar names ethylene, propylene, and butylene. A third series, the alkynes, has two triply bonded carbon atoms. Its most familiar member is acetylene, whose formal name is ethyne. All of these can be thought of as variants on the basic building block, methane.

See also CHEMICAL BOND AND VALENCE; NATURAL GAS.

Microanalysis

Advances in medical science have added immeasurably to the lives of millions of people around the world. In the area of diagnostic medicine, which involves determining what illnesses or conditions people suffer from or the presence or absence of certain chemicals in their system, microanalysis has been one of technology's greatest advances.

This technique, which allows physicians and technicians to take tiny amounts of tissue and subject them to tests for diagnostic purposes, is still evolving. Originally developed from traditional methods of physical chemistry, modern microanalysis or, as it is sometimes called, microchemistry has now been automated and perfected to a degree that was not even thought of just 20 years ago.

Origins of Microanalysis

The properties of chemical elements were largely uncodified until the late 1700s; modern analytical chemistry took another 70 years to be founded. Chemists seeking to create order out of the chaotic state of their knowledge began to develop

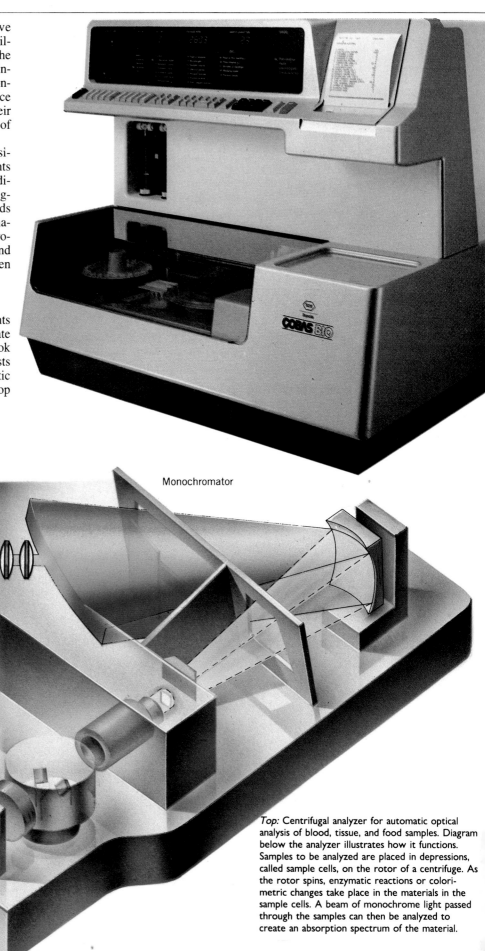

Top: Centrifugal analyzer for automatic optical analysis of blood, tissue, and food samples. Diagram below the analyzer illustrates how it functions. Samples to be analyzed are placed in depressions, called sample cells, on the rotor of a centrifuge. As the rotor spins, enzymatic reactions or colorimetric changes take place in the materials in the sample cells. A beam of monochrome light passed through the samples can then be analyzed to create an absorption spectrum of the material.

tests that would allow them to accurately determine which substances constituted a given sample.

The early tests required relatively large amounts of each sample—hair, tissue, or blood, for example. These samples, bit by bit, were dissolved in a beaker or test tube, as a given sequence of acids and bases was added. By this process, chemists attempted to make deductions about the substance itself.

The biggest problem with this method is obvious. It required a large sample, since a whole series of tests had to be conducted, and the more tests there were, the greater was the possibility of contamination. Once the tests were complete, a step of deduction—"this substance contains an excess of $\underline{x}$ because it reacted to tests a, b, c, and d in the following manner"—was required. Particularly with very sick patients, it was often inefficient and cruel, since large amounts of tissue had to be extracted, tests often had to be repeated because of contamination, and results could take weeks to achieve.

Modern Microanalysis

The two most important tools of microanalysis are the centrifuge and the gas spectrometer. Samples in tightly sealed containers are put in centrifuges and spun around, so that centrifugal force may magnify the sedimentation-inducing effect of gravity. This allows scientists to take an extremely small amount of tissue or fluid and quickly change its state. Solids in liquids are efficiently precipitated, or separated, from the solution; liquids of varying molecular weight form layers, which make further analysis easier; and concentrates are achieved from very small amounts of sample.

Gas spectrometers take the samples—often, but not always, after centrifuging—and analyze their constituent parts. A substance burned (pyrolyzed) at gradually increasing temperatures produces gases of different compositions, which are registered by the spectrometer. Since each substance evolved by pyrolysis has its unique "color"—color is a matter of the frequency of electromagnetic wavelength in the light that its burning produces—scientists are able to determine exactly what is in a sample by viewing its spectrographic emissions. Again, extremely small amounts can be used.

New Techniques

As in most technical fields, computers have played a great role in recent advances. Since analysis often calls for a comparison of present results with known patterns from the past, computers—which can store millions of pieces of information and quickly search through their files in a logical way—can aid doctors using microanalytic tools and methods.

All-in-one machines for microanalysis were invented in the early 1960s and are still being perfected. These machines can take very small amounts of substances, typically blood or urine, and subject them automatically to a series of tests, then print out and, if necessary, recheck the results—often in less than 5 minutes.

Below: Atomic absorption spectrophotometer for trace-element determination. As shown in box at right, the sample to be analyzed is vaporized in a flame. This excites the atoms in the sample so that they emit electromagnetic radiation at specific wavelengths. This radiation is then compared with the light emitted by a control bulb within the device that has a filament made of the same element being sought in analysis. The results are then printed out by a computer.

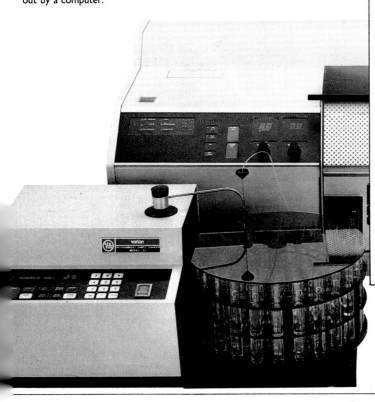

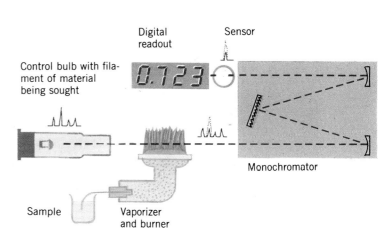

Control bulb with filament of material being sought

Digital readout

Sensor

0.723

Sample

Vaporizer and burner

Monochromator

Microcomputer

The era of microelectronics that we have entered promises to be as revolutionary as the machine age that was ushered in by the steam engine. One of the most important tools driving the rapid change from the mechanical-industrial age to a new electronic-information age is the microcomputer. Developed in 1974, the microcomputer is a descendant of the mammoth mainframe computers of the 1940s and 1950s and the filing-cabinet-sized minicomputers that emerged in the 1960s. Desk-top computers began appearing in the mid-1970s, and by the early 1980s, portable and hand-held computers with more computing power than many of their bulkier progenitors were on the market.

Computer-on-a-Chip

The basic building blocks of a microcomputer are located on a single chip of silicon the size of your fingertip. These components consist of thousands of microscopic transistors and circuits that are etched on the silicon wafer. Technically, a microcomputer consists of a microprocessor, a memory, and display circuits. It receives information (input), performs calculations, and then sends out the results (output). The microprocessor is the "brain" of a microcomputer—it performs the calculations on the information received and returns the results in proper order. The microprocessor has a control unit that synchronizes the sequences of operations performed on the incoming data and an arithmetic-logic unit that adds, subtracts, and reorganizes the data. Together, the control unit and the arithmetic unit are called the central processing unit or CPU. The two other basic parts of a microprocessor are a clock and the power supply. The memory stores incoming information and the instructions (program) as well as the temporary and final results.

The results of the processed information are displayed on an electronic screen or written out by a typewriter. The input device on a microcomputer is a keyboard that looks very much like a typewriter.

The microcomputer is a digital computer. It operates on a binary numbering system using only two digits, 1 and 0, which are called bits (from *binary digits*). All information fed into a microcomputer is converted into binary numbers through a code stored in the main memory. Each letter and number has a binary code equivalent. For example:

letter	binary code
A	1100 0001
B	1100 0010

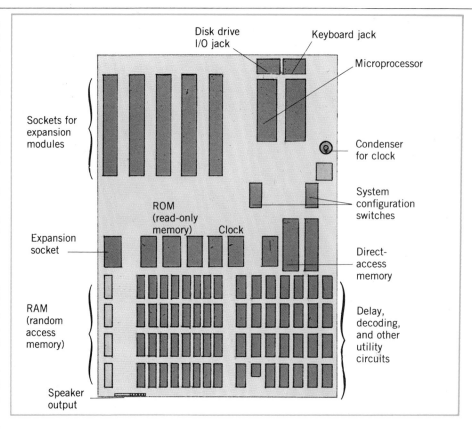

Above: Map of the main circuit board, or 'mother board,' of a microcomputer. The expansion sockets accept extra circuit board modules, or cards, which can expand the capabilities of the computer by boosting memory capacity, provide interfaces with peripherals, or supply the computer with operating systems and in languages contained in ROM (read-only memory).

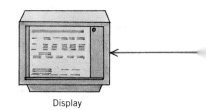

Display

Right: Schematic diagram of the relationship between the microcomputer's central processing unit and the input/output devices, called peripherals, with which it communicates. These latter normally include keyboards, video displays, printers, and plotters. The modem permits computers to communicate among themselves over an ordinary telephone line.

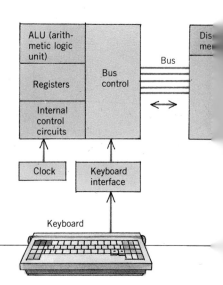

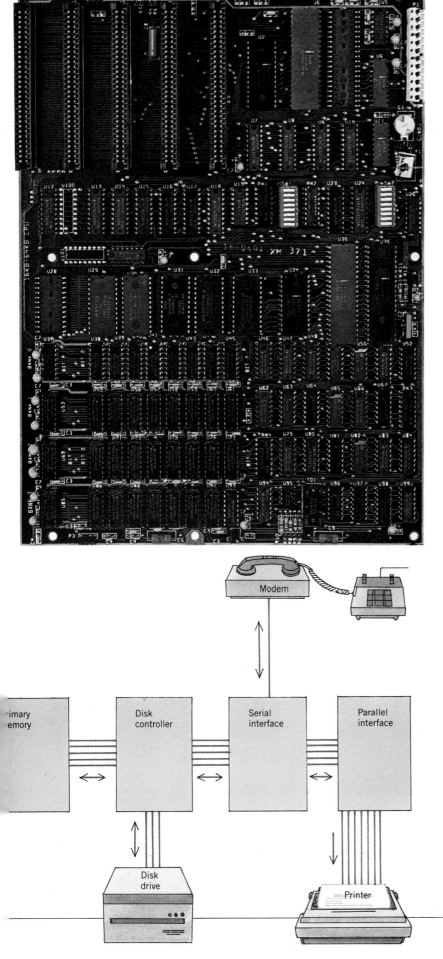

Left: Main circuit board of a popular microcomputer, the IBM PC. Its principal components are identified in the circuit board map at far left.

Using a Microcomputer

Like any computer, a microcomputer requires a program in order to operate. A program can be put directly into the computer memory by using appropriate language based on an assortment of ordinary words. But most microcomputer users are not skilled programmers and prefer to buy prepackaged programs, which are often called software. Software is usually stored on a floppy disk, or on a magnetic tape. The programs may be written in computer languages, such as BASIC (the most common), COBOL (for business applications), or FORTRAN (a math and engineering language). Software tapes or floppy disks, which are the size of a 45-rpm record or smaller, are simply inserted into a reading device connected to the microcomputer. Once the software for a specific application is activated, you can begin to enter your data on the keyboard.

Small home computers are starting to be used in thousands of applications. They are widely used by hobbyists, professionals, educators, researchers, and small-business people, among others. Some applications include accounting, record keeping, word processing, communications, information retrieval, learning, and teaching assistance.

Microcomputers also have opened the way to new forms of recreation. Video games controlled by microcomputers have become very popular. But microcomputers are also revolutionizing the arts. Music synthesizers are creating new musical modalities, and computer-assisted art is being explored.

Microfilm

The word "microfilm" conjures up images of old spy movies, in which top-secret information was always being handed from one spy to another at a late-night rendezvous. While microfilm may be useful in the world of espionage, such nefarious uses are by far the exception, not the rule. Librarians, it seems, are the largest users of microfilm—not spies.

History

The first patent for microfilm was granted in 1859. One of its first uses came in 1870, during the Franco-Prussian War, when small strips of film containing valuable information were strapped to the legs of carrier pigeons and sent overland. Such a clandestine use of microfilm may well have been responsible for its common association with espionage. Microfilm enjoyed its first major use in the 1920s, when 16-millimeter film was used to make file copies of checks in bank clearinghouses. Its use has expanded considerably since then, and it is now commonly used for storing business and legal records and for engineering and architectural drawings. Libraries use microfilm for storing copies of newspapers, directories, and indexes and in other areas where it is beneficial to have reduced-image copies.

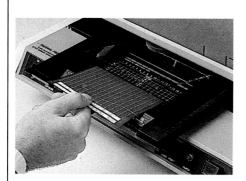

What It Does

A microfilm copy is a photographic reduction of printed material, kept on a film strip that must be optically enlarged before it can be read normally. Microfilm copies usually are made on 16- and 35-millimeter film and are reductions of from one-tenth to one-fortieth of the original document's size (a newspaper page, when microfilmed, can be reduced to the size of a postage stamp). For special purposes, pages may be reduced even more by using high-resolution film. The cameras used in the microfilming process are much the same as regular still cameras, although some are mechanized to feed documents automatically past the lens.

Like much of photography, microfilm copying first produces a negative, from which copies can be made. The microfilmed copy is viewed on special ma-

Above: Microfilm reader-printer. At top, the entire machine; left, slide tray into which the microfiche is placed; center, control panel and search function command switches; right, built-in photocopier, enabling the user to reproduce the microfilmed page in 'hard copy.'

chines that project an enlarged image (occasionally, even larger than the original) onto a glass screen.

Microfilm Today

The types of microfilm copies in use today are as varied as the uses to which microfilming is put. The two most common microforms are ribbon microfilm and microfiche. Ribbon microfilm is used extensively by libraries to store copies of newspapers and other materials of a serial nature. To store copies of an individual nature, ribbon microfilm may be cut into individual frames or groups of frames (unitized) and assembled on cards that can be easily indexed and retrieved. Copies of engineering and architectural drawings are kept in this manner.

A microfiche is a microcopy of material on a transparent sheet of film measuring approximately 3 by 5 inches (7.6 × 12.5 cm). On microfiche, each page of a document being copied is reduced to a small rectangle on the film sheet. Typically, one microfiche sheet has 60 or 70 pages of information. Microfiche copies can be read on projection machines similar to those used to read ribbon microfilm.

The benefits of storing material on microfilm are numerous. Microfilm is compact and easy to store (100 file drawers of documents can be reduced to two drawers of microfilm copies), it can be used to keep records of print materials that are deteriorating, and it is inexpensive.

The amount of information and material printed continues to grow each year, and even the most modern libraries are beginning to fill up, while some of the older ones simply have no more room for new acquisitions. Having microfilm copies made of materials is one of the best ways to save space. Now used primarily to store deteriorating items (such as newspapers) and bulky or little-used materials, in the years to come, microfilm may be the way by which all library collections are stored. There are problems with microfilming, however. Storage requirements are more stringent than for print copies, as microfilm must have greater protection against extremes in temperature and humidity and from dust and pollutants. Yet, with proper care, microfilm copies can last for a long time, ensuring that today's significant printed material will be readily available for study for future generations.

In addition to microfilm and microfiche, 2 other methods for storing reduced images are the mini-card and microcard systems. In these, the film is attached to a file card with identifying information and a die-cut window. In this way, the card is index and information all in one. Minicards generally use 35-mm film, while microcards employ the smaller 16-mm format, allowing the placement of more images on a single file card.

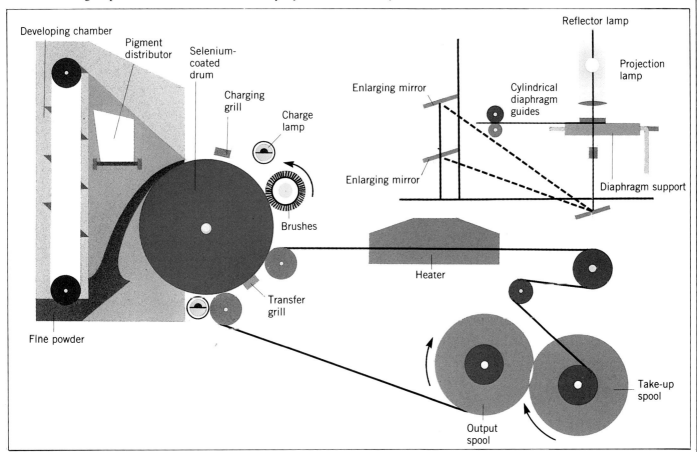

Above: Diagram of a continuous microfilm enlarging and printing machine manufactured by the Xerox Corporation. By using high-resolution lenses and sensitive film, originals can be reduced to 1/40 or less of their dimensions without loss of clarity or detail. A silver-coated film with a slow speed is used to achieve very high contrast, suitable for reproduction of both printed matter and photographs. In the case of old or yellowed originals, special filters are used. Films have also been designed with a built-in yellow filter for this use.

Micromanipulation

In almost every field of technology and science, modern techniques have allowed us to see, change, and make things that were once invisible, or at least untouchable. The first area where this trend became evident was in biology, with the invention of the microscope; the slow development of tools enabling us to work with biological material under the microscope has led to the techniques of micromanipulation, by which cells can be dissected, transplanted, and marked by tiny tools. The techniques have also been applied in the manufacture of electronic microcircuits and mechanical devices.

Elements of Micromanipulation

For biological applications, the first necessity for micromanipulation is a microscope with good illumination and an ample stage for mounting specimens. Next in importance are the micropositioners, which convert the inexact movements of the human hand into the precise movements necessary for operating on cells. Finally, we need the microtools, mounted on the micropositioners, which actually perform the operations.

Often, microscopes used in micromanipulation are especially designed to have a large, solid stage—a place for mounting exhibits—between illumination and microscope lens. Live cells are usually in liquid solution on special glass slides, which keep them moist and healthy.

Micropositioners are the most important elements of any micromanipulation system. They are, in effect, small clamps—often smaller than an adult's little finger—attached to a complex, geared mechanism that can move the micropositioner extremely small and precise distances. The micropositioner holds the microtools, which actually touch the cells and perform the important tasks of cutting, injecting, and marking tissue. These positioners must be exceedingly accurate, well-mounted, and reliable instruments.

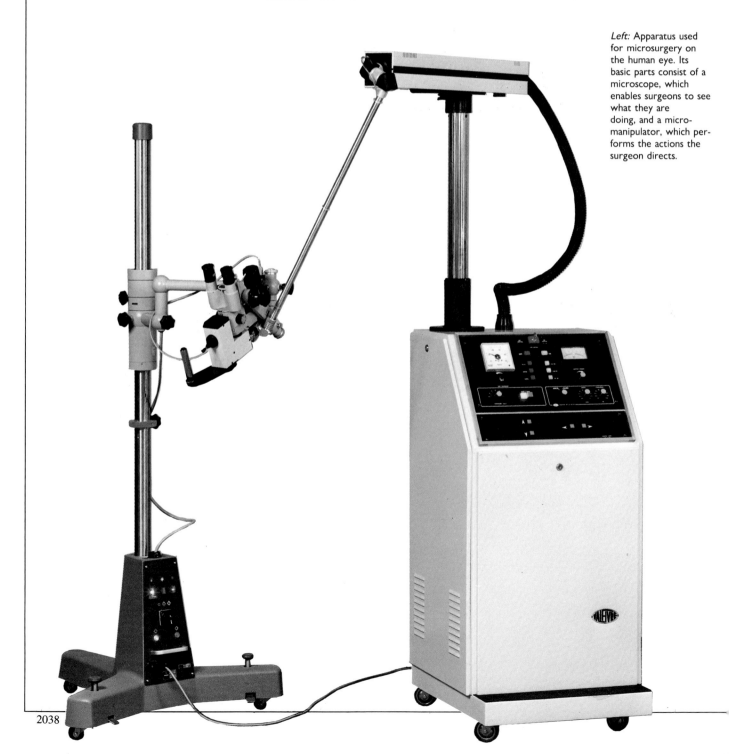

Left: Apparatus used for microsurgery on the human eye. Its basic parts consist of a microscope, which enables surgeons to see what they are doing, and a micromanipulator, which performs the actions the surgeon directs.

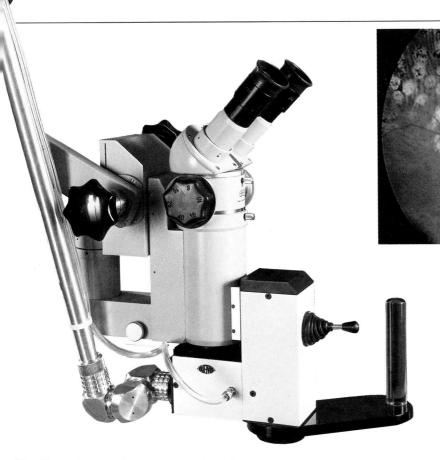

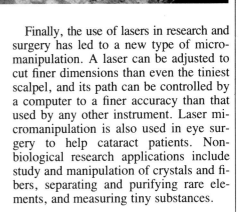

Finally, the use of lasers in research and surgery has led to a new type of micromanipulation. A laser can be adjusted to cut finer dimensions than even the tiniest scalpel, and its path can be controlled by a computer to a finer accuracy than that used by any other instrument. Laser micromanipulation is also used in eye surgery to help cataract patients. Nonbiological research applications include study and manipulation of crystals and fibers, separating and purifying rare elements, and measuring tiny substances.

The first micropositioners were activated by a screw mechanism—one turn of a given screw corresponded to a given movement—but every type of mechanical control has now been used, including pneumatic and hydraulic systems. Computer-controlled micropositioners are being used increasingly today. All micropositioners, regardless of type, have the ability to manipulate their attached tools accurately in three-dimensional space, whatever the means used to activate them.

The tools used in micromanipulation are similar to regular tools used in biological research, only much smaller. Often made of glass, they include scalpels, needles, pipettes, hooks, and forceps. Microtools must often be smaller in diameter than a human hair in order to perform with fine accuracy their work of manipulating the minuscule structures of cells.

Modern Trends in Micromanipulation

Though the basic elements of micromanipulation have remained the same since 1859, when they were first cataloged by Oskar Schmidt in *Microscopic Dissector,* the technology has changed, as has the uses to which it is put. Developments in medical knowledge have now made micromanipulative techniques applicable in cancer research and in certain surgical techniques, notably optical surgery and repair of damaged nerve fibers.

Above: Operating head of the microsurgery apparatus shown at left. The surgeon follows the operation he is performing through the binocular eyepiece. The surgeon directs the operation using a lever linked to servo-mechanisms that move a miniature scalpel. The servo-command is shown in greater detail below.

Top right: Microphotograph shows the retina of a human eye that has undergone laser microsurgery.

Microphone

It's hardly a sophisticated model, but two tin cans connected by a length of string can be considered a microphone. Simply remove the lid from each can and, after boring a hole through each bottom, tie one end of a string to the inside of both cans. Then you and another person each take one can and walk away from one another until the string is taut. When you speak into one of the cans, the acoustical energy of your voice will cause the bottom of the can to vibrate. The vibration passes into the string and is carried to the other can, where it causes the can bottom to vibrate in the same pattern as the bottom of the first can. When these vibrations reach the ear of someone holding the second can, they are converted to sound. Granted, the other person will hear a distorted reproduction of your voice, and if he is standing more than about 20 feet (6 m) away, you will probably hear nothing at all through the contraption; but however crude this device may be, it illustrates the principle on which the microphone functions.

Working Principles

Sound is the result of air molecules being deflected from their normally random motion. This happens, for example, when you clap your hands or shout; air molecules are forced to collide, bunch together, and, in the process, alternately expand and collide. Sound is the pressure on these air molecules; where there are a great many molecules in a cluster, the pressure is said to be high; where there are fewer molecules, the pressure is said to be low. Since air molecules expand and compress under pressure, sound energy is carried in waves. (Sound energy can be defined as variations in pressure.)

Sound waves can travel through air, liquid, and solid bodies. (They cannot, however, be transmitted through a vacuum.) In the crude tin-can microphone, the pressure of your breath disturbed the molecules in the can, causing the can bottom to vibrate. The molecules in the second can were then displaced by the pressure of the energy waves coming from the first can. The key to the functioning of the tin-can microphone is that the first can converts sound energy to mechanical energy, and the second can converts mechanical energy back into sound. The reason the tin-can microphone is not very effective is that mechanical energy cannot be improved, amplified, or otherwise modified. Electrical energy can be modified, and today's microphones convert sound energy into electricity.

Major Types of Microphones

A basic, rather uncomplicated type of microphone in use today is the carbon mike. Sound pressure from your voice (or a musical instrument, or whatever) passes through the mike head to cause the diaphragm—a thin metallic disk—to vibrate. These vibrations pass into a component called the button, which is a small cylinder containing closely packed carbon granules. Carbon conducts electricity, but not nearly as well as a metal such as copper. When you speak into the mike head, the carbon granules in the cylinder are compressed as the instantaneous air pressure increases, and then expand as the pressure decreases. When they are compressed together, the carbon granules can conduct electricity better than when they are allowed to expand, so that the electrical resistance of the microphone button varies in accordance with the sound waves striking the diaphragm. By allowing this varying resistance to control the amount of current flowing in the circuit in which the carbon microphone is connected, the sound energy is converted into modulated electrical energy. If necessary, this electrical signal can be directed into an audio amplifier, a device that magnifies the power of the original signal, but for some uses, such as local telephone service, the output of a carbon microphone can be made sufficiently strong so that no additional amplification is required.

A more sophisticated microphone is the dynamic mike, of which there are two varieties. The ribbon microphone (also called a velocity mike) consists of a thin, taut strip of metal (duralumin) ribbon, usually 2 to 4 inches (5-10 cm) long and a quarter-inch (6 mm) wide, suspended between the poles of a magnet. The ribbon, because it is directly in the magnetic field, will generate an electric voltage when it moves under the pressure of moving air molecules. Ribbon microphones also have a component called a transformer, which increases the very small voltage of the electrical signal induced in the ribbon, before it is fed to the amplifier, which this type of mike always requires. Though

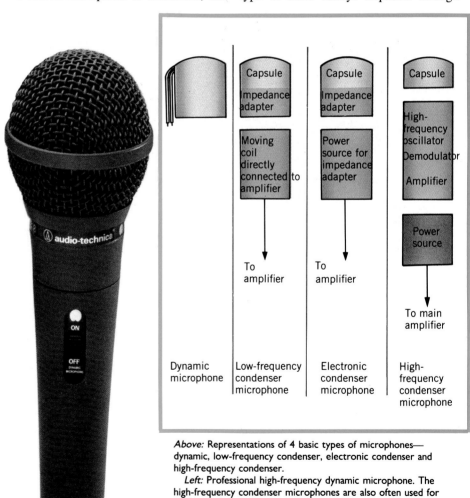

Above: Representations of 4 basic types of microphones—dynamic, low-frequency condenser, electronic condenser and high-frequency condenser.
Left: Professional high-frequency dynamic microphone. The high-frequency condenser microphones are also often used for professional recording, primarily because they filter out background noise. *Right:* Diagram illustrates how different shapes of microphones pick up sound from different directions.

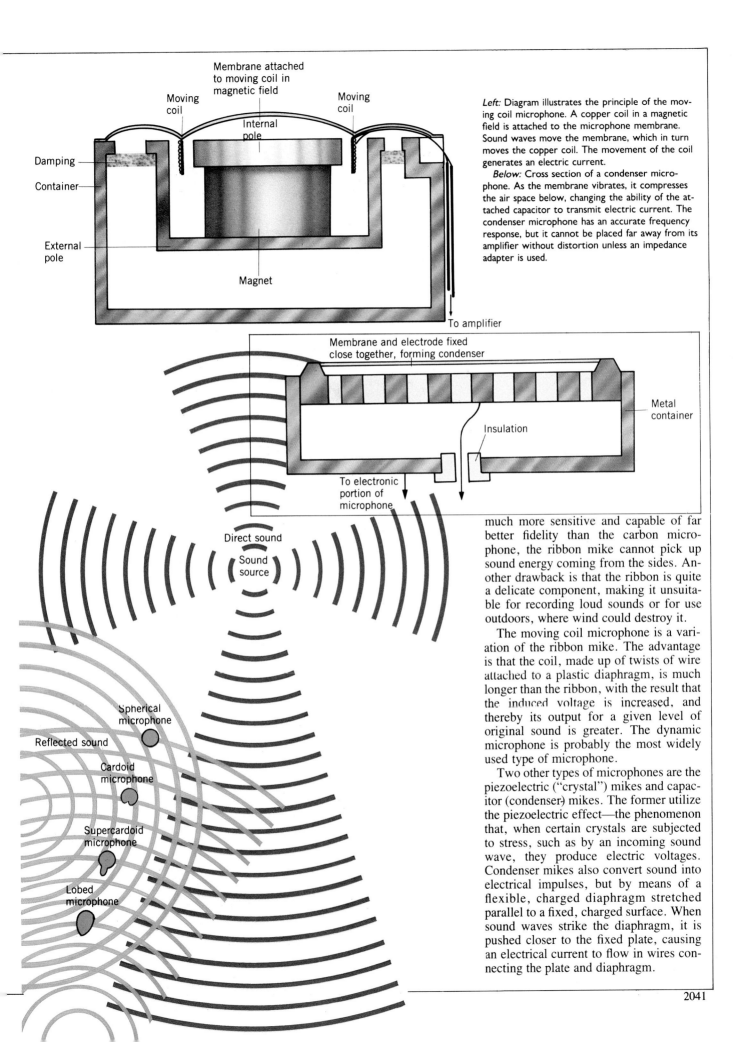

Moving coil

Membrane attached to moving coil in magnetic field

Moving coil

Internal pole

Damping

Container

External pole

Magnet

To amplifier

Left: Diagram illustrates the principle of the moving coil microphone. A copper coil in a magnetic field is attached to the microphone membrane. Sound waves move the membrane, which in turn moves the copper coil. The movement of the coil generates an electric current.

Below: Cross section of a condenser microphone. As the membrane vibrates, it compresses the air space below, changing the ability of the attached capacitor to transmit electric current. The condenser microphone has an accurate frequency response, but it cannot be placed far away from its amplifier without distortion unless an impedance adapter is used.

Membrane and electrode fixed close together, forming condenser

Metal container

Insulation

To electronic portion of microphone

Direct sound

Sound source

Spherical microphone

Reflected sound

Cardoid microphone

Supercardoid microphone

Lobed microphone

much more sensitive and capable of far better fidelity than the carbon microphone, the ribbon mike cannot pick up sound energy coming from the sides. Another drawback is that the ribbon is quite a delicate component, making it unsuitable for recording loud sounds or for use outdoors, where wind could destroy it.

The moving coil microphone is a variation of the ribbon mike. The advantage is that the coil, made up of twists of wire attached to a plastic diaphragm, is much longer than the ribbon, with the result that the induced voltage is increased, and thereby its output for a given level of original sound is greater. The dynamic microphone is probably the most widely used type of microphone.

Two other types of microphones are the piezoelectric ("crystal") mikes and capacitor (condenser) mikes. The former utilize the piezoelectric effect—the phenomenon that, when certain crystals are subjected to stress, such as by an incoming sound wave, they produce electric voltages. Condenser mikes also convert sound into electrical impulses, but by means of a flexible, charged diaphragm stretched parallel to a fixed, charged surface. When sound waves strike the diaphragm, it is pushed closer to the fixed plate, causing an electrical current to flow in wires connecting the plate and diaphragm.

Microscope

The human eye is a limited instrument. Beyond a certain size, objects are too small to be distinguished; they are, in effect, invisible. So people have invented tools to help sight reach beyond its normal limits. Instruments such as magnifying glasses and microscopes help one to see tiny objects by enlarging their images and sharpening the details.

Principles

When light is reflected from the surfaces of an object, the lenses of your eyes catch the rays coming from those surfaces and focus them into an image of the real object. This image is formed on the retina. The larger the retinal image, the closer the object appears; conversely, the closer the object is to one's eyes, the larger is its image on the retina. However, if the object is brought too close, the lenses of our eyes can no longer focus the image. (The least distance of distinct vision is approximately 6 to 15 inches [15 to 328 cm] from the eye.) This is why we cannot see very small objects. They must be very close to make an image large enough for you to distinguish details, but if they are too close, our eyes cannot focus on those details. An extra lens can solve this problem.

The lens of a magnifying glass forms an image that is larger than the object would appear to our retinas even at the closest possible distance on which the eyes' lenses could focus, but the image is formed at a distance to which the eyes can accommodate. The object seems larger because the magnifying glass lens makes a larger picture of it for the retina. The size of this enlarged image is the object's "apparent" size. The magnifying power of the enlarging lens is the ratio of the apparent size of the object to the size of the object as seen by the naked eye. The shorter the focal distance of the lens (the distance at which parallel light rays passing through the lens converge into the image), the more powerful is the lens. The strength of a magnifying lens is numbered according to how much it enlarges an object. A 10X lens, for instance, makes an image of the object 10 times larger than the object would appear to the naked eye.

Simple Microscopes

A simple microscope is a single lens (or system of lenses) that converges light rays with a very short focal length. The magnifying glass is one example. The best

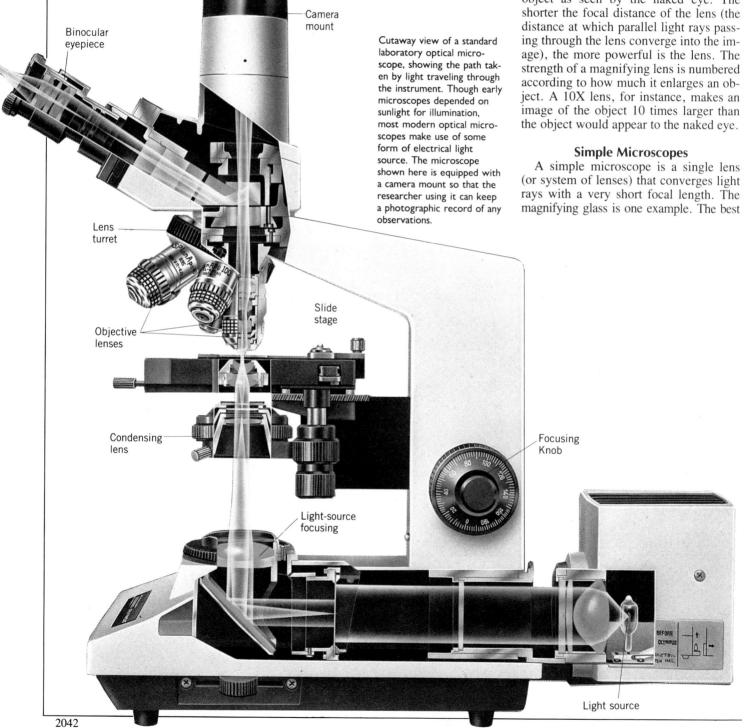

Cutaway view of a standard laboratory optical microscope, showing the path taken by light traveling through the instrument. Though early microscopes depended on sunlight for illumination, most modern optical microscopes make use of some form of electrical light source. The microscope shown here is equipped with a camera mount so that the researcher using it can keep a photographic record of any observations.

Binocular eyepiece

Camera mount

Lens turret

Objective lenses

Slide stage

Condensing lens

Focusing Knob

Light-source focusing

Light source

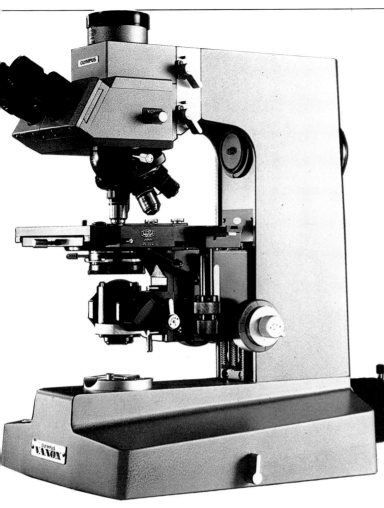

Left: Laboratory microscopes such as the one seen here are heavily built in order to dampen vibrations that could make viewing at high magnifications difficult.

Below: Microscope objective lenses, called nosepieces to distinguish them from the lenses of the eypiece.

Bottom: Micrometer slide stages permit precision manipulation of the object being viewed under the microscope; usually carried on a glass slide.

simple microscopes can magnify an object 10 to 20 times, but beyond 20X, the image becomes fuzzy. High-powered simple microscopes have several disadvantages. The short focal length means the lens must be placed very close to the eye. Because the object must also be very close to the lens, it is hard to illuminate it properly. Also, simple microscope lenses are prone to optical errors and aberrations that distort the image. Above 20X, compound microscopes are more effective.

Compound Microscopes

The device most people recognize as a microscope—the one used in a biology class, for instance—is a compound microscope. It has two lenses or lens systems, which magnify an image in two stages. The first lens—the objective—works like a simple microscope to make an enlarged image of the object. The second lens—the ocular—magnifies this image even more.

It is easy to assume that if two lens systems magnify the object better than one, several simple microscopes could be used in a line for an even better image. But in

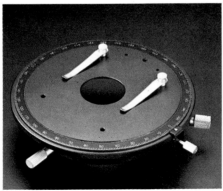

practice, the reflections and optical aberrations in the lenses limit the microscope to two systems.

The magnifying power of a compound microscope is the product of the magnifying power of the two lenses. A typical research microscope with an ocular of 10X and an objective of 10X would have a magnifying power of 100X. Microscopes often have two or three objectives of different powers, which can be moved into place as needed. Thus, the same research microscope with two more objectives of 45X and 100X would offer magnifying powers of 100X, 450X, and 1,000X.

The compound microscope makes the image sharper as well as larger. Sharpness, or "resolution," is the ability of the microscope to separate the closely spaced details of the specimen being studied. Only details larger than the wavelength of the light (the distance between the wave crests in the light rays) can be resolved. For all practical purposes, this limits useful magnification to about 2,000X. Beyond this, the separate points making up the image become too diffuse, and the image deteriorates.

Parts of the Microscope

Basic compound microscopes have three parts. First, there is the foot, which is the base on which the instrument stands. It is a heavy metal casting, usually a tripod or horseshoe-shaped, hinged to an arm that arches up, carrying the rest of the microscope. The body is the middle part of the microscope. It is hinged to the foot so that it may be tilted. The bottom of the body has a mirror attached to reflect light through the specimen being examined. Some high-powered microscopes have attached lamps to provide their own light sources. A platform called the stage is attached above the mirror and carries the specimen. In more powerful microscopes, a third lens system, the condenser lens, is often attached below the stage to focus light up through the specimen.

Attached to the body is a slide that holds a tube with both lens systems in it. The objective is at the lower end of the tube. When there are several objectives of different magnifying powers, they are mounted on a revolving nosepiece. The appropriate lens is swung into position along the optical axis. To use the microscope, you usually start with the lowest power objective, find the details you wish to study, and then focus on them with the more powerful objectives.

The ocular lens system is fitted into the upper end of the tube, and the whole tube with both lens systems can be moved up and down to focus on the specimen. Two adjustment knobs on the upper part of the body regulate the tube movement. The coarse-adjustment knob focuses the whole microscope first, and the fine-adjustment knob moves the tube small distances to complete the focusing.

High-powered compound microscopes have parts added to improve resolution, magnification, and mechanical accuracy.

Most objectives are dry lenses; light rays pass through air between the specimen and lens. Some microscopes use immersion lenses; the lens touches a drop of oil between it and the slide covering the specimen. This improves image resolution. High-powered immersion lenses require an immersion condenser, which is also connected to the specimen slide by oil, to pass light through to the objective.

Some research microscopes have a double, or binocular, tube that splits the light into two beams, letting you observe with depth-discerning stereoscopic vision like that of our naked eye. Trinocular tubes split the light beam into three—two for the eyes and one for a recording camera.

Types of Microscopes

There are many kinds of microscopes with different capabilities to fill the needs

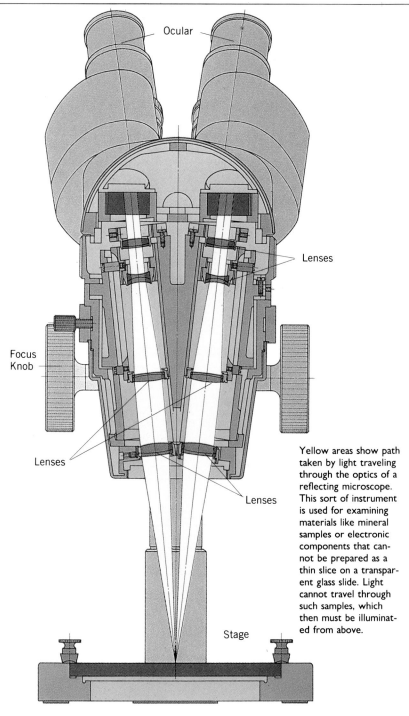

Yellow areas show path taken by light traveling through the optics of a reflecting microscope. This sort of instrument is used for examining materials like mineral samples or electronic components that cannot be prepared as a thin slice on a transparent glass slide. Light cannot travel through such samples, which then must be illuminated from above.

of research and industry. The basic microscope functions are modified to provide special indirect or split lighting, contrast, magnification, or divided images according to the special problems of the specimens. These specialized instruments include the stereoscopic microscope, polarizing microscope, reflecting microscope, fluorescence microscope, phase-contrast microscope, interference microscope, and darkground microscope.

Nonoptical Microscopes

The above-mentioned varieties of microscopes are all optical—that is, they use

some kind of light refracted through lenses to form an image. The magnifying power in such systems is limited by the wavelength of the light. Scientists have now found a way to use beams with the much shorter wavelengths of electrons so that the images of very small objects—such as bacteria or viruses—can be resolved. There are two basic types of electron microscopes, transmission and scanning. In the transmission electron microscope, the electrons are passed through the specimen. Some are absorbed, some are scattered, and the rest are focused onto a fluorescent screen or photographic plate

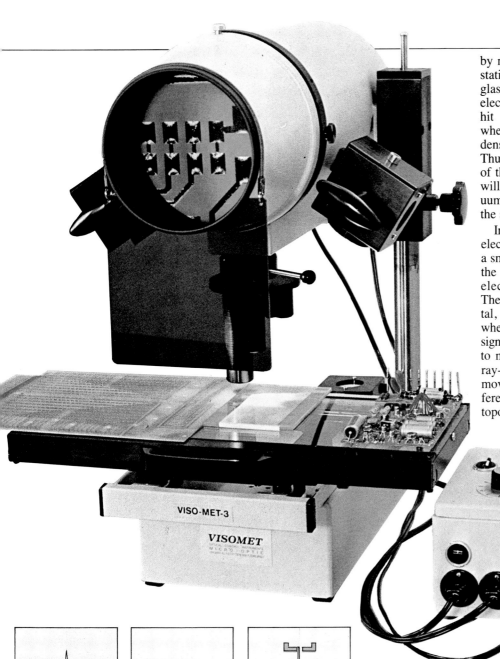

by magnetic lenses. Magnetic or electrostatic fields bend the path of electrons as glass lenses bend light rays. Where the electrons pass through the specimen and hit the screen, they make light spots; where they are held back or scattered by denser areas, the screen remains dark. Thus, the electron image shows the shape of the specimen. Any material, even air, will scatter electrons. Therefore, a vacuum is created in the tube, so that only the specimen can diffract the electrons.

In the scanning electron microscope, the electron beam is highly focused, striking a small area of the specimen. This causes the surface of the specimen to emit other electrons, called secondary electrons. These in turn activate a scintillator crystal, which produces tiny flashes of light when bombarded with electrons. Those signals are then amplified and finally made to modulate the brightness of a cathode-ray-tube (television) display. The beam is moved over the specimen to examine different areas. This builds an image of the topography of the specimen surface.

Above: Reflecting microscope equipped with a viewing screen used for performing quality-control checks on electronic components. *Left:* Schematic diagrams show the comparative structures of, left to right, an optical-transmission microscope, a conventional electron microscope, and a scanning electron microscope. The instruments all function according to the same principles, though the electron microscopes use a beam of electrons rather than a beam of light and so must use magnetic rather than glass lenses.

Transmission microscopes can resolve smaller images than scanning microscopes, but the scanning type gives a better picture of fine surface details.

The ion or field-ion microscope is the most powerful magnifier now in use. Using beams of helium atoms, it is able to enlarge up to 2 million times. It is used to examine metal atoms and their formation into crystalline structures. A needle made of the metal to be examined is pointed at a fluorescent screen. The tube is evacuated of air and then filled with helium gas. A positive charge between needle and screen attracts electrons from helium atoms. The remaining atoms lose their electrons, becoming ions. They are repelled from the positively charged needle toward the negatively charged screen. Where they strike the screen, it glows, creating an image of the material of the needle.

Microwave

Hundreds of telephone conversations can be carried simultaneously across space by one invisible microwave beam. Since this type of electromagnetic wave began to be used in the 1930s, it has been put to a wide variety of uses in military radio systems, communications satellites, radar, heating devices, and in a number of scientific applications.

The term "microwave" arose because, compared with commercial broadcasting waves, which are several hundred meters long, these waves are quite short. Microwaves range from about a foot (30 cm) to 1 millimeter in length, occupying a region on the electromagnetic spectrum between ultra-high-frequency television waves and

they set the cavities into oscillation. Once this has happened, the electrons return to the cathode, and the process is repeated. The magnetron has some limitations, however; for example, at higher frequencies, the cavities required for microwave generation are too small to be conveniently manufactured, and the weight of the magnet used in this device makes it impractical for some applications.

The klystron tube, on the other hand, does not require a magnetic field. In this tube, electrons follow a straight path from the cathode to a repeller plate and back, thereby passing through the cavity opening twice. However, the electron stream is broken up by cavity grids in such a way

that it only traverses the cavity at certain times. The stream of electrons is thus synchronized with the resonant frequency of the tubes, much the way a stream of air is sent through an organ pipe and resonated. The result is that the kinetic energy of the electron stream, and hence its electromagnetic radiation, is magnified until great power is developed.

Microwave Transmission

Microwaves can be beamed, focused, and reflected in much the same way as light. Like light, they travel in direct lines, along the line of sight rather than along the curvature of the Earth. As a result, they can only be transmitted over long

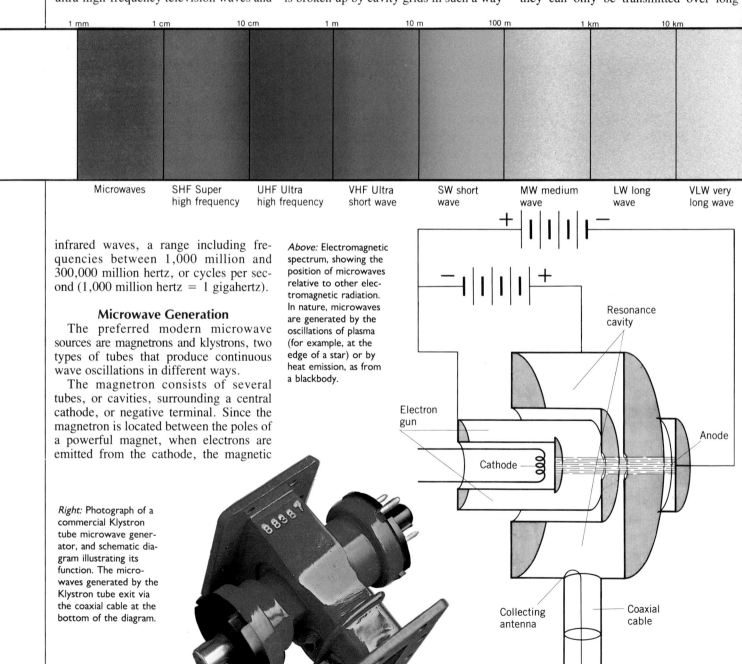

1 mm	1 cm	10 cm	1 m	10 m	100 m	1 km	10 km	1
Microwaves	SHF Super high frequency	UHF Ultra high frequency	VHF Ultra short wave	SW short wave	MW medium wave	LW long wave	VLW very long wave	

infrared waves, a range including frequencies between 1,000 million and 300,000 million hertz, or cycles per second (1,000 million hertz = 1 gigahertz).

Microwave Generation

The preferred modern microwave sources are magnetrons and klystrons, two types of tubes that produce continuous wave oscillations in different ways.

The magnetron consists of several tubes, or cavities, surrounding a central cathode, or negative terminal. Since the magnetron is located between the poles of a powerful magnet, when electrons are emitted from the cathode, the magnetic

Above: Electromagnetic spectrum, showing the position of microwaves relative to other electromagnetic radiation. In nature, microwaves are generated by the oscillations of plasma (for example, at the edge of a star) or by heat emission, as from a blackbody.

Right: Photograph of a commercial Klystron tube microwave generator, and schematic diagram illustrating its function. The microwaves generated by the Klystron tube exit via the coaxial cable at the bottom of the diagram.

Resonance cavity

Electron gun

Cathode

Anode

Collecting antenna

Coaxial cable

Left: Magnetron tube used to produce high-intensity microwaves. Unlike the Klystron tube, which can produce microwaves of varying frequency, each magnetron produces only microwaves of a single, predetermined frequency. Magnetron tubes are often used for radar applications, while Klystron tubes are more adaptable for laboratory use.

Below: Parabolic dish used for satellite radio communications at microwave frequencies.

antenna. Dish-shaped or parabolic antennas are best suited for picking up faint signals. Electronically "steered" antennas contain many small elements whose interconnections can be switched so as to render the unit sensitive in any given direction; thus, these antennas do not have to be mechanically aimed.

Although the microwave-transmission system, consisting of antennas, towers, transmitters, and receivers, involves a substantial capital investment, the capacity of this system for the simultaneous transmission of thousands of telephone calls and many television programs brings down the cost per unit considerably.

Microwaves have a variety of applications. Apart from their role in communications systems (both terrestrial and satellite), their uses include industrial and scientific applications such as atomic and space research. In recent years, the microwave oven, in which food can be cooked in a short time without heating up the surrounding air, has come to be used in many homes as well as in airplanes, trains, and restaurants.

field forces them into a circular path at a speed that allows them to hit the cavity openings at timed intervals. In so doing, terrestrial distances by making successive hops. Microwave transmission over distances requires a series of repeater stations mounted on hilltops or towers at intervals of about 30 miles (50 km). They are electronically amplified before retransmission at each stage. For overseas communication, active-repeater satellites are now used, which receive, amplify, and retransmit microwave signals to ground stations all over the world.

Ordinary wire cannot efficiently transmit microwaves. Coaxial cables, consisting of an insulated inner wire and a cylindrical outer "shield" conductor, are best suited for transmitting microwaves up to several thousand million hertz. At higher frequencies and with large amounts of power, waveguides are usually used to transmit microwaves. Waveguides are pipes, usually rectangular or circular in cross section, through which microwaves travel as a result of the waves' alternating electric and magnetic fields, much the way electromagnetic waves travel in free space.

Microwave antennas come in many different sizes and shapes. Directivity is increased by enlarging the diameter of the